SOURCES FOR MODERN BRITISH HISTORY

General Editors: Kathleen Burk, John Ramsden, John Turner

REAL OLD TORY POLITICS: The Political Diaries of Robert Sanders, Lord Bayford 1910–1935
Edited by John Ramsden. 1984

THE DESTRUCTION OF LORD ROSEBERY: From the Diary of Sir Edward Hamilton, 1894–1895
Edited by David Brooks. 1987

THE CRISIS OF BRITISH UNIONISM: The Domestic Political Papers of the Second Earl of Selborne, 1885–1922
Edited by George Boyce. 1987

LABOUR AND THE WARTIME COALITION: From the Diary of James Chuter Ede, 1941–1945
Edited by Kevin Jefferys. 1987

THE MODERNISATION OF CONSERVATIVE POLITICS: The Diaries and Letters of William Bridgeman, 1904–1935
Edited by Philip Williamson. 1988

THE CRISIS OF BRITISH POWER: The Imperial and Naval Papers of the Second Earl of Selborne, 1895–1910
Edited by George Boyce. 1990

MY DEAR MAX

The letters of Brendan Bracken to
Lord Beaverbrook, 1925–1958

Edited with an introduction by
RICHARD COCKETT

Introductory matter © Richard Cockett 1990
Brendan Bracken's letters © Churchill Archives Centre,
Churchill College, Cambridge
Lord Beaverbrook's letters © the Trustees of the Beaverbrook
Foundation

British Library Cataloguing in Publication Data

Bracken, Brendan
  My dear Max: the letters of Brendan Bracken to Lord Beaverbrook, 1925–1958. (Sources for Modern British History).
  1. Great Britain. Journalism. Bracken, Brendan
  2. Journalism. Beaverbrook, William Maxwell Aitken, Baron 1879–1964
  I. Title   II. Beaverbrook, William Maxwell Aitken, Baron 1879–1964   III. Cockett, Richard   IV. Series
  070.92
  ISBN 0–9508900–9–X

PUBLISHED BY THE HISTORIANS' PRESS
9 DAISY ROAD, LONDON E18 1EA

Typeset at the University of London Computer Centre
Printed in Great Britain by Antony Rowe Ltd

CONTENTS

Acknowledgements		vii
1	Brendan Bracken	1
2	Lord Beaverbrook	18
3	Bracken and Beaverbrook, The Correspondence	28
The letters:		
4	The inter-war years, 1925 – 1939	34
5	The War, 1939 – 1945	48
6	Toiling under the yoke of Socialism, 1945 – 1951	55
7	Winston's return, 1951 – 1955	126
8	Eden and Suez, 1955 – 1956	180
9	The last hurrah, 1956 – 1958	202
Recommended Reading		215
Index		217

For PNC and OPR

Acknowledgements

I owe a major debt of gratitude to the Trustees of the Beaverbrook Foundation and the Clerk of the Records of the House of Lords for their kind permission to let me publish the letters of Lord Beaverbrook and I am equally indebted to Mr Corelli Barnett, Keeper of the Archives at the Churchill Archives Centre, Churchill College, Cambridge, for his permission to publish the letters of Brendan Bracken.

I must also record my gratitude to the following persons and institutions for their help in shedding light on some often very obscure references in the Beaverbrook/Bracken correspondence: Mrs Jean Ruse of the English-Speaking Union, Mr Andrew Burns of British Steel, Mr Robert Rhodes James M.P., the *Daily Express*, the National Farmers Union, the Public Information Office of the House of Commons, as well as the libraries of the London embassies of the United States of America, Canada, Jordan, Jamaica and Argentina. Needless to say, any errors that remain in the text or footnotes are my responsibility alone.

The production of this volume would not have been possible without the encouragement and support of Dr John Turner, and I would also like to thank the other editors of *Sources for Modern British History*, Dr Kathleen Burk and Dr John Ramsden, for their interest in the project. Mrs Camari Ward battled unflinchingly with my handwriting to produce the typescript. Finally I must record my debt to my parents, in whose beautiful garden the work was composed during the summer of 1989.

Royal Holloway and Bedford New College
May 1990

The Historians' Press acknowledges the unfailingly professional assistance of the University of London Computer Centre during the production of this book.

1
BRENDAN BRACKEN

It was wholly in keeping with the air of mystery that Brendan Bracken liked to cultivate about himself that his faithful chauffeur should spend a good part of the week after his master's death shovelling Bracken's private papers into the grate at 8 Lord North Street, Bracken's elegant Georgian house in Westminster. Aley, the unfortunate chauffeur, had consulted an old friend of Bracken's, Sir Patrick Hennessy, beforehand; but both were later reproached by the likes of Churchill and Beaverbrook for committing Bracken's life to the flames and thus perpetrating an act of historical vandalism. Yet that is what Bracken had requested and it was an act that was entirely in character, for behind the noisy, bustling, gregarious facade that Bracken presented to the world was an innermost self held aloof from other men. He was a man of many friends — and many enemies — but no intimates. It was thus hardly surprising that a man who had taken such pains to conceal his real self from the prying eyes of an inquisitive world while he was alive should endeavour to do the same after he was dead. We shall, therefore, never have a complete picture of Brendan Bracken — which is as he would have wished.

Nonetheless, Bracken has been fortunate in having attracted the attention of two particularly diligent biographers, as a result of which we now have at least a partial account of Churchill's 'faithful Chela'. Both Andrew Boyle (*'Poor, Dear Brendan', The Quest for Brendan Bracken* [Hutchinson, 1974] and Charles Lysaght (*Brendan Bracken* [Allen Lane, 1979]) have done enough to provide the historian with the bare bones of Bracken's life. Their task was complicated by Bracken's own habit of offering juicy morsels of self-revelation and personal history to his friends and companions: nearly all of it was pure invention, self-contradictory, or both.

He was born on 11 February 1901 in the village of Templemore, Ireland, into a comfortably-off family. His father, a staunch republican, died when he was three years old. He ran away from school, a Jesuit College in Mungret; and in 1916, his family apparently resigned to the young Brendan's delinquency, he was shipped off to stay with relations in Australia. In 1919 he returned to Ireland, where he found himself unwelcome and thus immediately set sail for England, where he arrived in the spring of 1920. Probably due to the unpopularity of the Irish at the time, but also perhaps due to the resentment he felt towards his inhospitable family, he posed as an Australian — and was never subsequently to disclose his Irish roots to anyone. Bracken's first task in England was to equip himself with an English public school education and to this end he presented himself for an interview with the headmaster of Sedbergh School a few days after term had started in mid-September 1920. Legends abound about this remarkable interview between Bracken, presenting himself as an orphaned Australian three years younger than he actually was, and the rather perplexed William Weech. As Weech hesitated about accepting this extremely unorthodox 'boy', Bracken produced a cheque book and offered to pay for a term in advance. Having passed a set of oral and written tests, Bracken was cautiously accepted into the school and thus began a life-long connection with Sedbergh, Weech becoming the first and most altruistic of his mentors. However, Bracken stayed only three months, departing as mysteriously as he had arrived.

There followed a series of teaching jobs at public schools, most notably Bishop's Stortford. But London and the world of politics and journalism beckoned and Bracken now began to ingratiate himself with the literary and political élite. One of the first people to spot his talent — or at least his endearing impudence — was J.L. Garvin, the venerable editor of *The Observer*, and it was at his house, Gregories in Beaconsfield, that Bracken first met Winston Churchill in early 1923. It was not in Brendan Bracken's nature to sit back and enjoy the verbal dexterity of the already famous statesman, and he so impressed Churchill with his precocious intelligence and conversational skill that Churchill demanded to see him again. For his part, Bracken immediately set about making himself as useful as possible to Churchill. At the age of 22, Bracken became Churchill's campaign manager in the 1923 election for the constituency of West Leicester. He threw himself into this campaign with enormous gusto and energy; he might not have impressed the electors of Leicester, who returned a Labour M.P., but he certainly impressed Churchill. Their political destinies were now inseparable. As Bracken informed his mother in 1922, 'I've decided to hitch on to a political star. The name of the star is Winston Churchill.'[1]

It was Baldwin who described Bracken as Churchill's 'faithful chela' — although, like many of that statesman's more celebrated pronouncements, it probably owed more than he cared to admit to his cousin Rudyard Kipling. Churchill became the one fixed star in Bracken's otherwise frequently shifting firmament of friends and colleagues. Unlike many other younger men who at one time or another considered themselves to be acolytes or political followers of Churchill — such as Robert Boothby, Archibald Sinclair, or Anthony Eden — Bracken never nursed any political ambitions of his own. The others, however close, were all essentially political allies of Churchill, harbouring their own political hopes and aspirations. As far as Bracken was concerned politics rose or fell with Winston Churchill. There is no evidence that Bracken ever had any substantial political ambitions of his own; nor did he ever disagree politically with his self-elected chief. In 1929, however, Bracken was elected M.P. for North Paddington. He did nothing to disavow the contemporary local newspaper reports that he was 'a graduate of Oxford University', 'of considerable wealth' and the owner of four houses; he was returned as an M.P. with adequate, if not handsome, majorities in every election until 1945 when he was one of the early victims of the great Labour landslide.

In the House of Commons, his policy was one of unflinching support for Churchill. As the latter became gradually more isolated in the ranks of his own party as a result of his controversial stands on India, the Abdication Crisis and the growing menace of Nazi Germany, so what little support he had once enjoyed in Parliament all but melted away. Bracken and Boothby alone retained their faith in him and as the attacks on Churchill became harsher as the 1930s progressed, so Bracken became proportionately more obdurate in support of the embattled statesman. Of course, they

---

1 Andrew Boyle, *Poor, Dear Brendan; The Quest for Brendan Bracken* (Hutchinson, 1974), p. 101.

were yet to have their finest hour in 1940; but it required a great act of faith, some would say blind loyalty, to remain so confident in Churchill's ultimate destiny during the 'locust years'. But this loyalty should not be interpreted as mere sycophancy, for such unflinching support earned Bracken the right, which he frequently exercised, to argue with Churchill as few other men dared. This was especially so during the years of Churchill's premiership, when the rest of the Cabinet tended to cower under the weight of the towering personality in their midst. It was thus often left to Bracken to shout some sense into Churchill when the latter's judgement seemed to falter. Churchill would take such treatment from no-one else but Bracken. Ronald Tree, Churchill's wartime weekend host at Ditchley, was astounded by Bracken's outspokenness in front of his leader; 'He was the only man I knew who would openly stand up to Churchill in an argument if he thought him to be in the wrong. I have often seen him in the library at Ditchley engaged in a furious struggle, with Churchill glowering at him but gradually backing down'. When Churchill proposed an otherwise worthless old Harrovian for a vacant office, Bracken shouted at the Prime Minister 'You only want him because he was at that bloody old Borstal of yours'.[2] Yet Bracken could also laugh Churchill out of his tendency to moodiness and introspection — the 'Black Dog'. At one of the most crucial moments of Churchill's career, just after his debilitating stroke in 1953, Lord Moran, Churchill's physician, recorded that 'Tonight Brendan dined with us. He can draw the P.M. out, and has a kind of explosive cheerfulness which seems to help'.[3]

Although Bracken was destined, through his own choice, to spend his entire political career in the shadow of Churchill, at the same time he also carved out an independent career in the field of financial journalism. His achievements in this field were, if anything, greater than those in the political field. In 1923 he started working for the reputable but undynamic family firm of Eyre and Spottiswoode, publishers of the Prayer Book and the Bible, having been introduced to Simon Crosthwaite-Eyre by Evan Frederick Morgan, heir to Lord Tredegar. Bracken was put in charge of revitalising their magazines, such as *Illustrated Review* which was

---

[2] Charles Lysaght, *Brendan Bracken* (Allen Lane, 1979), p. 179–180.
[3] Lord Moran, *The Struggle for Survival* (Constable, 1967), p. 413.

re-launched in January 1924 as *English Life*. The circulation of *English Life* trebled within three years. By 1926 he was appointed to the board of Eyre and Spottiswoode and at the tender age of 25 could be seen rushing between the great country houses of England in the back of a gleaming Hispano-Suiza with a liveried chauffeur, formerly in the employ of the Churchills. It was also at this time that the Crosthwaite-Eyres agreed to install him on a long lease at 8 Lord North Street, Westminster, where he could readily indulge his passion for fine Georgian decoration and furniture. Romney's portrait of Edmund Burke, Bracken's other political hero, adorned the mantlepiece.

In 1926, recognising that the City was the only remaining 'profession' that lacked a trade magazine, Bracken launched *The Banker*, which quickly prospered. In the same year, he persuaded the always cautious Eyre and Spottiswoode to buy the *Financial News* and in 1928 they also acquired, under Bracken's direction, the *Investor's Chronicle* and the *Liverpool Journal of Commerce*. In 1928 came perhaps his greatest coup when he bought a half-interest in *The Economist*, sharing the paper with Sir Henry Strakosch, the head of Union Corporation (a South African mining concern) who was to become a great friend and supporter of Brackens' career. By 1928 he had joined the select ranks of the 'Press Barons'.

However, unlike other examples of the breed — such as Lord Beaverbrook — Bracken was very much a 'hands off' proprietor, respecting the editorial independence of his editors. This was especially true of the liberal-inclined *Economist*, whose editor had initially been very wary of the young, ostensibly Tory newspaper proprietor. Neither Sir Walter Layton, nor his successor Geoffrey Crowther, ever had any cause for complaint about editorial interference. Bracken, did, however, take a rather closer interest in the editorial content of the *Financial News*. In tandem with the patient and long-serving journalist Paul Einzig, Bracken used the paper to attack the threatened economic domination by Germany of South-East Europe that was a natural concomitant of the policy of appeasement. During the war, Einzig himself felt the harsher side of his proprietor's tongue when he dared to start criticising Churchill's government. Nonetheless, as a rule Bracken was content to 'manage' his papers and, even despite the depression, his efforts met with conspicuous success. His own commercial and financial acumen also gave him a much needed platform of independence and security in his dealings with amicable, but much older characters, such as Beaverbrook, Churchill, Strakosch, Garvin and Lord Camrose (the proprietor of the *Daily Telegraph*).

So what sort of a man was the Bracken of the 1930s and 1940s, when he was in his prime? The *Financial Times* (which Bracken had taken over in 1945) printed an obituary which gives as accurate a picture as any:

> Vigour was an outstanding characteristic, instantly striking at the first moment of meeting him. His large, robust frame was surmounted by a mass of red hair, silvery in his later years, but always vivid. He spoke and gestured incisively. Great powers of aggression were at the service of a rapid, leaping mind, which sometimes moved too fast for slower interlocutors. Circuitous processes of logic were no obstacle to him; he took great pains to see that they were translated into action.

Of his first years in the House of Commons:

> A member of Parliament at that time recalls the startlingly tall, carrot-topped figure, sitting high up at the very back of the back benches. His strength in the House of Commons lay in interjection and in repartee.... The formal speech on the set occasion suited him less well than the clash of debate. At answering hecklers he was in his element, and at provoking members of the party opposite most adroit.

Robin Barrington-Ward, the wartime editor of *The Times*, noted that Bracken had 'all the better qualities of the Buccaneer'.[4] This was indeed true. Everybody was drawn to his energy, his humour, his ceaseless flow of conversation. He was extremely indiscreet, and a lot of what he said was pure invention. Sir John Colville, ever a shrewd judge, summed up Bracken very neatly on first encountering him in full flow across the dinner table in May 1940: 'Bracken is a cad, "slick" and amusing and quite likeable in his way; but rather too talkative and apt to make the most ridiculous pronouncements.'[5]

Bracken was in his element engaging in heated and prolonged political debate with champagne, whisky and cigars to hand — which made him such a welcome guest at the tables of Beaverbrook and Churchill. His favourite foil was Nye Bevan; it was

---

[4] R. Barrington-Ward to G. M. Young, July 21st 1941, Times Archive.
[5] John Colville, *The Fringes of Power*, Vol. I (Sceptre, 1985), May 18, 1940.

Bracken who coined the soubriquet 'Bollinger Bolshevik' of Bevan. Michael Foot has written of these evenings at Cherkley, Beaverbrook's country house, with Bracken declaiming and '...gesturing as he went somewhat in the manner of a domesticated orangoutang.' Foot describes the scene:

> ...the assorted company, the polemical free-for-all, the deluge of drink and journalism and politics, the orang-outang manner, the absolute rule that no holds were barred; indeed, customarily, an incitement from the host that the more eminent his guests, the more ferocious should be the cross-examination or the raillery.[6]

Politically, he was only nominally a Tory. He could perhaps be more accurately described as a liberal imperialist without the moral self-righteousness. He was a self-made man and believed in the ethics of self-help, free enterprise and competitive individualism. He was essentially an outsider and an anti-establishmentarian; he had no time for the *noblesse oblige* of the Tory gentry or the guilty conscience of the middle classes. He was, to use more modern nomenclature, a quintessential 'Thatcherite'. That much is abundantly clear from his correspondence with Lord Beaverbrook. As such, he found himself increasingly out of step with the 'spirit of the age', which, in the 1940s and 1950s, tended towards the Keynesian policies of full employment through demand management and nationalization and the principles of feudal socialism embodied in the Welfare State. He railed against the planners and Keynesian economists who saw the salvation of British industry in central planning and high direct taxation. As he warned the Royal Empire Society in February 1945, a few months before the Socialist deluge in the General Election:

> If research, risk-taking and enterprise are not discouraged there is no reason for pessimism about the future of British industry...we can steadily improve the standard of living in Britain. To do this we must keep an ever watchful eye on the people who believe there can be a curse of plenty. Those restrictionists are to be found among unenterprising leaders of employers and employees. Timidity makes them live with their hands on the brake. They see salvation in an eternity of restrictions and controls. Britain's salvation can only be found in expansion and freedom.

For Bracken, Keynes, the economic guru of his generation, was the man who had 'made inflation respectable' and it was the

---

6 Michael Foot, *Debts of Honour* (Poynter, 1980).

old, defiant Bracken who, only three years before his death, resigned from the Institute of Directors when he heard that Frank Cousins, the General Secretary of the powerful Transport and General Workers Union, was due to address them.

Yet there was also little doubt that Bracken's main interest in politics, besides Churchill, was the drama that it provided. He thrived on the excitement and the intrigue. Lord Winster wrote on Bracken's death that:

> the political machine, not politics, interested him. Intrigue was in his blood. If he had any political affinities they were with the Whigs of the eighteenth century.'[7]

More than anything else, Bracken's letters to Beaverbrook sparkle with the sheer fun of politics. It was the best and biggest game of all.

Yet behind the exuberant and remorselessly self-confident exterior, all his contemporaries noticed his basic sensitiveness, his loneliness and melancholia. Bracken's *Financial Times* obituarist observed that:

> He was reserved, too, in other habits of life. He would disappear into the country, on walking and fishing expeditions — Scotland was a favourite retreat — without letting even his intimates know where he was staying. Indeed, though he had many friends he disclosed to no-one the full circumstances of his life. His gregarious conviviality was mixed with a more melancholy strain, and his innermost self held aloof from other men. There were times when he shut himself up in his house, seeing and speaking to no one. At heart, he was a lonely man. He never married...he hid great sensitivity behind his gutsy manner.

His enduring love was for Lady Penelope Ward. But, as her mother later recalled for the benefit of Andrew Boyle:

> ...I've met hardly anyone who could match his radiant vitality and marvellous powers of conversation. Maybe he was preternaturally shy or felt that he was too ugly or inadequate, but never once did he display the slightest sign or gesture of affection to Penelope. My daughter grew attached to him but couldn't understand his inability to relax and be completely at ease with himself when alone with her.... His reluctance to talk freely and openly about himself was an extremely sore point. I could swear that he felt more at

---

7 *Brendan Bracken : Portraits and Appreciations* (Eyre and Spottiswoode, 1958) p. 35

home in my company than in Penelope's, possibly because I was older and therefore safer to be with.⁸

Those who took his brash and seemingly philistine exterior at face value were often in for a rude awakening when they discovered that the man they liked to denigrate as an arriviste thug was an expert on Georgian art and literature, could recite virtually the whole of *Crockford's* clerical directory from memory and was possessed of an encyclopaedic knowledge of the public schools of England. Colville was one who was more than a little surprised at finding Bracken defending Christianity with his customary vehemence at a dinner party in 1941:

> Brendan invited Vincent Sheean [an Irish-American] and Duncan Sandys to dinner and there ensued a violent religious argument, Sheean being an atheist and Brendan and Duncan, rather surprisingly, both being stalwart partisans of Christianity.... Brendan is very sensitive to any anti-religious opinion and has, I think a religious temperament beneath his blasphemous exterior. The level of argument was not very high, but there was a compensating intensity of feeling.⁹

Robert Bruce-Lockhart, a close friend of Bracken's, also became gradually more intrigued by Bracken's contradictory nature, remarking in the privacy of his diary that Bracken:

> ...was a strange mixture — violent in language, kind in heart, in many respects a buccaneer, yet full of artistic knowledge and considerable taste.¹⁰

However, Bracken was also possessed of all the less attractive qualities of the buccaneer in bountiful quantities. He could be bullying, rude, overbearing and boorish. To those who crossed his path, he had few endearing qualities. Hugh Dalton, who clashed with Bracken over foreign propaganda during the war, found him an impossible colleague — as did Dalton's staff. Recording one Political Warfare Executive Meeting in his diary, Dalton reflected that Bracken was '... back towards his old form — reckless rudeness. He is, as Gladwyn [Jebb] says, simply a guttersnipe.'¹¹

---

8 Boyle, p. 199.
9 Colville, 24 June 1941, it Fringes of Power, I, 483–4.
10 Kenneth Young, *The Diaries of Sir Robert Bruce-Lockhart, 1939 – 65* (Macmillan 1980), 20 March 1947.
11 Ben Pimlott, *The Second World War Diary of Hugh Dalton* (Jonathan Cape, 1986), 3 Feb. 1942.

For his part, Bracken heartily reciprocated Dalton's animosity and warmed to the fight. Bruce-Lockhart recorded in his diary a story heard at the Foreign Office:

> Very funny about Dalton...Brendan...had had Gladwyn Jebb to dinner. Brendan had made some remarks about Dalton...and Jebb had repeated them to Dalton who complained to Winston. W.S.C. sends for Brendan: 'Is it true that at dinner the other night you attacked . . . Dalton's work?' 'What I said was that Dalton was the biggest bloodiest shit I've ever met!' Winston laughed.[12]

The historian of the *Financial Times* has written of Bracken's not altogether helpful presence in the offices of the paper during the post-war years, and in particular his behaviour at the paper's Tuesday lunches, which he had instigated:

> On these occasions he would stride into the dining room rather late, help himself to a gin and martini and start abusing someone from the assembled company, which usually consisted of the rest of the board, the editor and one or two journalists, with perhaps a distinguished guest. The bullying was blatant and of a mental rather than physical nature. Indeed, it would be fair to say that the staff as a whole of the post-war FT, in as much as it came into contact with Bracken, loathed and feared him in about equal proportions.[13]

At the same time, if Bracken pledged his loyalty to someone — or something — that loyalty would be unwavering. Whether it be to Churchill, Sedbergh and Ampleforth Schools, the *Financial Times* or Beaverbrook, Bracken would perform countless acts of — often unrecorded — kindness on their behalf. It was Bracken who secured the contract for Churchill's war memoirs that finally relieved the aging statesman of any financial worries. Even those whom he liked to snipe at in private, such as Anthony Eden, could count on Bracken's support, especially in times of adversity. Bracken liked to refer to the handsome foreign secretary as the 'Robert Taylor' of politics; but when Eden's world had crashed around him in January 1957 and he was sailing from Southampton for a recuperative holiday in New Zealand, his political career at an end and the shrill condemnation of the world still ringing in his ears, he was nonetheless pleased, as he recalled in his memoirs, that:

12 *Bruce-Lockhart Diaries*, 8 August 1941.
13 David Kynaston, *The Financial Times; A Centenary History* (Viking, 1988), p. 161.

Friends came to see us off, at dockside, on board ship and at the locks. At one of these, my wife and I were looking casually over the side when a tall figure came running through the fog. It was my kind friend, Lord Bracken, who had missed us at our sailing and headed us off this way to say good-bye.[14]

The already critically ill Bracken was just able to throw a box of cigars on board.

The war was undoubtedly Bracken's 'finest hour'. Having endured the wilderness years with Churchill, in September 1939 Bracken started reaping his reward by becoming Parliamentary Private Secretary to Churchill who found himself recalled to Government as the new First Lord of the Admiralty. When Chamberlain's government failed to command the confidence of a sufficient number of Conservative M.P.'s during the famous parliamentary debate on May 8, 1940, it was Bracken who sensed that if Churchill now played his cards right, he would soon be Prime Minister. Bracken's crucial intervention was to persuade Churchill to remain silent at the vital meeting of Chamberlain, Halifax and Margesson (the Conservative chief Whip) on May 9 to decide on Chamberlain's successor. Bracken knew that out of his instinctive loyalty Churchill would volunteer to serve under the uninspiring Lord Halifax; but when it came to it, Churchill remained silent and Halifax duly made it clear that he was not willing to serve as Prime Minister. Some have attributed the advice on 'silence' to Kingsley Wood, but it seems much more likely that it was Bracken who tendered this crucial counsel.[15]

Once Churchill was installed in Number 10 Downing Street, Bracken moved in as the new Prime Minister's Parliamentary Private Secretary, symbolically taking over Sir Horace Wilson's old room, from which Chamberlain's most powerful Civil Servant had helped to direct the ultimately disastrous policy of 'appeasement'. Bracken, Beaverbrook and Lord Cherwell, Churchill's scientific adviser, now formed Churchill's 'Kitchen Cabinet'. These three were supposed to wield awesome power, far more than any of

14 Anthony Eden, *Full Circle*, (Cassell, 1960), p. 584.
15 Kingsley Wood is credited with giving the crucial advice by Anthony Eden in *The Reckoning* (Cassell, 1965), pp. 96–97; Boyle outlines the case in favour of Bracken in *Poor, Dear Brendan*, pp. 246–248. Churchill himself testified to his famous 'silence' in his memoirs, *The Second World War* (Vol I, 1948), pp. 523–524.

the Cabinet. It was after midnight over drinks that Churchill and his inner coterie met to debate, analyse and criticise the overall conduct of the war. As Beaverbrook later recalled: 'the Prime Minister, Brendan and I used to meet every evening; we settled most things.'[16] Charles Lysaght has described Bracken's role at this time:

> In the highly personalized administration that Churchill ran, these two cronies [Bracken and Beaverbrook] were believed to wield more political power than any member of the rubber-stamping War Cabinet. In Bracken's case the detail or character of his influence is particularly elusive. No tell-tale minutes survive. More mysteriously, Bracken, alone among Churchill's wartime aides, received no accolade and little mention in the latter's war memoirs. Contemporary estimates of his importance varied. He was dismissed by some as a court jester, a retailer of tit-bits of political gossip to beguile the Prime Minister's leisure hours, but most realised that he had a more substantial role even if it remained true that on important matters Churchill let no man take decisions for him.[17]

It was thus not surprising that Bracken should resent being plucked from this cosseted position of much power and little responsibility to become the new Minister of Information in July 1941. The Ministry of Information, housed in the London University Senate House building in Bloomsbury, had already been the political graveyard of three successive Ministers since the start of the war and Bracken himself was under no illusions as to the task awaiting him, writing to his old mentor J. L. Garvin:

> This is one of the toughest jobs which has ever fallen to the lot of man! And I think that in a very short time I shall be joining the happy band of ex-Ministers of Information.[18]

The basic problem for the MOI was its relations with the other Whitehall Ministries. The MOI struggled to assert its independence; but all the other departments of government maintained the final say in the release of their own news — thus effectively denying the MOI any autonomy at all. The 'Battle of Bloomsbury', as this struggle was only half-jokingly called in the corridors of power, had been going on ever since the beginning of the war; Bracken's immediate predecessor, Duff Cooper, had resigned after

[16] Moran, p. 75
[17] Lysaght, p. 179.
[18] Lysaght, p. 191.

the loss of the latest round in that battle. However, as the official historian of the MOI has written, his replacement by Bracken was

> a master-stroke. Bracken possessed everything his predecessors had lacked: excellent press relations, a very close friendship with the Prime Minister, bustling confidence in tackling the Ministry's adversaries, and a scorn for the exhortation of the British public. Under his — initially reluctant — stewardship, the Ministry of Information became efficient and unobtrusive.[19]

Bracken threw himself into the task of gaining more powers for the MOI from the other Whitehall departments with his customary zest and energy. He genuinely believed in press freedom, and saw an autonomous, powerful MOI as a guarantor of that freedom. The press rallied to his side, recognising that at last they had a Minister who would fight vigorously for the release of more news from the Service Departments and the Foreign Office — which Bracken collectively called 'the oysters'. In asserting the rights of the MOI, Bracken was prepared to take on every one — with the crucial advantage of knowing that Churchill would always back him up. He thus entered into a long and heated correspondence with the First Lord of the Admiralty to assert the MOI's rights for more news from the 'Silent Service' and, more famously, he conducted a long and acrimonious battle of attrition with Hugh Dalton of the Ministry of Economic Warfare to win the control of foreign propaganda for the MOI. Neither was he prepared to kow-tow to the Foreign Office and in 1944 engaged in lively exchanges with Anthony Eden over the question of cable censorship. In all these rather byzantine Whitehall power struggles, there is no doubt that Bracken always came out with most of what he had been seeking. For this, Bracken earned the undying gratitude of the propagandists at the MOI who had news with which they could propagand, and the press, who now had news with which they could fill their papers. He also earned the grudging admiration of his fellow politicians who recognised that he was a good deal more than just a lightweight toady of Churchill's.

There is no doubt that fighting Churchill's war was the halcyon period of Bracken's life. But there were signs before the end of the war that even his seemingly boundless reservoirs of energy

---

19 Ian Mclaine, *Ministry of Morale* (George Allen and Unwin, 1979) p. 7.

were not inexhaustible. In November 1944 Robert Bruce-Lockhart was already noting in his diary:

> ...My own feeling is that Brendan wants to get out of the Ministry as soon as possible. He is not well, has a bad heart, and seeing Lord Moran regularly....I think and have thought for a long time that Brendan is far from well. No man can stand the pace which he sets himself. When he is well, he is decisive, quick in perception, and brilliantly intuitive. He is also kindness itself. When he is ill or under the influence of alcohol, which he takes to keep him going, he does no real work, is unpunctual and erratic, and altogether difficult to handle.[20]

With the ending of the coalition in May 1945, Bracken became First Lord of the Admiralty in Churchill's brief caretaker government. To those unacquainted with Bracken's declining powers, he now seemed to be on a par with Eden, Butler, Lord Woolton and other Conservative leaders in the race for the richer pickings in Churchill's expected post-war government after the general election of July. But all these expectations were confounded by the Labour landslide on July 26. Not only did Churchill find himself out of office, but his 'faithful chela' found himself without a seat as the electors of North Paddington plumped for the Labour candidate, Mason MacFarlane, instead. Bracken's result was, perhaps, the inevitable consequence of six years of benign neglect of his constituents. There was certainly nothing marginal about the result as he was defeated by 6,500 votes.

This was undoubtedly a grave blow for Bracken. Nonetheless, it apparently left his zest for politics undiminished as he now returned to the House of Commons in one of the first by-elections of the new Parliament. In November 1945, Bracken was elected as the M.P. for Bournemouth, one of the safest Tory seats in the country. In Parliament, he warmed to the task of attacking the aggressively self-confident Labour government and won laurels from the Tories for his spirited attacks on Labour, especially during the debates on the nationalization programme. He specialised in shadowing the Minister for Fuel and Power, and was thus at his best in his assault on the bills that nationalised the gas industry and the iron and steel industry. Nonetheless, in terms of political philosophy he now found himself increasingly detached from the more progressive younger generation in the party, to

---

[20] *Bruce-Lockhart Diaries*, 20 Nov. 1944.

say nothing of his contemporaries like Butler and Macmillan who favoured greater government control of industry and higher state spending. Bracken fought within the Party to try and stem the rising tide of the 'charter-mongers', but there was little he could do. Moreover, it became increasingly clear that he did not have the required *gravitas* to become a first-rank politician. As Disraeli wrote: 'The British people being subject to fogs and possessing a powerful middle class require grave Statesman'. Bracken was not 'grave'; there lurked the suspicion in many peoples' minds that his rollicking attacks on the Labour party, which were often very wide of the mark, were done chiefly for his own amusement.

By 1948 his political star was waning. But what finally put paid to any political aspirations that he might still have entertained was illness. His sinus problems, which had plagued him all his life, got steadily worse and by 1950 it was clear that he could not go on. He won the Bournemouth seat for the Tories in both the 1950 and 1951 elections, but it was plain to all his friends that he no longer had the appetite for politics that had sustained him for the previous two decades. Their worst fears were confirmed when he refused to accept office in Churchill's new government in 1951, despite all the Prime Minister's most persuasive pleadings. In November 1951 he resigned his seat in the House of Commons and in the 1952 New Year's Honours Bracken was elevated to the peerage as Viscount Bracken of Christchurch, although he never took his seat in the House of Lords.

With his political career at an end, Bracken concentrated on his business interests. A new outlet for his energies was the chairmanship of the Union Corporation. Sir Henry Strakosh had presided over the Union Corporation until his death in 1943. He had decided that Bracken was the best man to succeed him and thus Bracken became chairman in 1945, borrowing money from Beaverbrook to buy the extra preference shares in the Union Corporation that were necessary. He was an active chairman and made a point of flying to South Africa several times a year to inspect the mining side of the business on the ground. However, as his health deteriorated in the early 1950s these visits to South Africa became increasingly rare.

It was his role as a newspaper proprietor that chiefly occupied him in the post-war years. In 1945 Bracken completed his most significant business manoeuvre by buying the *Financial Times* from Lord Camrose; the *Financial News* and *Financial Times* were amalgamated into one paper, the *Financial Times*, under his management. The new paper went from strength to strength and by 1947 onwards pre-tax profits on the *Financial Times* were running at half a million pounds a year. *The Economist* also prospered. It was in the 1950s that the paper was transformed from a parochial organ of financial comment into a serious weekly political paper with an international reputation.

Bracken also had the added incentive of writing the weekly 'Men and Matters' column which appeared in the *Financial Times* every Monday from 1946 until Bracken's death under the pseudonym of 'Observer'. Alan Hodge, Bracken's assistant on this column, has described Bracken the columnist at work:

> The Scribe [i.e. Hodge himself] was asked to produce a list of targets for attack. Invariably these were shot down by Bracken in withering terms. This was part of a process of warming up by which he got into his stride. He would then pace about, talking explosively, jumping from one subject to another, from the problems of coal miners to Impressionist painters, from technological education to the needs of St. Paul's Cathedral, from politics and business in the United States, about which he was deeply informed, to the beauty of Georgian country houses, on which he was no less an expert. 'Polymath' was a word that he liked to apply to men of far- ranging interests and varied knowledge. The word fits him.[21]

The 'Men and Matters' column was witty and pugnacious and reflected Bracken's increasing despair at the economic management of Britain by both Labour and Conservative governments. In July 1952, he warned that:

> leading men on both front benches know perfectly well that we are living on what is left of our thrifty Victorian ancestors and on the savings of industry, which ought to be applied to replacing well-worn plant and equipment.

On Harold Wilson's resignation in 1951, Bracken wrote:

> Of Mr Wilson it may be said that he was over-promoted and has now been over-demoted.

And on the designs for the proposed Royal Festival Hall:

> In appearance the new hall will be like a Zeppelin on stilts. Its facade might not look out of place among the gas-holders of Beckton

---

21 Kynaston, p. 360

or the factories that line the Great West Road. Concert-goers will have to try to concentrate on their music amidst the roar of trains on Charing Cross Bridge, which is only a few yards away.

As the 1950s progressed, Bracken's interest in the paper declined and he became increasingly hard to deal with. Gordon Newton, editor of the *Financial Times* from 1949 to 1972, recalls of the 1950s:

> What kind of man did Bracken become? He kept until near the end that commanding presence and that ability to talk in company on almost any subject. But the ebullience gradually left him. He became withdrawn and morose. He lived increasingly in the past to such an extent that some of those close to him must have know the inner history of the war by heart. And most important so far as the paper was concerned he became fearful of the future. As the confidence ebbed so it became more difficult to obtain a decision from him, so it became practically impossible if as a result money had to be spent.[22]

In his last years, he found solace in his financial and moral support for his old school, Sedbergh, where he would frequently spend weekends. He gave money for the new Library, over the entrance to which are inscribed the words 'Remember Winston Churchill'. He also took an active interest in Ampleforth, the Yorkshire Roman Catholic public school run by the Benedictine monks. In 1950, he launched a new monthly magazine, *History Today*. He was also active as a Trustee of the Churchill Trust and helped in the initial financing of Churchill College, Cambridge. Bracken did Beaverbrook a similar service by acting as trustee for scholarships for Canadian students in Britain funded by the University of New Brunswick at Fredericton, of which Beaverbrook was Chancellor. One of his last acts was to persuade Francis Mathew, the Manager of *The Times*, to purchase Eden's memoirs for serialization, thus guaranteeing Eden a measure of financial security in his retirement.

In January 1958, Bracken was diagnosed as having throat cancer. To the modern medical mind this was, perhaps, not surprising, as Bracken had once calculated with Robert Bruce-Lockhart that at an average rate of consumption of 4 cigars and 40 cigarettes daily, by 1944 alone he had smoked 28,000 cigars and 280,000 cigarettes — 'We did not get down to his bottles of whisky and

---

22 Kynaston, p. 214.

champagne.'[23] Despite cobalt treatment his condition quickly deteriorated and by May it was clear that he was dying. In July he asked to be moved to Sir Patrick Hennessy's flat overlooking St. James's Park. It was there that he died on 8 August. His estate totalled £142,032. The main beneficiary of his will was, appropriately enough, Churchill College, Cambridge.

2

LORD BEAVERBROOK

Beaverbrook was the most celebrated of that peculiar breed of men — the 'Press Baron'. Accused by Baldwin of wielding 'power without responsibility', Beaverbrook aroused a degree of resentment and mistrust amongst politicians and civil servants that has rarely been equalled among public figures in modern British history. To a certain extent he deserved this; presbyterianism and an impish sense of mischief were the two guiding lights of his life.

Like Brendan Bracken, Beaverbrook was a self-made man born in a British dominion and was thus essentially an outsider in the charmed circle of British, and particularly Conservative, politics. Born in 1879 to a Church of Scotland Minister who had emigrated to Canada in 1864, Max Aitken (he was created Lord Beaverbrook in 1916) liked to think of himself as a 'son of the manse'. Like the young Churchill, Max Aitken proved himself to be 'incurably idle' at school, but considerably better at achieving things in the real world. During the years 1906 to 1910, he assiduously amassed a fortune through business deals in Montreal and Toronto. Having made several millions of dollars, in 1910 he set sail for England to enter the world of politics in the capital of the Empire, never to take up permanent residence in Canada again — but retaining the rasping Canadian accent to the end. It is easy to see what drew Bracken and Beaverbrook together. They were both essentially buccaneers, self-made men who believed in the ethical and

[23] *Bruce-Lockhart Diaries*, 27 September 1944.

moral values of competitive capitalism from which they had both benefited so spectacularly. Michael Foot's description of Beaverbrook, culled from a long and deep friendship, could equally well be applied to Bracken:

> he was a rampaging individualist — no one could ever question that — and he always favoured the rumbustious, marauding private enterprise system which had enabled him to become a multi — or, as he would call it, a maxi-millionaire.
> But he brought with him too, in those pre-1914 days, inherited from his Covenanting ancestors or blown across to him in the Continent of his birth from the tradition of American populism, a detestation for the stuffiness and stupidities and snobberies of the English Establishment. He was an instinctive radical.....[1]

Max Aitken's political career blossomed in London through the patronage of his fellow-Canadian Andrew Bonar Law, leader of the Conservative Party. It was through Bonar Law that Aitken found the seat of Ashton-under-Lyne, which he held for the Conservatives until raised to the peerage in 1916. Much as Bracken hitched his star to Churchill, so Aitken hitched his star to Bonar Law. This first phase of his political career was when Aitken earned his reputation as a political intriguer; he was rightly credited as the 'kingmaker' who persuaded Bonar Law to pull out of Asquith's coalition government in December 1916, thus paving the way for the accession of Lloyd George. Having failed to gain office in the new government, Aitken was compensated by being raised to the peerage as Lord Beaverbrook. However, in February 1918 Beaverbrook was appointed Minister of Information and Chancellor of the Duchy of Lancaster, a post he held until the end of the War. More importantly, though, he continued to act as Bonar Law's 'faithful chela' and the height of his political influence was secured when Bonar Law became Prime Minister in November 1922 with a thumping Conservative victory at the polls. However, dreams turned to ashes as after only 100 days of the new government Bonar Law was forced by ill-health to resign; he died in October 1923. Beaverbrook was never again to enjoy the same kind of power and influence that he had experienced from 1916 to 1923, even under Churchill.

However, as though to compensate for his political isolation, Beaverbrook began to focus his energies on his nascent newspa-

---

[1] Michael Foot, *Debts of Honour* (Poynter, 1980), p. 75.

per empire and it was in his role as a newspaper proprietor that he was to become most widely known. In November 1916 he acquired control of the *Daily Express*, an ailing, minor publication that within 10 years had been transformed into Britain's biggest-selling daily newspaper, peaking at a circulation of 2,329,000 in 1938. The other papers in the Beaverbrook stable were the *Evening Standard*, the most famous feature of which were the cartoons by Low, and the *Sunday Express*. As he explained to a surprised Royal Commission on the Press in 1947, Beaverbrook ran his papers 'to propagand'. It was through his papers that Beaverbrook sought to establish his position as an independent political force, once he became increasingly estranged from the inner sanctum of Conservative Party politics after the death of Bonar Law. In doing so, he was hardly unique; Lord Rothermere tried to do much the same with his newspapers, principally the *Daily Mail* — often in tandem with Beaverbrook.

The Beaverbrook papers thus came to reflect their master's voice. There is no doubt that Beaverbrook had considerable gifts as a journalist — his staccato prose, which he employed on everything from Cabinet memoranda to his private correspondence, was essentially the prose of a popular newspaper leader writer, a style that has hardly changed to this day. However, Beaverbrook was also fortunate in acquiring the services of two technically outstanding journalists who gave the *Daily Express* the edge over all its rivals, namely Arthur Christiansen, editor of the *Daily Express* from 1933 to 1956, and E.J. Robertson, general manager of Express newspapers from 1921 to 1955. In Christiansen's own words 'the policies were Lord Beaverbrook's job, the presentation mine.'[2]

And of Robertson, A.J.P. Taylor, Beaverbrook's official biographer, has written:

> Unlike Northcliffe, Beaverbrook rarely went to the office, and he had no experience on the technical side. He never supervised his own articles on the Stone or set a page. He operated from afar, sometimes stimulating, sometimes criticizing. He knew that he could rely on Robertson, and his faith was abundantly justified. Beaverbrook's newspapers rested on the firm foundation of Robertson for more than a generation.[3]

Beaverbrook kept a strict control on the political content of his

[2] Arthur Christiansen, *Headlines All My Life* (Heinemann,1961), p. 144.
[3] Taylor, p. 172.

papers, and editors were likely to be pursued by messages and memos from around the world as the peripatetic proprietor scrutinised their every action. Beaverbrook also became famous for fostering a coterie of very able left-wing journalists on his papers, such as Francis Williams, Michael Foot, Frank Owen, Frank Buchman and David Low. These journalists were attracted by the radicalism and vigour of Beaverbrook and the latter frequently courted the displeasure of Conservative Central Office by harbouring such dangerous subversives on his newspapers. However, the alleged independence of such journalists was somewhat of a myth; all were obliged to move on to newspapers with which they felt a greater degree of political sympathy. As Michael Foot, editor of the wartime *Evening Standard*, diplomatically put it in his letter of resignation to Beaverbrook in 1944:

> I know you never ask me to write views with which I disagree. But as this works out it is good business neither for you or for me. The leaders which I now write are hardly worth writing since they are non-committal and from my point of view I am associated with a newspaper group against whose policies (but not against the proprietor) I am resolved to wage perpetual war.... The compromise worked and certainly to my advantage. But I do not see how it could work very much longer. The business of maintaining allegiance to my own political ideal and to a newspaper which fundamentally must be opposed to them is too difficult.[4]

Did Beaverbrook succeed in influencing the course of politics through his newspapers? Tom Driberg entitled his 1954 biography of Beaverbrook *A Study in Power and Frustration*, which is a fairly accurate summary of Beaverbrook's career as a newspaper proprietor, for it remains incontrovertible that he achieved far more as a behind-the-scenes manipulator in the days of Bonar Law and under Churchill during the Second World War than when he ran his more public and independent crusades in his papers. His greatest campaign — for Empire Free Trade — failed; and it was during the public controversy over this campaign that Baldwin, under attack from both the Rothermere and Beaverbrook presses, uttered his fateful words about the 'Press Barons' exercising 'Power without responsibility — the prerogative of the harlot through the ages'. Beaverbrook was a staunch defender of the appeasement policies of Chamberlain, which ended in disaster for the country

---

4 Taylor, p. 172.

and considerable embarrassment for Beaverbrook when *The Daily Express* declared that 'Britain will not be involved in a European War' only three weeks before war actually broke out. It was during this period that his friendship with Churchill all but ceased, as Beaverbrook aligned himself firmly with the Chamberlainites in trying to 'appease' Nazi Germany — even to the extent of secretly subsidising the Home Secretary, Sir Samuel Hoare, to the tune of £2,000 p.a. from 1938 to 1940 in the hope that Hoare would duly succeed Chamberlain and thus Beaverbrook would find himself restored to his cherished position of influence in Downing Street.[5] During the war, his papers vigorously campaigned for a 'Second Front Now' in 1942 to relieve the pressure on the Russians, but to no avail. Towards the end of the war the Express newspapers railled without success against the Bretton Woods financial agreements of Keynes's making, and the papers also fought a vigorous campaign on behalf of the Conservative Party in the general election of 1945 — which if anything persuaded people to vote Labour. In the post-war world the Beaverbrook press embraced the cause of friendship with the Soviet Union, which seemed to impress neither the British public nor the Soviet Union and during the 1950s the Beaverbrook Press championed the cause of Empire whilst the nationalist currents that had been unleashed since 1945 ensured that Britain was obliged to divest itself of most of its Imperial obligations during that period. From the 1920s on, Beaverbrook found himself swimming against the tide of domestic and international politics at every corner; it was indeed a case of 'power and frustration'.

Beaverbrook obtained the stature that he did not because of his sometimes erratic and often perverse independent forays into politics via his newspapers, but through the magnanimity of his old friend Winston Churchill, who took Beaverbrook into his wartime Cabinet in May 1940 as the new Minister of Aircraft Production. Having fought against Churchill's anti-appeasement politics throughout the late 1930s — even to the extent of relieving Churchill of his column in the *Evening Standard* — Beaverbrook now once again found himself in the centre of things, and together with Bracken and Professor Lindemann (later Lord Cher-

---

[5] See Richard Cockett, *Twilight of Truth* (Weidenfeld & Nicolson, 1989), pp. 57–59.

well) formed Churchill's midnight 'kitchen cabinet'.

Beaverbrook's energy and his impatience with conventional procedures were exactly suited to the task of creating the Ministry of Aircraft Production from scratch and then producing enough planes to fight off the imminent invasion of Britain. That he succeeded in his task so brilliantly was without doubt Beaverbrook's crowning achievement. Of Beaverbrook during those anxious, yet glorious, summer months Churchill later wrote: 'He did not fail. This was his hour'.[6] In April 1941 Beaverbrook was created Minister of State, with a brief as general overlord of production. It was in this job that Beaverbrook undertook his famous mission to Moscow in September 1941 in order to arrange the long-term supply of the Russian Armies. He subsequently became the Cabinet's most outspoken supporter of Soviet Russia — for once aligning himself with some of the more left-wing journalists on his own papers. In December he completed a similar trip to Washington to galvanise the recently combatant America into increasing their war production. It was largely due to Beaverbrook's urgent and inspiring promptings that Roosevelt was persuaded to arbitrarily increase his projected output figures by 50% in his 'victory programme' announced to Congress on 7 January 1942.

However, the strain and stresses of almost two years of working flat out had taken their toll on the 63 year old 'Press Baron'; Harold Macmillan, parliamentary secretary to the Ministry from 1941 to 1942, later wrote that by 1942:

> Beaverbrook had undergone tremendous strain for twenty arduous months. His exertions at the Ministry of Aircraft Production were almost superhuman. His recent journeys to Moscow and Washington under the harsh conditions of travelling in war-time, had affected him severely. His asthma had grown daily worse. The frame had become too weak to sustain the flame of the spirit.[7]

Beaverbrook's ministerial life was also plagued by constant disputes with the most powerful Labour member in the Cabinet, Ernest Bevin. As Minister of Labour, Bevin resented Beaverbrook's encroachments on what he saw as his own ministerial brief by Beaverbrook in his role as 'Production Supremo'. Matters came to a head in the winter of 1941-2. In January 1942,

---

6 Churchill, *The History of the Second World War* (London, 1949) Vol.II, p. 286.
7 Harold Macmillam, *The Blast of War* (Macmillan, 1967), p. 144.

Beaverbrook became the Minister of Production, but such were the inter-departmental conflicts that this caused, especially at the Ministry of Labour, that by February 28 Beaverbrook had resigned from the government.

> Writing to Eden three days later, Beaverbrook put his three reasons [for resignation].... (a) Asthma; (b) Attlee's anti-Russian policy; (c) responsibility without power as minister of production.[8]

After his resignation, Beaverbrook appointed himself as leader of the 'Second Front Now' campaign for the rest of 1942. Such was his undoubted personal popularity at the time, and the public association of him with Russia at the height of that country's wartime popularity, that he might also have entertained hopes of succeeding Churchill as Prime Minister, as the occupant of Number 10 Downing Street's fortunes fell to their lowest ebb with the fall of Tobruk in June 1941, following hard on the heels of the fall of Malaya, Singapore and other military disasters. There is no doubt that the continuing military failures of Churchill's government contributed to considerable political uncertainty during 1942 — Sir Stafford Cripps was another name widely canvassed as a successor to Churchill — but the Prime Minister's position was irrevocably restored by the victory at El Alamein in October 1942.[9]

In September 1943, Beaverbrook returned to the government as Lord Privy Seal. He had no department to run, so could thus pick and choose the issues in which he might interfere. A.J.P. Taylor has written with some justification that:

> The twenty-one months which Beaverbrook spent as Lord Privy Seal were the most agreeable of his political life. He was once more on the inside. He knew everything that was going on in war, international and home politics. But the storms which blew around others did not reach him.... He saw the war cabinet papers without the harassment of attending its meetings. He was again intimate with Churchill, providing advice and entertainment in full measure."[10]

---

[8] Taylor, p. 518
[9] See Kevin Jefferys, ed., *Labour and the Wartime Coalition: from the diary of James Chuter Ede 1941–1945* (Historians' Press, 1987), pp. 37–92 for an account of the various intrigues within the government during this period.
[10] Taylor, p. 548.

Like Bracken, Beaverbrook thoroughly enjoyed power and the privilege of being so near to the centre of it as an intimate of Churchill. It was during the war that the two became soul mates, delighting in the unconventional, buccaneering and energetic spirit in which Churchill's highly personalised administration was run. Bracken and Beaverbrook delighted in having fun at the expense of their more staid and establishment-minded socialist coalition colleagues such as Hugh Dalton and Clement Attlee. They shared a similar outlook towards the Tory party, unafraid to criticize the Tory 'grandees' such as Lords Halifax, Salisbury and Derby. Sir John Colville, himself educated at Harrow and a scion of an old English family, recorded his observations of a dinner he attended with Harold Balfour, the 11th Marquis of Queensberry and Beaverbrook and Bracken:

> Before dinner there was an incident which was indicative of the strong social chip on Lord Beaverbrook's shoulder. In the course of attacking Eden he said that the latter owed his success to his birth and education. He then turned on the assembled company and said that true men of quality, like Harold Balfour, Brendan and himself had worked their way up from nothing by sheer hard work and ability, whereas Lord Queensberry and I were like Anthony Eden and had only got where we were because of the circumstances in which we were born... we had an excellent dinner with a magnum of champagne and lots of brandy, followed by a rotten film. When Balfour and Queensberry had gone, there followed a long political conversation.... The evening was fun, with real buccaneering, racketeering atmosphere. Of course, they are both utterly mischievous and will do the Conservative Party countless harm, at this election and afterwards.[11]

For many, Colville's prediction was to seem to be all too accurate. During the last year of the war Beaverbrook began to take an increasing interest in the general election that he knew must come at the end of the war. He threw himself into the election campaign of June 1945 with his customary gusto, and was thus held to be largely responsible for the debâcle that followed. This was not altogether fair, for although his newspaper campaign was clumsy and superficial, Beaverbrook did not have anything to do with Churchill's notorious 'Gestapo Speech' which opened the Conservative campaign and from which the party never recovered. The general election of 1945 was a watershed for Beaverbrook,

11 John Colville, *The Fringes of Power*, Volume II, May 27, 1945.

for it marked his ultimate departure from British politics, and, come to that, from Britain as well. He had no contacts in the new Labour government and had little sympathy for their policies. His position with the Conservatives was not much better, as many continued to hold him responsible for the 1945 defeat; and as time went by he found himself as far out of sympathy as Bracken was with the new 'progressive' Conservatism of Eden, Butler and Macmillan.

The nineteen years left to him were spent in a regular migration from one Beaverbrook house to the next in search of peace and sun. In 1946 he bought Cromarty House at Montego Bay, Jamaica; and Aitken House at Nassau in the Bahamas was bought in 1947. His house at Nassau became his regular winter bolt-hole. The autumn was spent in Fredericton, New Brunswick, where he was appointed Chancellor of the University in May 1947. He attended every annual degree ceremony in October from then until 1963; 'Fredericton became the most fixed point in his restless life'.[12] In the spring and early summer he returned to England, maintaining his house at Cherkley and a flat in Arlington House in St. James's Street. In the summer he departed for his house at La Capponcina, at Cap d'Ail near Monte Carlo where his yacht was moored. During these annual peregrinations he kept in daily contact with his Express editors in London, often telephoning them several times a day to dictate leaders and suggest stories. He never ceased to take an active interest in his papers, but after 1945 his mind turned to other things.

He delighted in his duties at the University of New Brunswick and as well as endowing scholarships to the University he also founded the Beaverbrook art gallery at Fredericton and bequeathed numerous smaller gifts. So impressed were the burghers of New Brunswick by this deluge of patronage that in 1962 they established 25 May as Beaverbrook Day and a provincial holiday. He also turned his hand to writing several historical books during the 1950s and early 1960s, including accounts of Lloyd George (1963), his Canadian friend Sir James Dunn (1961), R. R. Bennett (1959), his own *Early Life* (1964) and the *Abdication Crisis* (1966). He spent considerable time in cultivating the Presbyterian Church and also spent considerable energy on maintaining his

---

12 Taylor, p. 577.

friendship with Churchill. Although Beaverbrook had no political influence on his old friend any more, he was assiduous in making Churchill's life as easy as possible, even to the extent of installing a lift at La Capponcina for Churchill's use during the latter's frequent sojourns there. But his links with political Britain were gone; he relied on Bracken's letters for his inside political information.

Beaverbrook died on 9 June 1964. His son, Max Aitken, a distinguished fighter-pilot during the Battle of Britain, renounced the hereditary title; there could only be one Lord Beaverbrook.

3

BRACKEN AND BEAVERBROOK — THE CORRESPONDENCE

The correspondence of Bracken and Beaverbrook is, above all, a record of their friendship. As such, it reflects both the ups and downs of a relationship that was never without its strains; it could hardly be otherwise with two such individualistic and cantankerous characters.

They probably met for the first time in 1923, through J.L. Garvin or Churchill. Beaverbrook was already the famous 'kingmaker' and 'Press Baron', Bracken the young and mysterious adventurer. There is a story, possibly apocryphal, about Beaverbrook's method of satisfying himself that the brash social and political climber was as fearless and ingenious as he liked to make out. It is told by Andrew Boyle:

> Beaverbrook is said to have requested [Bracken's] help, claiming that he had been having trouble with the Foreign Secretary. Curzon, it appeared, was insisting that part of a public speech he had recently delivered, and which had been extensively quoted in Express newspapers, did him, Curzon, a grave injustice. The original text had been revised beforehand, so that the offending words had never been uttered. Beaverbrook confessed that he disbelieved Curzon's tale for two reasons; first the Marquis took some swallowing at the best of time, but second and more important, he, Lord Beaverbrook had gained possession of the notes which Curzon used on the day he spoke.
> 'What I want', said Beaverbrook, 'is Curzon's own signature on his own handiwork. Will you get it for me?'
> It was a madly quixotic proposition. Yet Bracken often boasted later that he thought nothing of it, carrying it off perfectly and without turning a hair. According to his own account, he reconnoitered Curzon's official residence, noting when the policemen changed shifts, when the doors were locked and the lights put out at night, and when the same doors were opened (and by whom) in

the morning.... He proposed to 'effect an entry' as soon as the sleepy servant unbarred the front door to put out the cat and haul in the milk before breakfast. Bracken did so with despatch, bounded up the stairs before the startled retainer could stop him, and made straight for Curzon's bedroom. The layout of the house, he claimed, had been conveniently provided for him in advance; and he had, of course, memorized it. The Marquis had not yet risen, but he was disturbed by the unceremonious descent on him of a person who did not even bother to knock first. The glazed look in his eyes when he saw Bracken seemed to reflect horror as well as astonishment, as though he had been expecting a footman with a tray of tea instead of a well-dressed, aggressive stranger who thrust a document under his nose and said 'Sign here'.

'Who knows?' commented a friend of Bracken's who heard all about the alleged incident at second hand. 'Maybe the Marquis in the moment of waking feared that some thug from his vice-regal days had come liquidate him'.

At any rate, Curzon in his shocked condition did as he was told, scrawling his signature across the paper with the intruder's fountain pen. Then Bracken left the room, prudently refraining from going out the way he had come in. By now, he realized, the alarm would have been raised by the servant he had stepped over at the front door. So he opened a first floor side-window, lowered himself to a convenient drainpipe, and shinned down to safety. According to Bracken, Beaverbrook laughed uproariously when he received the document and learnt in detail how Curzon's signature had been obtained.[1]

It has the ring of truth to it. However, their friendship never flourished during the inter-war years. Their great bond, of course, was Churchill; but whereas Bracken always willingly operated in Churchill's shadow, Beaverbrook pursued his own political lines during the 1920s and 1930s, and most of the time he found himself opposed politically to Churchill. Just as his relations with Churchill cooled, so his earlier interest in Bracken never flowered. The lack of correspondence between the two in the 1930s testifies to this. In 1935, an ugly quarrel erupted between them when the *Sunday Express* published a story about how the reluctant Bracken was forced to produce his birth certificate during the North Paddington campaign of 1929. There was certainly a lot of criticism of Beaverbrook in Bracken's newspapers, which Beaverbrook repaid in kind; so much so that on one occasion Bracken threatened to bring a law suit against the Canadian 'Press

1 Boyle, p. 107–108.

Baron'. It was during this period of estrangement that Beaverbrook also decided to satisfy himself about Bracken's mysterious past, despatching a reporter called Percy Hoskins to Ireland to unearth Bracken's roots. Hoskins duly ran the Bracken family to ground, but at the time Beaverbrook refrained from using information about which Bracken was so sensitive. However, it was not like Beaverbrook to resist the temptation to play with this gem of historical knowledge and it duly appeared in the *Evening Standard* on 23 June 1944. This article also related how Bracken's Fenian father had once been refused a gun licence. The enraged Minister of Information used his powers to excise this passage from the later edition, thus casting a temporary cloud over their friendship.

Such pranks showed how difficult it was to maintain a solid friendship with the 'Beaver'. Beaverbrook's sense of mischief was not easily suppressed. Lysaght has correctly observed that Bracken's friendship with Beaverbrook was preserved

> more by mutual entertainment than by mutual trust.... Despite an age difference of over twenty years, Bracken and Beaverbrook had much in common. They both ranked good conversation and good writing among the great delights of life. They were both aggressive British patriots. They were both cynical and irreverent in manner, yet possessed of a measure of genuine idealism deep down. Bracken acquired many of the older man's mannerisms as a newspaper controller, although never his essential style.[2]

In the end, such shared 'joie de vivre' triumphed over Beaverbrook's unpredictable enthusiasm for mischief.

However, during the late 1930s their friendship warmed considerably and was irrevocably cemented by their shared experience in Churchill's 'kitchen cabinet' during Britain's 'Finest Hour' in 1940–41. Churchill was the great link in their life, and he dominates their correspondence to a considerable degree. Beaverbrook's relationship to Churchill was more complex than Bracken's. As Beaverbrook always aspired to an independent political position of his own, he was always bound to view Churchill as much as a rival than as a friend. This was especially true of the 1930s when Beaverbrook and Churchill diverged politically and saw very little of each other. In 1942, Beaverbrook might even have hoped to supplant Churchill as war premier — there

2 Lysaght, p. 149.

is certainly some evidence to support this thesis. But it was only after the war, with the collapse of all Beaverbrook's own political causes and ambitions in the ruin of the 1945 election, that Beaverbrook became the firm and dependable boon companion that has passed into legend. This is clearly evident from the correspondence. Before 1940 their correspondence about Churchill is fractious, whereas after 1945 they both bask in the warm memories of a more heroic age with Churchill at the helm. Bracken's relationship with Churchill was, of course, straightforward. His letters are testimony to the warmth and affection that he held for Churchill and of the numerous services, both large and small, that he undertook on Churchill's behalf.

The only reason that so few letters survive from the war years is that during this period of high drama Beaverbrook and Bracken must have seen each other at least several times a day. Whereas the lack of correspondence during the inter-war years testifies to the coolness of their relationship, the lack of correspondence during the war years testifies to a warm friendship. Moreover, Beaverbrook and Bracken found themselves increasingly united in political opposition against their fellow Conservatives who in the later years of the war were drifting towards the planned economy and the Welfare State. Having formerly been friends, they now found themselves to be intimate political allies as well. They were both firm believers in private enterprise and the market economy and fought their corner in the Conservative Party. Their post-1945 correspondence remains an excellent analysis of the failings of the 'Butskellite' consensus policies that they laboured so hard against; just as it remains an excellent testimony to the survival of a free market critique within the ranks of the Conservative Party. In the domestic political context their correspondence is an intriguing 'Thatcherite' analysis of Britain's post-war economic ills. After 1945, their friendship never paled.

Bracken wrote to entertain as much as to inform. His letters give a hint of his conversational skills which endeared him to so many. The 2nd Earl of Birkenhead later wrote:

> To receive a letter from Bracken was a two-fold pleasure. The contents were always pungent and stimulating because he was incapable of boredom, and secondly he wrote an exquisite and meticulous hand. Equally striking was his dominion over the English language, and one of the delights of his conversation was its

obvious spontaneity.[3]

Beaverbrook, on the other hand, was not a wordsmith. Bracken spoke and wrote as much as for his own amusement as anything else. Beaverbrook, as Lord Moran, Churchill's Boswellising physician, noted 'is only concerned with the bare drama of events'. Beaverbrook did not share Bracken's (and Churchill's) delight in exploring the possibilities of the English language; Lord Moran shrewdly noted that 'The Beaver' was 'a miser about words'.[4] If this seems a strange thing to write about a man whom many considered to be England's pre-eminent journalist, it was, nonetheless, true.

As Bracken had all his papers incinerated, not all of Beaverbrook's letters to Bracken survive. However his secretaries made copies of the vast majority of them, but it does mean that their correspondence is therefore not complete. The entire surviving correspondence can be found in files 56 to 59 of the Beaverbrook Papers at the House of Lords Record Office, London. The Bracken letters in these files are almost all typed copies of his original, handwritten letters. They were copied by a secretary in the Beaverbrook library, established after Beaverbrook's death. On the break-up of the Beaverbrook library in 1975, the albums of original letters to Beaverbrook from people such as Bracken and Churchill were sold privately and some correspondence was later auctioned at Southeby's. Only a handful of Bracken's original letters survive, written in his much admired hand.

About 95 per cent of the correspondence in the House of Lords Record Office is published here. I have omitted very few letters in their entirety; those that are omitted relate to obscure matters such as Bracken's recommendations for Beaverbrook's church funding in Scotland and Beaverbrook's more bland reports of happenings in Jamaica and Canada. The only passages in the letters that I have consistently excised refer to the University of New Brunswick — I have left out most of their exchanges on the minutiae of administering the University and its scholarship programme, with which Bracken and Beaverbrook were closely involved. Nonetheless I have included some passages relating to this subject to afford the reader a flavour of their discussions on

---

[3] *Brendan Bracken: Portraits and Appreciations*, p. 41.
[4] Moran, p. 9.

these matters. I have also omitted a little of Beaverbrook's more obscure social gossip from his letters from Jamaica and the South of France. Otherwise their correspondence is published in total.

At the end of the last file of their correspondence, there is a typewritten note by Beaverbrook:

> .... There is something to be said for a life of Bracken. It's a wonderful story of the bare foot, brought up in conditions reverse of Empire, subversive of Empire's associations. And yet going up from bare foot boy to such importance in the empire that he was... possibly second only to Churchill.[5]

---

5 House of Lords Record Office, Beaverbrook Papers C/59.

4

THE INTER-WAR YEARS: 1925–1939

Bracken to Beaverbrook
4 May 1925

English Life,
1 & 2, Goldsmith Street,
Fleet Street, E.C.4

Dear Lord Beaverbrook,

I enclose a copy of English Life[1] and a reproduction of Sargent's drawing of Winston. Despite the black fourpence you might like to have it.

Yours very truly,
Brendan Bracken

Beaverbrook to Bracken
5 May 1925

Dear Bracken,

Very many thanks for your letter of 4th and for the enclosure. I am very glad to have the reproduction of Sargent's drawing.

My opinion of Winston has not altered. I knew from the beginning he would give in to the Bankers on the Gold Standard, which I think is the biggest sin in this Budget.[2]

Yours sincerely

---

1 Published by Eyre and Spottiswoode. Bracken had been editor of the magazine since January 1924.
2 In his first Budget as Chancellor of the Exchequer, on 25 April 1925, Churchill announced the restoration of the Gold Standard; a policy for which Montague Norman, the powerful Governor of the Bank of England, was largely responsible.

Beaverbrook to Bracken
14 January 1931
My dear Brendan,
I write to let you know that you made a fine impression on the Newspapers Proprietors' Association at their meeting the other day.

Altogether apart from the line you took up, you impressed everybody by the cogency of your argument and the strength with which you stressed your viewpoint.

Don't bother to answer this letter.

Yours sincerely,

Bracken to Beaverbrook   8, Lord North Street,
14 January 1931   Westminster
Dear Lord Beaverbrook,
It may seem odd that one of the smallest of political tyros should attempt to persuade a master of politics to interest himself in a great public affair. But the memory of the agreeable lunch you gave me not long ago encourages me to write to you about the India Conference.[3] This wretched Government, with the aid of the Liberals and some eminent Tories, is about to commit us to one of the most fatal decisions in all our history, and there is practically no opposition to their policy.

Disagreeing, as I did, with much of your Empire Free Trade policy,[4] I could not but admire all the force and resources which you put into your campaign, and I believe that if those great talents were devoted to combatting defeatism, it would still be possible to preserve the essentials of British rule in India.

Yours sincerely

---

3 The Round Table India Conference, 12 Nov. 1930–19 Jan. 1931, was chaired by Prime Minister Ramsay MacDonald and decided that India would be allowed to advance quite rapidly towards self-government. It was a policy to which Churchill, and hence Bracken, were much opposed.
4 From 1929–1931, Beaverbrook openly campaigned against the Conservative Party leadership for a policy of tariff reform, or Empire Free Trade.

Beaverbrook to Bracken
9 December 1931
My dear Brendan,
 I have heard very bad news about you this morning.
 I am told that you dined with Lady Cunard[5] last night.
 If you continue in this course you will have to give up walking in Parnell's[6] footsteps.
 I have no doubt that her ladyship is the most estimable of London's fashionable hostesses.

                Yours ever,

Bracken to Beaverbrook   20, Bishopsgate,
9 December 1931   London, E.C.2.
My dear Max
 Many thanks for sending me the letters from your minions. As the Daily News, the Morning Post and a number of other papers published similar material, it is no use singling out the Sunday Express for invidious criticism.
 In any event, the affair is really petty, but as the public have quite rightly stirred themselves up about buying British and using British services, some temporary damage may have been done to Winston. But as his reason for travelling to America by the Europa was a righteous one, he deserves much credit.[7]
 We must meet soon.

              (Sgd) Yours ever
                 BRENDAN

Bracken to Beaverbrook
8 April 1936 (Telegram)
Mr Baldwins political life is passing unpeacefully to its close.[8]

                  Bracken

5 Lady Cunard (1896–1965); Society hostess to political and literary London.
6 Charles Parnell (1836–1891): Irish Nationalist leader.
7 On 5 December 1931, Churchill set sail for America on board the German liner *Europa*, which aroused some hostile criticism in Britain amidst the depths of the depression.
8 Stanley Baldwin (1867–1947). Prime Minister 1923–4, 1924–9, 1935–7. This is probably a reference to the turmoil created by Hitler's invasion of the Rhineland in March and the continuing crisis in Abyssinia,

Beaverbrook to Bracken
8 April 1936
(Telegram, Cannes)
I have ordered my top hat with mourning coat and black gloves so please see I'm not disappointed. Wish you would come here for Easter to stay with me.

Max

Bracken to Beaverbrook   8 Lord North Street,
May 1936   Westminster
My dear friend
  On arriving from a journey in Devonshire I got the news that a return of asthma has blown you back to Cannes.
  To one who looks upon your company as one of the happiest things in life, this news is grievous.
  You have a spirit stronger to bear your hardships than I have to think of them. And so I tell you unless you come home quickly and in good health, I will add to your woes by visiting you in Cannes.

Brendan

Bracken to Beaverbrook   20, Bishopsgate,
22 September 1936   London, E.C.2.
My dear Max
  You might like to look at the balance sheet of West Australian Newspapers Limited. Profits for the last financial year, after providing £15,000 for taxes, were £69,883. Pretty good.
  Western Australia is a very small place. The profits earned by the leading newspapers in the states of Victoria and New South Wales are very much greater. I am told that the average annual profits of the Sydney Morning Herald for a period of ten years amount to a quarter of a million pounds a year.
  Australia is indeed a good country for the newspaper owner. Keith Murdoch,[9] who runs the biggest group of newspapers in

---

which Mussolini had invaded in 1935. In fact, Baldwin's fortunes were to be restored by his masterly handling of the Abdication Crisis in December 1936 and he did not resign until May 1937.

9 Sir Keith Murdoch, Australian newspaper proprietor, father of Rupert

Australia is, I think, in England.

A.G.Millar[10] to Bracken
24 September 1936
Dear Mr Bracken,
 Lord Beaverbrook returns the Tenth Report of the Directors of West Australian Newspapers, Ltd. He is very much obliged to you for showing it to him.
 Lord Beaverbrook looks forward to an early visit from you to Cherkley.
 He went to see Mr Churchill yesterday and lunched with him at Westerham.

Bracken to Beaverbrook   8 Lord North Street,
14 January 1937   Westminster
Much Missed Max,
 How are you? And is Arizona doing the work left undone by that tribe of English, foreign and oriental doctors who have been let loose upon you during the last year?
 While you've been resting from your labours your works are mightily following you. The S. Daily Express has made Camrose[11] meet his Culloden. That nobleman has been wise in his decision to retire from what is called popular newspapers. Poor old R[12] — who is getting more and more like Lady Houston[13] in his handling of controversies — has been encouraging his papers to make ponderous attacks on Layton.[14] Your Express figures must have made

   Murdoch.
10 A. G. Millar was Beaverbrook's secretary. He is described by A. J. P. Taylor (*Beaverbrook*, p. 580) as 'The perfect secretary.... The key figure in Beaverbrook's life.'
11 1st Viscount Camrose (1879–1954). Newspaper proprietor and owner, together with his brother Viscount Kemsley, of the *Daily Telegraph* and a string of national and local papers
12 1st Viscount Rothermere (1868–1940). Younger brother of Viscount Northcliffe and proprietor of the *Daily Mail*, the *Evening News* and other papers.
13 Lady Houston (1857–1936). Notable for her extreme wealth and eccentricity of manner.
14 Sir Walter Layton (1884–1966). Economist, editor of *The Economist* and editorial director of the Liberal national daily news paper the *News Chronicle*.

R and his satraps wince. We shall witness the N. Chronicle[15] beating the Mail's circulation. Northcliffe's[16] brothers are very much like Napoleon's.

Nothing much has happened since you left us. Baldwin is still looked upon as the re-incarnation of William the Silent. Our electro-plated Cromwell wd be wise to clear out before he takes another pluperfect political pearler. Your Neville Chamberlain[17] is no showman. He has just returned from a holiday in France. In his luggage were a pair of crutches. 'I took them as a precaution — luckily I had not to use them,' said the 68 year old heir to Baldwin's place!

Mr Simpson[18] is suing a lady named Mrs Sutherland who is said to have asserted that he got a dowry.

Our prim Runciman[19] is on his way to America. I'm glad you're there to keep an eye on him. He and Hull[20] are Siamese twins — the only true begotten Cobdenites left on earth.

Bless you dear Max. Come home soon. I'm finding it hard to play alone.

Brendan

Bracken to Beaverbrook   Villa Thalassa,
Late August 1937   La Croix,
                                                       Var

Max

What fun you gave us at Deauville. You are indeed the best of hosts & companions.

Preliminary twinges of depression begin to assail me when I

---

15 The *News Chronicle*.
16 1st Viscount Northcliffe (1865–1922). 'The Napoleon of Fleet Street' was the elder brother of Rothermere and founder, in 1896, of the *Daily Mail*. He was the first and most powerful of the 'Press Barons'.
17 Neville Chamberlain (1869–1940). The son of Joe Chamberlain; Minister of Health 1924 – 9, Chancellor of the Exchequer 1931–7, Prime Minister 1937–40.
18 Mr Edward Simpson was divorced from Mrs Wallis Simpson (later the Duchess of Windsor) in October 1936, thus precipitating the Abdication Crisis.
19 Walter Runciman (1870–1949). Liberal politician, President of the Board of Trade 1914–16, 1931–37. Mediator between the Czechoslovak Government and the Sudeten Germans, 1938.
20 Cordell Hull (1871–1955). Secretary of State of the United States of America, 1933–44.

think of your departure to Jamaica. You can hardly understand how greatly you will be missed.

Best wishes & thanks.

Brendan

The D.M[21] is a reformed paper. No mention of newsprint in four successive issues!

Bracken to Beaverbrook 8 Lord North Street,
17 December (1937) Westminster
Max

Your letter describing the delights of Miami & Nassau arrived on the coldest day known to London for many a year. Were Merrill here you might have seen an impetuous & expensive guest.

As the days passed one became hardened to this brutal climate. Though your invitation tempted me to escape it, I can't leave what you rightly called a feast or famine business. Famine is now the operative word. It doesn't daunt us, but we of the F.N.[22] must work hard. And so here I must remain grasping the moth eaten coat tails of the money changers.

The only happy memory I have of Charleston airfield is the remembrance of a well conditioned Max flying to the sun. Your selfish friend thought that London would be a cheerless place without you. Time sharpens the truth of that foreboding.

I send you the new supplement of the D.N.B.[23] Don't neglect to read Tom Jones[24] on Bonar Law & Dawson[25] on Northcliffe. Strange stuff in parts. The piece on Balfour is a small masterpiece. As an Imperialist you should read Goldie Biography.[26]

Bless you and how I miss you.

B.

---

21 The *Daily Mail*.
22 The *Financial News*.
23 The Dictionary of National Biography.
24 Dr Thomas Jones (1870–1955). Deputy Secretary to the Cabinet 1920–30. Confidant of Lloyd George and Baldwin.
25 Geoffrey Dawson (1874–1944). Editor of *The Times* 1912–19, 1923–41.
26 Sir George Goldie (1846–1925), a colonial trader who was credited as 'the founder of Nigeria' because of his chairmanship of the National African Company.

Bracken to Beaverbrook   8 Lord North Street,
24 January 1938   Westminster

Max

Your letter describing the joys of the Deep-South fills me with envy. The South bred Calhoun, America's greatest Presbyterian, & he became the father of secession. Go thou and do likewise. New life will be spring in England when we substitute taking for giving.

Our Brummagem Prime Minister[27] & his Minister of Agriculture[28] are now glorying in defeatism. They have made it crystal clear that the Government will prosper the great wens, at the expense of the farmers who feed them. Your loyal Frank Owen[29] attacks them. But the most of the press encourage their complacency.

London is livelier. When you departed the Hyde Park Hotel it descended into dullness. It has been awakened by four bright young West End gentlemen who used its hospitality to cudgel one of Cartier's directors bearing a parcel of jewels. Their leader is an old Etonian, a scion of an ancient family of bankers & the winner of a slander action against a young lady who said he was a giver of venereal disease.

More news from the gangster front. Cunningham Reid has begun his suit to sustain Marylebone's relations with Cassell's estate. If his spouse repeats in Court what she says in private society, there will no falling off in newspaper sales.

Our low trade is also brightening up. As you will see from the enclosed cutting Lord Kemsley[30] has launched an attack on the Daily Mirror. He wd be a better moral censor if he ceased to publish the Empire News. You will be surprised by the news that the staid Investors Chronicle is again attacking the Ostrer fraternity for linking football pools with films....

27 Neville Chamberlain had succeeded Baldwin as Prime Minister on 28 May 1937.
28 W. 'Shakes' Morrison (1893–1961) Minister of Agriculture and Fisheries 1936–39.
29 Frank Owen (1905–79). Beaverbrook journalist, Editor of the *Evening Standard* 1938–41, Editor of the *Daily Mail* 1947–50.
30 1st Viscount Kemsley (1883 – 1968). Proprietor of the *Sunday Times*, *Daily Sketch* and a string of provincial papers.

I wish you wd lighten the darkness of Stornoway House.

Bracken to Beaverbrook 20 Bishopsgate,
24 August 1938 London, E.C.2.
Max

Here is the Report on Germany's Economic Developments. I should like to return it on Monday.

You will not need to be told that any report on German economic conditions which emanates from Berlin is unlikely to be an objective document. But this Report is worth reading in so far as it shows the trends of Nazi industrial and financial policy, if as voluminous as some of the late lamented Mr Kreuger's Swedish Match Reports. And for all I (or anybody else in London) know, it may be equally disingenuous.

It is difficult — perhaps impossible — for outsiders to discover the real factors about the industrial and financial position in Germany. Anti-Nazis assert that Germany is drifting into an industrial and financial collapse. They say that the budget is fraudulent and that the good employment and trade figures are products of a hectic inflation. The Nazis usually claim that their economic system is as excellent as it is new. But they have to admit that their financial affairs are wrapped in mystery. This admission means much to any considering man. Mysterious finance is almost always crooked!

This Report cannot conceal the fact that Germany has little Gold and no credit. And since this Report appeared, the German Government have imposed further swingeing taxes on industry, and have ordained a ten-hour working day for German labour. These stark decisions rub the bloom off much of the Report.

Bracken to Beaverbrook 20 Bishopsgate,
16 December 1938 London, E.C.2.
Max

I've promised to stay with a friend in the country for Christmas. But as I have just heard that he is having a party of some twenty people staying with him, I am anxious to extricate myself from his hospitality. If I can do this, you know how delighted I shall be to spend Christmas with you.

While you have been away, there has been a hell of an underground row in the Government. Hudson[31] (of the Department of Overseas Trade), Dufferin,[32] and Strathcona,[33] and another Under-Secretary, who have access to certain papers of the Committee of Imperial Defence, denounced Belisha[34] for making unjustifiable statements regarding progress in certain re-armament departments. One of them tackled Inskip[35] about more statements, and that old gentlemen most surprisingly admitted the charge. He is also said to have roughly criticised Belisha.

The four Under-Secretaries interviewed the Prime Minister and threatened to resign. Chamberlain held a parley with them, in which they showed some firmness. They declared that they could not stay in the Government unless Belisha and Inskip were sacked. And they took the opportunity of telling the Prime Minister that they were most disheartened that an old gentleman like Runciman should be re-imported to the Cabinet. In view of Chamberlain's bleak character, one would have assumed that he would have told these rather impertinent Ministers to go to the devil. He was surprisingly patient. He told them that if they resigned a General Election in January was unavoidable. The Government, he said, had been through many trials and were being constantly attacked by ill-conditioned supporters in the House of Commons. If the four Ministers were to resign, the cause of their resignations could not possibly be concealed from the public. And the Government would be gravely discredited as their re-armament programme was widely, but unfairly regarded as being in a state of chaos. Chamberlain added that Central Office had made a canvass in the key constituencies and that Hacking[36] had assured him that it was improbable that the Government would poll more votes than

31 Robert Hudson (1886–1957). Secretary of State at the Department of Overseas Trade.
32 4th Marquess of Dufferin and Ava (1909–45). Parliamentary Under-Secretary for the Colonial Office.
33 Lord Strathcona and Mount Royal (1891–1959). Parliamentary Under-Secretary of State for War.
34 Leslie Hore-Belisha (1896–1957). Liberal politician. Secretary of State for War, 1937–40.
35 Sir Thomas Inskip (1876–1947). Minister for the Co-ordination of Defence 1936–39.
36 Douglas Hacking (1884–1950). Chairman, Conservative Party Organisation, 1936–42.

the socialists if an election were held in January.

Chamberlain also said that some of the allegations against Belisha took him completely by surprise. And added: 'I give you my word that I shall conduct a most thorough investigation into the matters you have brought to my notice'. The Under-Secretaries were thus persuaded to hold their hand until January.

Chamberlain must look upon Belisha as a most restful colleague![37]

Bracken to Beaverbrook 20 Bishopsgate,
Wednesday (Spring 1939) London, E.C.2.

Max,

Miller gave me your message. Kingston was the division wooed by Belisha. Admiral Royds,[38] the sitting member, has announced that he will not fight again.

Belisha, without consulting the Co-ordinating Committee set up by the Tory, Nat Liberal and Nat Labour organizations, approached one Mr Hendricks who is the Chairman of the Kingston Tory Association. Hendricks was both flattered and alarmed. He consulted the big shots of his committee and found that they were rigidly opposed to Belisha's candidature. The fact that Belisha was willing to abandon his present party label did not surprise or please them. They looked upon Belisha as a person willing to give up any principles for much less than 30 pieces of silver!

Hendricks was advised to say that Belisha was quite unacceptable.

Minister Morrison's[39] transfer to the Dominions Office is under review. The argument for transferring him to this sinecure is that he has had a fearful time during the last few years. And so he ought to be put out to grass for a bit. His suggested successor

---

37 A full account of this episode (from Hore-Belisha's point of view) can be found in R. J. Minney, *The Private Papers of Hore-Belisha* (London, 1960), pp. 161–166.
38 Admiral Sir Percy Royds (1874–1955). He was M.P. for Kingston-upon-Thames from 1937 to 1945.
39 William 'Shakes' Morrison (1893–1961). Minister of Agriculture and Fisheries, 1936–1939 and subsequently Minister of Food, Postmaster-General and Minister of Town and Country Planning. His successor as Minister was Dorman Smith, formerly President of the Farmer's Union.

would make you rage against the cynicism of the Government. When are you coming home?

Bracken to Beaverbrook 20 Bishopsgate,
16 March 1939 London, E.C.2.
Max

.... Your hero Chamberlain took a pluperfect pearler yesterday.[40] Instead of telling Parliament that Hitler had broken the promise he made at Munich, he entered into a protracted legalist argument worthy of Uriah Heep or Simon,[41] or both.

Chamberlain's political success during the last six months (and they have been very great) were due to the feeling that Munich was a landmark of peace. The crude destruction of what was left of Czechoslovakia must inevitably create doubts in Chamberlain's judgement in the constituencies. He told the public that he brought them peace in our time. He also declared that Hitler had assured him that the truncated Czechoslovakia State would be allowed to live in peace. Germany had no desire to obtain control of alien populations!

Now that Hitler has incorporated about eight million aliens into the Reich, the worth of his promises is evident even to the stupidest elector. One of the Coroner's[42] principal colleagues declared to me today that a National Government was inevitable, and that an effort should be made to retain Chamberlain's services by offering him the Lord Presidency of the Council! As I grow older, I become increasingly distrustful of emotional reactions, and to me Chamberlain appears a tough old gentleman who will fight for all his might against any 'real National Government' in which he will not hold the first place. He is greatly advantaged by the fact that most of his Parliamentary colleagues are subservient and stupid. Unless he has a succession of bad by-election reverses he can mould them according to his will.

It was very stupid of him to issue his declaration on Friday that

---

40 On 15 March German troops marched into Prague and occupied what was left of Czechoslovakia after the Munich agreement. In the afternoon Chamberlain made a statement in the House of Commons on Hitler's flagrant breach of the Munich agreement.
41 Sir John Simon (1873–1954). Liberal politician, lawyer and Chancellor of the Exchequer 1937–40, Lord Chancellor 1940 – 45.
42 Chamberlain.

European tension was decreasing and that the German Government were becoming more moderate, and that the public might hope for a disarmament conference before the end of the year.[43] This is the fourth time that an optimistic declaration by him has been followed by ructions in Europe. Poor little Sam Hoare's efforts to support his master have been even more unfortunate.[44] He told us that the golden years were coming. He suggested that Chamberlain, Daladier and the three European Dictators should join together in bringing us peace and plenty. Sam's stock is now quite unsaleable!

War talk is beginning again, and will probably deepen the slump that has been with us since 1938. In my humble judgement, the fear of war is negligible if we push on with our rearmament programme and avoid internal political quarrels. My optimism is not solely based on our strength. The real hope for peace lies in the fact that the Nazi gangsters in Germany are all so conscious of their own weakness in the event of a war in which the first class powers are engaged. The Nazi bosses now live on the fat of the land. If war broke out the grim German General Staff would take command, and some of the blood and thunder Nazi bosses would be drafted into the front line trenches. The leaders of the Nazi Party have an unappeasable appetite for blackmail, but I am sure that they will stop short of war.

The other great hope for peace is, of course, that Germany is without any of the financial, raw material and industrial resources necessary for a nation which launches a European war. She has collected a good deal of booty in Czechoslovakia, but that country contains none of the metals necessary for a sustained conflict.

We rely on you to keep your noble and sharp eye on Mussolini.[45] And to organise all the croupiers, income tax dodgers, billiard markers, and other notable citizens of Monaco into an

---

43 On 9 March, Chamberlain had given a very optimistic survey of the prospects for the future peace of Europe at an 'unattributable' lobby briefing at Downing Street; his remarks were widely reported in the press the next day.

44 The following day, 10 March, the Home Secretary, Sir Samuel Hoare (1880–1959), had at Chamberlain's behest made a notorious speech in which he predicted the imminent dawning of a 'golden age' of peace and prosperity in Europe.

45 Beaverbrook was staying in Monte Carlo at the time.

effective opposition to the march on Nice! It may or may not be known to your lordship that during the Munich crisis, the British General Staff ordained that the Tenth Lancers (now mechanised) were to be stationed in Monte Carlo. If you will take charge of Monte Carlo, this very able Regiment can be utilised to defend the more vulnerable parts of the ever-expanding British frontiers.

Bracken to Beaverbrook 8 Lord North Street,
25 March 1939 Westminster
Max,

If war comes and the organization described by Hoare[46] starts up any newspaper man would covet the job you outlined.

As I am what is called an able-bodied man my duty in times of war must be to go off with the soldiers. No one knows better than I how incompetent a warrior I shall be. But there will be lots of prentice recruits.

I am most grateful for the suggestion you made. It will be the best of jobs for somebody.

---

46 As Home Secretary, Hoare had ministerial responsibility for setting up the Ministry of Information that would come into being on the start of war.

5
THE WAR 1939–1945

Britain declared war on Germany on 3 September 1939 after the German invasion of Poland on 1 September. Churchill was immediately recalled to the Government as First Lord of the Admiralty, and Bracken went with him as his Parliamentary Private Secretary. Beaverbrook was somewhat less than enthusiastic about a war that he believed Britain should never have entered — he believed Britain should remain barricaded behind the bastions of the empire and not entangle herself in European affairs — and he stayed sulkily on the sidelines throughout the 'Phoney War'. He even flirted with proponents of a negotiated peace in the Spring of 1940 — efforts that were to rebound on him later as his letter to Bracken of 20 June 1942 indicates.

However, with the German invasion of North France on 9 May the 'Phoney War' ended. Churchill became Prime Minister and Beaverbrook was brought into the War Cabinet to start the Ministry of Aircraft Production from nothing. In doing this he gloriously fulfilled, and even surpassed, everyone's expectations of him.

Bracken to Beaverbrook   Admiralty,
20 November 1939   Whitehall
Little Lord Max and how do you do!
    I hope that the South has rid you of asthma and that we shall see you soon.
    Despite the heavy labours of Lord Macmillan[1] I can send you no news. You probably heard the coroner's broadcast and now clearly understand our war and peace aims. The old gentleman's remarks about international trade were worthy of Cobden. For

[1] Lord Macmillan (1873–1952). First Minister of Information.

21 July 1941   *The War*   49

many years the Tories have been stealing the Socialists' clothes. Surely the coroner is now after Archie Sinclair's[2] kilt.

There is still plenty of chatter about peace aims. Attlee[3] and Greenwood[4] want a sort of re-hash of President Wilson's fourteen points. But I am told that Horace Wilson[5] has not yet decided his peace aims.

I asked yr Mr Robertson[6] to stir up yr boys to consider the implications of the enclosed cutting from today's Times. It should help to make the coroner realize the folly of retaining an ossific M. of Information which neglects our vital interests and disheartens our friends in all parts of the world.

Yrs,
Brendan

On 20 July 1941, Bracken reluctantly accepted the post of Minister of Information in Churchill's government. Although Bracken approached his new responsibilities with considerable trepidation, he was to become as good a Minister of Information as Beaverbrook had been a Minister of Aircraft Production in 1940. On Bracken's first day at his new office in Bloomsbury, Beaverbrook wrote to him:

Beaverbrook to Bracken
21 July 1941
My dear Brendan,
In the ordinary way, it would be looked on as a sarcastic or even an unfriendly act to offer a man congratulations on becoming Minister of Information.

2 Sir Archibald Sinclair (1890–1970). Liberal Politician, Leader of the Liberal Party 1935–45. In his youth, a political acolyte of Churchill.
3 Clement Attlee (1883–1967). Labour Politician, Leader of the Labour Party 1935–55. Deputy Prime Minister, 1940–45, Prime Minister 1945 – 51.
4 Arthur Greenwood (1880–1954). Deputy Leader of the Labour Party.
5 Sir Horace Wilson (1882–1972). Permanent Secretary to the Ministry of Labour 1921–30, Chief industrial advisor to the Government 1930–39, Permanent Secretary to the Treasury 1940–42. He was Chamberlain's most trusted official and was one of the chief architects of the Government's appeasement policies.
6 Mr. E. J. Robertson (1882–1960). General Manager of Beaverbrook's newspapers.

In your case this is not so. You are going to make a great success in this office. Your gifts of imagination and energy will be given a scope they have never enjoyed before.

And the glory you win will be all the brighter because it shines in a dark and dismal sky.

Yours ever,

Bracken to Beaverbrook   Ministry of Information,
Malet St.,
W.C.1

My dear Max,

Your letter was a great encouragement to me.

I have no illusions about this job. And I would not have taken it without your backing. You know all that need be known about how to run this Ministry. And as I shall be wanting your help, you will curse the day that you pressed me to come here! For you are already overworked, and have little time for the affairs of other Departments.

Bless you.

(sgd) Yrs,
Brendan

Beaverbrook to Bracken
20 June 1942

My dear Brendan,

Our conversation today left me in considerable anxiety about the future.

I feel that personalities are interfering with the best results.

I hope that there is some contribution I can make to the conflict on behalf of our beloved Empire as well as Great Britain.

But these stories about my seeing Stokes[7] continually and other rumours (I include, of course, the story about the American Ambassador) disturb me.

I send you a copy of my correspondence with Stokes and an assurance that I have not seen him or talked with him, in person or

---

7 Richard Stokes (1897 – 1957). Labour MP for Ipswich. Beaverbrook had communicated with Stokes and other left-wing politicians in 1940 about the possibilities of forming a 'peace-front' in the spring of 1940; these furtive flirtations with pacifist socialists came back to haunt Beaverbrook in 1941–42. See A.J.P. Taylor, *Beaverbrook*, ps. 403–406.

by telephone — I have had no communication with him whatever, direct, or indirect, since I left the Government.

It has been a long series of rumours that I have been called on to deny, and I am tired out now.

Do you think that any part of the fault lies with me?

Yours ever,

Bracken to Beaverbrook   Ministry of Information,
23 June 1942   Malet St.,
           W.C.1.

My dear Max,

Many thanks for your letter of June 20.

Like all lively men you are pursued by a band of snapping critics. They have been chasing after you ever since you established the Ministry of Aircraft Production and liquidated some of the incompetent vested interests with which they were concerned.

Other critics are people who got sore shins during your reign at the Ministry of Supply.

Until the undertaker frees England from them you will have to bear with the barking of a number of old Edwardian frumps who have never forgiven you for offending the squirearchy by making Bonar Law leader of the Tory Party. But I do not think these critics count for much. They were out of touch with life in England before the war. Now they can be looked upon as troglodytes.

I am quite certain Winston would never allow them to make mischief. I know too that he is also pursued by an odd assortment of critics who would like to do everything in their power to secure your aid.

When Winston returns I shall, with your permission, show him your letter.

Yrs,
B.

On 12 June 1944, Lord Beaverbrook, then Lord Privy Seal in the Government, received the following, which he forwarded for advice to Brendan Bracken.

My Dear Max   *12 June 1944*

                                           Stow Vicarage,
12 June 1944   King's Lynn,
                                                       Norfolk.

My Lord,

    I know you have many pressing problems at present, but can you spare a few moments for this one:

    England is still largely country: conditions in country parishes are very different from those in town parishes, yet not one of the bench of bishops (our natural leaders) has any experience as a country clergyman.

    Could you find time to discuss this matter with the Prime Minister? His usual channels of advice in this direction are all townspeople, the country parsons would be immensely enheartened if they could have one bishop who had sympathy and understanding because he had been a country clergyman himself.

    If you would like me to come and see you to talk this over, I should consider the journey to London well worth while.

                                                     Your Lordship's
                                                    obedient Servant,
                                                    Gordon Quinion.

Bracken's secretary replied to Beaverbrook's secretary, on behalf of the Minister of Information:

                                   Ministry of Information,
22 June, 1944   Malet St.,
                                                          W.C.1.

Dear Miss Hogg,

    Mr. Bracken has read with interest the Rev. Gordon E. Quinion's letter to Lord Beaverbrook which has been forwarded to him and which I return herewith. He sees no prospect of Mr Quinion's being made a Bishop. He remarks further that as Lord Beaverbrook has bought several benefices in the Church of England His Lordship might of his charity award one of these to his correspondent.

    Mr. Bracken also suggests that you should aid him by telling His Lordship that he thinks there is now a good case for disestablishing the Church of England. He considers it the ripest of scandals that a bigoted Presbyterian should become a Patron of Church livings. Were it not for the flying bomb, the weather and

18 April 1945   *The War*   53

the reading of Mr. Lyttelton's[8] speeches he would have reported this matter to the Archbishop of Canterbury.

Yours sincerely,
(Sgd) A. S. Hodge

Beaverbrook to Bracken
7 April 1945

Dear Minister of Information,

I see that you are paying for busts of Mr Ernest Bevin,[9] M. Maisky,[10] and Lt. General Cunningham.[11]

As a tax-payer, laying down 19/6d in the £, I find it difficult to countenance this expenditure.

If I were an M.P. I would ask a question. And if I were a voter in North Paddington,[12] I would ask my Member to put a question down.

Yours sincerely,
Beaverbrook

Bracken to Beaverbrook   Ministry of Information,
18 April 1945   Malet Street,
A 529/38   W.C.1

Dear Lord Privy Seal,

The Minister of Information is honoured by your letter of 7 April about busts. He is generally responsible for the doings of the War Artists Advisory Committee. But he is not obliged to approve or veto the subjects that this Committee may choose. In January 1942 at the height of pro-Russian feeling in Britain they commissioned Jacob Epstein[13] to deliver a replica of the bust he had already made of the Russian Ambassador to England. In May 1942 the Committee also commissioned Epstein to deliver a modelled head

---

8 Oliver Lyttleton (1893–1972). Conservative politician, Member of the War Cabinet, 1941–45.
9 Ernest Bevin (1881–1951). Trade Unionist, founder of the Transport & General Workers Union and Labour politician. Minister of Labour 1940–45 and Foreign Secretary 1945–51.
10 Ivan Maisky (1884–1975). Russian Ambassador to Britain 1932–43.
11 Lt. General Sir Alan Cunningham (1887–1983). Military Commander who had particularly distinguished himself in North Africa.
12 Bracken's parliamentary constituency.
13 Sir Jacob Epstein (1880–1959). Sculptor.

of the General who had conquered East Africa. Bevin's head was commissioned in March this year just in time to avoid political controversy.

6

TOILING UNDER THE YOKE OF SOCIALISM 1945–1951

Brendan Bracken was defeated in the 1945 General Election, but was re-elected to Parliament as M.P. for Bournemouth after a by-election in November 1945. Bracken thus retained a very active interest in politics and was considered to be one of the Conservative leaders in Parliament. Beaverbrook, in contrast, gave up all immediate interest in British politics and divided his time between his residences in Jamaica, the Bahamas, Canada, the South of France and England. His most intimate link with British politics was Bracken, who proceeded to write the absentee 'Press Baron' a regular report of the British political scene.

At home, the landslide victory of the Labour Party ensured a majority Labour Government for the first time in Britain's history. Led by the 'big five', Attlee, Morrison, Bevin, Cripps and Dalton, Labour energetically started putting into operation their vision of a planned economy — based on nationalization of the 'commanding heights' of the economy — and a Welfare State that proved very popular with the British people at the time. The first two years of the Labour Government, 1945–47, were halcyon years for the Labour movement. In 1947, the Government hit the economic rocks that several of their critics had seen lurking just beneath the unruffled waters of Socialist advance and it was left to Sir Stafford Cripps to carry them into the 'age of austerity'.

For the Conservatives it was a time of anxious re-examination of their own principles and policies.

Beaverbrook to Bracken
20 June 1946
My dear Brendan,
 The Federation of British Industries without making any application to the Daily Express, asked Trevor Evans,[1] their principal radical writer, who is strongly in favour of public ownership and hates every form of private enterprise, to become their Publicity Agent.
 They offered him an advance on the pay he gets from the Daily Express. Evans refused.
 Evidently Sir Clive Baillieu practices the gentle art of Whistler; in other words how to make friends and influence people.
Yours ever,
P.S. When Evans turned down the F.B.I., the negotiator said that since he had found a resting place in the Daily Express, which was truly in favour of free enterprise, surely he could handle his subjects in the same way for the F.B.I.
 That is not a verbatim account of what transpired between the F.B.I. and Trevor Evans: It is a paraphrase.

Bracken to Beaverbrook Princes House,
27 June 1946. 95, Gresham Street,
London, E.C.2.
My dear Max
 I read your letter about the F.B.I.'s clumsy approach to Trevor Evans.
 If the F.B.I. were not peopled by such bone-heads they would understand that it is better for British industry that a man like Evans should work under the control of the Express than as a P.R.O. for the F.B.I.
 If the F.B.I. had any sense they should be cunningly endeavouring to plant people of their own picking on to the newspapers instead of trying to steal staff from Fleet Street!
 The trouble about the F.B.I. is that they have neither brains nor stuffing. The Socialists have a lot of luck. One of their best windfalls is the F.B.I. and its Chairman!

---

1 Trevor Evans (1902–81). Industrial Correspondent of the *Daily Express* from 1930 to 1967. He was knighted in 1967.

Beaverbrook to Bracken
11 July, 1946
Dear Mr. Bracken,
Lord Beaverbrook sends you the following message:
Matthew (Chapter 25. Verse 29)

> For unto every one that hath shall be given, and he shall have abundance: but from him that hath not shall be taken away even that which he hath.

Yours sincerely,

Bracken to Beaverbrook   Princes House,
22 September 1946   95, Gresham Street,
   London, E.C.2.

My dear Max,

Thank you very much for sending me such fine whiskey and wine. It will brighten up the gloomy winter ahead of us.

Harriman[2] is delighted by his new job. He owes it, he says, to Hannegan[3] and Ed Flynn.[4] That crafty pair have done something to improve their Boss's reputation as a dispenser of patronage.

Our newspapers are full of praise of Harriman as the last of the New Dealers and the understanding friend of Russia! Though our Averell does not quite fit this description, he ought to be a good Secretary of Commerce. That is a pleasant post. The terms of the American loan[5] to Britain will help Harriman to become the greatest stimulator of exports in American history.

Eden[6] has been showing W.S.C.[7] a speech on foreign affairs

---

2 Averell Harriman (1891–1986). U.S. Ambassador to Russia 1943–46, Ambassador to Britain 1946, Secretary of Commerce 1946–48.
3 Robert E. Hannegan (1903–49). Chairman of the Democratic National Committee, 1944–49.
4 Ed Flynn (1906–72). Trade Unionist.
5 In 1945, the British, facing national bankruptcy at the end of the war, had borrowed $3,750 million from the Americans on what many in Britain considered to be unnecessarily harsh terms; Beaverbrook and Bracken were both fiercely opposed to the loan.
6 Anthony Eden (1897–1977). Conservative Politician. Foreign Secretary 1935–38, 1940–45, 1951–55. Prime Minister 1955–57.
7 Winston Spencer Churchill.

58   *My Dear Max*   22 September 1946

which he is to fire off tonight. It has infuriated our friend who calls it 'lousy and Wallacey'.

Yrs
B.

Bracken to Beaverbrook Princes House,
7 October, 1946 95, Gresham Street,
London, E.C.2.

My dear Max

The Tory Conference is over. It was an interesting affair.

The neo Socialists, like Harold Macmillan,[8] who are in favour of nationalizing railways, electricity, gas and many other things, expected to get great support from the delegates who are supposed to be greatly frustrated by the result of the General Election and successive by-elections.

Rab Butler[9] and the other moles engaged in research to produce a 'modern' policy for the Tory Party believed that Blackpool would be a paradise for the progressives.

It turned out that the neo Socialists were lucky to escape with their scalps. The delegates would have nothing to do with the proposal to change the Party's name.[10] They demanded a real Conservative policy instead of a synthetic Socialist one so dear to the heart of the Macmillans and Butlers, and it gave Churchill one of the greatest receptions of his life.

I know not whether the Tories' return to their ancient faith is likely to get us more votes at the four forthcoming by-elections. It certainly won't lose us any. Of course, if Mr. Harry Pollitt[11] and his braves were really to run candidates, the Tories' fortunes

8 Harold Macmillan (1894–1986). Conservative politician. Minister Resident in the Mediterranean 1942–45, Minister of Housing 1951–54, Minister of Defence 1954–55, Foreign Secretary 1955–56, Chancellor of the Exchequer 1956–57, Prime Minister 1957–63. He was created Earl of Stockton in 1984.
9 R. A. Butler (1902–82). Conservative politician. Under-Secretary of State at the Foreign Office 1938–41, President of the Board of Education 1941–45. Director of the Conservative Research Department 1946–51, Chancellor of the Exchequer 1951–55, Leader of the House of Commons 1955–61, Home Secretary 1957–62, Foreign Secretary 1963–4.
10 Some Conservatives did flirt with the notion of changing the name of the Party to the 'New Democratic Party' or 'Union Party'.
11 Harry Pollitt (1890–1960). Secretary of the British Communist Party

would move in a big way. But Mr. Pollitt is uncooperative. He is not even willing to run a candidate at Rotherhithe.

I expect the Government is going to have a rough ride at the Annual Conference of the T.U.C. Jack Tanner[12] and company have put down what amounts to a Vote of Censure on Bevin's foreign policy. All the big Unions are agreed in pressing for a wage policy and the National Union of Railways is pressing for the appointment of working-class socialists to the Boards which are to control transport. The Steel Unions are going to do plenty of hatchet work as a protest against the appointment of the slippery Forbes to the headship of the Steel Board.[13] And all the Unions are demanding a forty hour week.

During the last eleven months the Government have spent no less than £529,000,000 in rigging the gilt-edged market!

Our sinuous friend, Lord Portal,[14] is in a great state of dither. The Government have offered Leathers[15] the Chairmanship of the Board which is to control all transport. He has refused. Morrison[16] asked him whether Portal was fit for the job. The reply was 'certainly not'. Game, venison and other delectables are now pouring into Downing Street from Laverstoke. And the Lord is declaring that he has never been in sympathy with the Conservative Party but his long experience of South Wales has taught him to hold the Socialists in high honour! The greedy little eyes of our porcine friend are certainly fixed on the main chance.

1929–56.
12 Jack Tanner (1889–1965). Prominent Trade Unionist, President of the Amalgamated Engineering Union 1939–54.
13 The Iron and Steel Board was set up as a prelude to full nationalization. Sir Archibald Forbes was Chairman of the Board, 1946–49 and 1953–59.
14 Lord Portal (1995–1949). Owner of Laverstock House, Hampshire. He occupied a number of minor Government posts during the war. As well as being Chairman of the Bacon Development Board, Portal had briefly been Regional Commissioner for Wales under the Civil Defence Scheme in 1939. He did not succeed to the post in question.
15 Lord Leathers (1883–1965). Minister of War Transport 1941–45, Secretary of State for the Co-ordination of Transport, Fuel and Power 1951–53.
16 Herbert Morrison (1888–1965). Labour Politician, Home Secretary 1940–45, Lord President of the Council and Leader of the House of Commons 1945–51, with special responsibility for Labour's nationalization programme. Foreign Secretary, 1951.

I see that Clare Luce[17] is to become one of the sponsors of a monthly magazine called 'Plain Talk'. With Clare in charge it ought to live up to its title!

(Sgd) Yours ever
Brendan

Bracken to Beaverbrook
16 October 1946

Princes House,
95, Gresham Street,
London, E.C.2.

My dear Max,

You must be glad that your academic exercises are over. It is a great honour to be Chancellor of the University[18] but such an office must inevitably expose you to bores.

Some of the newspapers say that the House of Commons has re-assembled in a chastened mood. I can see no signs of chastening in the serried ranks of the Socialists. On the contrary, many of them have returned from subsidised missions to all parts of the world more than ever seized of their own importance.

In the new session we shall have Bills to nationalize the railways and electricity. As these Bills are a fulfilment of some of the pledges given at a General Election they will be enthusiastically supported by the back-benchers of the Socialist Party. The Tories will fight them. But, as you and I remember the attitude taken up by Crookshank[19] and Butler to the Morrison sponsored scheme for nationalizing electricity there is not likely to be much convincing opposition from the most of our Front Bench. And I am told that before the war Macmillan wrote a book in which he approved of the placing of railways and electricity under State control.[20] The Socialists have, apparently, compiled some elegant extracts from this work which Morrison can be counted upon to use effectively.

Winston is in very good fettle and is determined to continue to lead the Tory Party until he becomes Prime Minister on earth or Minister of Defence in Heaven.

Eden has accepted an invitation to visit the antipodes. He plans

---

17 Clare Luce: American playwright, magazine publisher and politician
18 Beaverbrook was invited to be the Chancellor of the University of New Brunswick at Fredericton, Canada; he was installed in May 1947.
19 Harry Crookshank (1893–1961). Conservative politician, served in a number of junior government posts from 1934 to 1945 and 1951–55.
20 *The Middle Way*, published in 1938.

to be away for several months.

The House of Lords passed the Bill nationalizing Cables and Wireless yesterday. Cranborne[21] declared that it had been approved by the previous Government. That is news to you and me and Sir Edward Bridges![22]

(Sgd) Yours ever,
Brendan

Bracken to Beaverbrook   8 Lord North Street,
30 October 1947   Westminster
My dear Max,

Boss Morrison staged his debate on the Press in the House of Commons yesterday.[23] The first debate in this Parliament on a Private Members motion: it was particularly well attended. Foot[24] and his friends mercilessly ridiculed Kemsley. And of course you were also abused. No new epithets.

Bill Brown[25] made the best speech of the debate. It was an admirable blend of satire and cogent reasoning. Perhaps it was a shade too long and slightly marred by his King Charles' head obsession about the closed shop. But these small blemishes count for nothing when compared with the vast merits of the speech.

That ponderous old Wilson Harris[26] for once made a fine speech — one which greatly angered the government. Your Max[27] made his best speech so far. Very good it was.

21 Lord 'Bobbety' Cranborne, 5th Marquess of Salisbury (1893–1972). Grandson of 3rd Marquess of Salisbury. Secretary of State for Dominion Affairs, 1940–42, Lord Privy Seal 1942–43, Secretary of State for Dominion Affairs 1943–45, Leader of the Conservative Party in the House of Lords.
22 Sir Edward Bridges (1892–1969). Secretary to the Cabinet 1938–45; Permanent Secretary at the Treasury 1945 – 56.
23 The debate on the Royal Commission on the Press, which sat from 1947 to 1949.
24 Michael Foot (1913–). A Beaverbrook journalist and Labour M.P. for Devonport 1945–55, Ebbw Vale 1960–83, Blaenau Gwent since 1983, leader of the Labour Party 1980–83.
25 William Brown (1894–1960). Journalist and Independent M.P. for Rugby 1942–50.
26 H. Wilson Harris (1883–1955). Editor of the *Spectator* 1932–53; M.P. for Cambridge University 1945–50.
27 Max Aitken (1910–1985). Beaverbrook's eldest son, M.P. for Holborn 1945–50.

James Stuart[28] picked Maxwell-Fyfe[29] to speak for the Tory Front Bench without of course telling me. When I objected he declared that he thought that as I had a 'personal interest' in the Press it might be inappropriate for me to speak. I replied by saying that most of the Socialist speakers had 'personal interests',[30] and that big farmer Hudson was never prevented from speaking on agriculture because of his 'interest'.[31] Nor did I suppose that Macmillan and Ashetton (sic)[32] would refrain from opposing the nationalization of transport because of their railway directorships. He professed to have been full of regrets but could make no change as he had announced the choice of Fyfe to the 1922 Committee![33] Winston tried to put things right by telling me that it never occurred to him that I had not been asked to speak for the opposition. And he had not remembered that on a private members day only one speech could be made from each of the front benches.

I think both had forgotten that I spent over 4 years in the Ministry of Information! A personal interest indeed!

One must get over these disappointments.

Kemsley was very upset. Her Ladyship now says that owing to the monstrous conduct of Socialist speakers Gomer[34] must forthwith sell all his papers. I am very sorry for them. For they are not made for controversy.

I am still being mauled by doctors. When they almost succeeded in curing one leg the other resenting their lack of attention has started up painful and festering sores. It is all very depressing. I doubt if the doctors really know what is wrong. That consoling

---

28 James Stuart (1897–1971). Joint Chief Whip of the Coalition Government 1940–45; Opposition Chief Whip 1945–48
29 Sir David Maxwell-Fyfe (1900–1967). Barrister and deputy Chief Prosecutor at the Nuremberg War Crimes Trial, Home Secretary 1951–54, Lord Chancellor 1954–62.
30 Almost all the Labour M.P.s speaking in the debate were journalists by profession.
31 Robert Hudson (1886–1957). Farmer and Minister of Agriculture and Fisheries, 1940–45.
32 Ralph Assheton (1901–1984). Conservative MP and Chairman of Conservative Party organization 1944–46; his railway interests are not listed in Who's Who.
33 the Committee of Conservative back-bench M.P.s.
34 James Gomer Berry, 1st Viscount Kemsley.

man Bruce Lockhart[35] tells me that the symptoms are exactly the same as his when his tiresome disease first began to afflict him.

I am afraid my dear friend that I shall not have the happiness of spending Christmas with you in Jamaica. I shall probably have to spend it in gloomy journey to and from Harley Street.

There has been no political excitement during the last few weeks. Attlee's broadside against the Communists has obviously upset many of the Trade Unions and almost all the lively shop-stewards. But as you well know the Communists are careful about replying to frontal attacks. They organize their retaliation underground. Doubtless they will strike back hard when they find the right opportunity....

Winston has written about 150,000 words of his War book.[36] It will run into five volumes. If Uncle Joe[37] continues to attack him the History will probably be dedicated to Messrs Attlee and Bevin....

I miss you greatly

Yours ever,
Brendan

Bracken to Beaverbrook   8 Lord North Street,
3 November 1946   Westminster
My dear Max,

I have withdrawn my objections to nationalizing the doctors. I now think it too mild a treatment. A bill to send them to the knackers would be warmly supported by me.

My sudden conversion is due to the careful chart I have kept since I bumped a shin against a step in the House of Commons. The chart is short and divided into three parts.

I

The doctors decided that a little touch of penicillin would heal the bruise.

II

The result of the application was a boiling up of the bruise and the spreading of blisters all over me.

---

35 Sir Robert Bruce-Lockhart (1887–1970); diplomat and writer, a close friend of Bracken and fellow sufferer.
36 Churchill's *History of The Second World War*, published in 6 volumes 1948–1951.
37 Josef Stalin (1879–1952).

III

The doctors declared that I am one of the unlucky allergic to Penicillin. To cure the consequences of their first cure they dosed me with iodide. That stuff stirred up my antrum and irritated the Penicillin blisters.

I am now allergic to doctors. Job was radiantly happy by comparison with your humble servant. Day and night do I itch and curse.

Why! Oh why! did I press for an honour for Sir Alexander Fleming[38] and help to raise money for St. Mary's Hospital. Despite Bruce Lockharts' infallible knowledge and experience I do not think I have been afflicted by his speciality.

That this illness is very boring is proved by the length of this letter.

All political news amounts to a monotonous account of Ministerial shortcomings. Strachey[39] is again fearful of food shortages. He blames the wicked Americans for abandoning inter-Governmental purchases.

Shinwell[40] is full of woe. Dog racing and horse racing are the great enemies of the production he planned.

The oily Wilmot[41] is in a spin. He cannot make the deliveries he so confidently promised industry. And so he is being bitterly criticised by industrialists and by our great exporter Stafford Cripps.[42]

Though muddle and more muddle marks the doings of this Government their popularity or acceptability does not wither. The

---

38 Sir Alexander Fleming (1881–1955). The discoverer of Penicillin, Fleming was Professor of Bacteriology at St. Mary's Hospital Medical School 1928–48.
39 John Strachey (1901–63). Minister of Food 1946–50, Secretary of State for War 1950–51.
40 Emanuel Shinwell (1884–1986). Minister of Fuel and Power 1945–47, Secretary of State for War 1947–50, Minister of Defence 1950–51.
41 John Wilmot (1895–1964). Minister of Supply.
42 Sir Stafford Cripps (1889–1952). Lawyer and Labour politician. Solicitor-General 1930–31, Ambassador to Russia 1940–42, Minister of Aircraft Production 1942–45, President of the Board of Trade 1945–47, Minister for Economic Affairs 1947, Chancellor of the Exchequer 1947–50. As much as for his own austere lifestyle as his tight handling of the economy as Chancellor he earned the soubriquet 'Austerity Cripps'.

result of the Municipal elections strengthens them and discourages the Tories.

The Windsor lady[43] must have been sadly disillusioned by her husband's interview with Attlee. Nothing could have been more stark than his declaration that no Governmental employment will be given to the Ducal democrats. I am sorry for them.

Yours ever
Brendan

Bracken to Beaverbrook Princes House,
12th November 1946 95, Gresham Street,
London E.C.2.

My dear Max

I have no lively news for you from this town.

The Socialist Ministers, who were such great promisers at the last Election, have now become exhorters. A blinding flash of inspiration makes them preach the stop press truth, that if workers do not produce enough they cannot enjoy an abundant life. It is going to be rather difficult to persuade workers of the truth of this message. For twenty-five years Socialist Ministers have been telling the workers that the Government can pay for anything voters deem desirable, and that by soaking the rich, lush benefits can be conferred on everyone, save, of course, the rich. Above all, the employers are incompetents and exploiters. I think Attlee and his Ministers will find it very difficult to get the workers to un-believe all the sort of propaganda they put out in the past in order to attract votes.

Winston is well and hopes to collect a vast supply of dollars from Harpers for the libel they published in 'Dinner at the White House'.

Mary's engagement was cyclonic. She only met her young-man a few weeks ago. I will give you my impressions of him after I meet him tonight.[44]

Your son Max is working very hard. He chases after me in the hope of picking up a little news from Wednesday morning until Saturday night. Alas, he is constantly disappointed as I can find none. In fact, I should like a little news in order to fob off Bruce

---

43 The Duchess of Windsor, formerly Mrs. Wallis Simpson.
44 Mary Churchill, Winston's daughter, married Christopher Soames on 11 February 1947.

Lockhart who is always belly-aching for a piece for his column and I am finding it a hard job to fill up the Observer column in the Financial Times. I am going to carry the war into little Max's camp by ringing him up and asking him for some news!

I am still aching all over as a result of my penicillin cure. There seems to be no shortage of bandages and ointments and it is an agonising process taking them off and putting them on.

The Manchester Guardian says that Hore Belisha has come to the conclusion that the Tory Party can never win an election on its own account. He wishes to bring the succour of his presence into a Coalition!

(Sgd) Yours ever
Brendan

Bracken to Beaverbrook   8 Lord North Street,
16 November 1946   Westminster
My dear Max

The long deferred fight between Socialists over Bevin's foreign policy has begun in a big way.[45]

The Attlee-Morrison Government will of course win the first rounds. To say that they are angry and apprehensive is an understatement of their feelings. They are shrewd politicians who see the menace behind the decision of sixty Socialist Members to put down an amendment to the Address which is nothing but a vote of censure on the Foreign Secretary. The Government know full well that the daring sixty have the sympathy of at least fifty other Members. And that the Unions & constituency associations are deeply divided on foreign policy.

I doubt if this breach between Government & their followers or masters can be repaired unless Bevin departs & is replaced by a more malleable Foreign Secretary. As Attlee could never throw over Bevin & the artful Morrison is anathema to the very left all that is open to them is to use the big stick against their more determined 'followers' & exploit all the resources of patronage in dealing with the rest.

And so a long, intensely bitter fight lies ahead of the Govern-

45 On 12 November 1946, 57 Labour M.P.s from the Left of the Party tabled an amendment to the Address that was strongly critical of Bevin's foreign policy which they saw as unduly subservient to Washington.

ment — a fight which may change the face of politics in Britain.

This Socialist split naturally increases the confidence of the Tories. It may even moderate the ardour of the planners in the party who would like to fasten a policy on us derived from Fabianism & the Primrose League.[46] These gentlemen seem to be sublimely unaware of the fact that Messrs Attlee & Morrison are in a better position to do this.

I remain the writhing victim of the bungling doctors. I know of nothing more irritating than the long drawn out daily dressings inflicted upon me. Nor am I much comforted by being told a great improvement will occur in a few weeks.

I hope you are getting plenty of sun.

Yours ever,
Brendan

Bracken to Beaverbrook
5th December 1946

Princes House,
95, Gresham Street,
London, E.C.2.

My dear Max

Our two Socialist professors have had a bad week. Joad lost his deposit in the Scottish Universities By-Election[47] and Laski has lost a good deal more than his money in the case he brought against the newspapers.[48]

Cripps and Morrison are running around the country making woe, woe speeches. The former declares we may come a cropper when the American loan runs out. And Morrison holds that unless we can greatly increase production our whole standard of living is in jeopardy. I know not the motive behind these dreary

---

46 The Fabian Society was founded in 1884 by the Webbs and G.B. Shaw to propagate Socialist thinking. The Primrose League was founded in 1883, mainly by Lord Randolph Churchill. It grew out of the 'Fourth Party' and was dedicated to the memory of Disraeli and Tory Democracy.

47 Dr Cyril Joad, the eminent Socialist academic, came second but lost his deposit in the by-election for the Combined Scottish Universities seat. Polling took place between 22 and 29 November 1946, and Walter Elliott was returned for the Conservatives.

48 Harold Laski (1893–1950). Labour theorist and academic, Chairman of the Labour Party during the 1945 general election. In 1946 Laski brought a libel action against, among other papers, the *Daily Express* for alleging that he had advocated violent revolution; he lost and had to pay £16,000 in costs.

speeches. It is much too simple to assume that the Government are merely reporting the facts of life to an unthinking community. I shall not be surprised if the Government have some plan to secure greater power for the direction of labour.

Many of the Tories are becoming restive about the industrial policy which is being sedulously advocated by Macmillan and his friends. Speaking for the Party in the Debate on The King's Speech, Macmillan said that the State should have greater powers to intervene and to manage industry. He also said that discipline in factories should be left to the workers. I think the latter thought is even too ambitious for the T.U.C. though it will certainly meet with the hearty approval of Mr Harry Pollitt.

I have been irritated beyond description by the wearying treatment I have been given to get rid of the ill effects of penicillin. I am getting better and I have now made up my mind to take a holiday. Davis (sic)[49] and his tribe are against my going to such a hot place as Jamaica or Florida, as it might re-start the irritation caused by penicillin. My plan is to set off in the Queen Elizabeth on December 27th. I shall have to spend the first week of January in New York as we have some important contracts with the American Metal Company which require revision. When I get freed from business I shall go to Baruch's[50] quiet old plantation in South Carolina for a week or ten days. I expect I shall then be feeling much better and more than willing to disregard Davis' advice by going to Jamaica, for there is no better tonic than your company.

(Sgd) Yours ever
Brendan

Bracken to Beaverbrook
(January 1947)
My dear Max,

Thank you very much for all your hospitality. My stay with you was a pleasure beyond all telling.[51] I am counting the days

49 Sir Daniel Davies (1899–1966). Bracken's physician and close friend; also Nye Bevan's doctor.
50 Bernard Baruch (1870–1965). American *eminence grise* and financier; a very close friend of Winston Churchill and confidant of successive American Presidents.
51 Bracken had stayed at Beaverbrook's house at Montego Bay, Jamaica,

between now and your return to our Socialised Isle.

The news from England is very gloomy. But even if this Government put all the people into hair shirts there would be no change in Downing Street....

The doctors have got hold of me again.

Yours ever
Brendan

Bracken to Beaverbrook Princes House,
5 March 1947 95, Gresham Street,
London, E.C.2.

My dear Max,

If there are any lights amid the encircling gloom which surrounds Britain they are carefully concealed from me. Conditions here are worse than any we knew in the darkest days of the War.[52]

The coal crisis which has shut down most of our industries and kept all homes in darkness for many hours every day, would have come in March for the stocks of the Power Companies were becoming lower and lower. An exceptional spell of cold weather brought the power crisis in February, and with it the Government fell into the worst of panics. They slashed production everywhere and knocked the bottom out of the export drive for which the country has sacrificed all its efforts for more than eighteen months.

Shinwell's hysteria disgusted Attlee and, indeed, all of his colleagues. He would have been removed from office were it not for the fact that notice was served on Downing Street by Mr Horner[53] that if Shinwell were removed the miners would go on strike.

Though it is snowing heavily today the Air Ministry declare we are in for a spell of warm weather. If this optimistic calculation proves right we shall have a temporary respite from our power crisis but the intelligent leaders of the electricity industry declare that a worse one awaits us next winter and what is even more serious, we shall be confronted with an almost insolvable transport hold-up. We are also given the grim news that many of our factories may have to shut down in the winter for the want of

during January 1947.
52 Bracken was writing during the most severe part of the notoriously cold winter of 1946–47.
53 Arthur Horner (1916–68). General Secretary of the National Union of Mine Workers 1946–59.

raw materials. The purchasing agencies of the Ministry of Supply have muddled everything they touched. We might have recovered from the havoc they have created if we had a good supply of hard currencies. But the conditions attached to the American loan which makes Sterling convertible into dollars are likely to diminish our dwindling hard currency resources.[54]

Meanwhile the Government have lost whatever grip they have had. Their only solution for our troubles is to force the House of Commons to pass through immensely complex nationalization Bills without any opportunity for free discussion. For the first time in our history the guillotine has been introduced into the Committee stages of the important Bills.

You and I never needed any telling that the Socialists would muddle our affairs. But in our most pessimistic moods we could hardly have imagined that Attlee and his colleagues could make such a mess of things. England has resisted and survived many bad governments. Under this one the public is listless, not to say helpless. The very large part of the population who believe in Socialism seem to pity rather than to criticise their rulers. And above all, they champion them against their Tory critics. Unless our people are fundamentally changed there ought to be a lively re-action against the muddlers in Downing Street. The only question is whether it will come in time. The sellers' market is passing away and we must face tremendous competition from the Americans and other big exporting countries. And although the government may ration the community until they live like famished eskimos, we cannot produce the raw materials necessary to employ a working population of twenty million who live on a speck in the Atlantic Ocean with no raw materials save coal, which will be rationed for years to come.

Returning from New York to London is like a journey from pre-War Vienna to Belgrade. Neglect and decay all around one sees and no one seems to have the vitality to challenge the proposition that fair shares of a declining production must kill our hopes of restoring prosperity to our much afflicted people.

The Government which is putting out fires in our hearths is even more determined to quench fires in the bellies. And that is

---

[54] This indeed proved to be the case when sterling became convertible in July 1947.

22nd April 1947   *Toiling under the yoke*   71

what we need to save us in these hard times.

I have not seen enough of my dear political colleagues to give you any interesting political news. Most of the energies of the tory leaders are given over to an attempt to produce an industrial policy which will not offend the Planners.[55]

I shall be spending most of the week in the House of Commons and this perhaps will enable me to give you some political news.

(Sgd) Yours ever
Brendan

Bracken to Beaverbrook   Princes House,
22nd April 1947   95, Gresham Street,
London, E.C.2.

My dear Max,

As our curious Ministers have plenty of snoopers listening in to the transatlantic telephone conversations I think we should deprive them of the pleasure of listening to our talks on politics.

The central weakness of the present Government is not the record, bad as it is, of a Minister like Shinwell, for there are plenty of other incompetent Ministers. The truth is that the Prime Ministership is beyond Attlee's capacity. He chirps in Downing Street and believes so long as he is there that all is right with Britain.

.... Attlee has no real control over his Cabinet. Cripps and Dalton[56] are pursuing conflicting policies. The Morrison/Bevin feud will, of course, flare up if both are able to remain in the Government.

Alexander's[57] bolt on conscription finished him. What a fool he was not to remain buried at the Admiralty until he could get a Ministerial pension or a job like High Commissioner to Canada!

The Cabinet just drifts along in the vague hope that something will turn up to redeem their fortunes. Their paymasters of the T.U.C. are constantly pushing them into the worst of fixes and

---

55 Conservative industrial policy was formulated by a comittee under R.A. Butler and published as the *Industrial Charter* in May 1947.
56 Hugh Dalton (1887–1962). Economist and Labour politician. Minister of Economic Warfare (where he frequently crossed swords with Bracken) 1940–42, President of the Board of Trade 1942–45, Chancellor of the Exchequer 1945–47. One of the major figures in the post-war Labour governments.
57 A.V. Alexander (1885–1965). Labour politician, First Lord of the Admiralty 1940–45, 1945–46, Minister of Defence 1947–50.

they dare not stand up to these bosses.

I doubt if we have had a worse Government since the days of Lord North's.[58] That nobleman had a king behind him who controlled more than a hundred Members of the House of Commons. His control was very unpopular in the country. But I have no reason to believe that the T.U.C. control of far more Parliamentary votes than King George III possessed is unpopular. I think a large part of the electorate is content to put up with all sorts of shortages if they are quite certain that the privileged are being grilled. And who can doubt that they are!

We Tories ought to pray that the Socialist Ministers will be glued to the Treasury Bench at least for another year. Given that space of time it is not foolish to expect that the public will become tired of being pushed around by muddled Socialists. Meanwhile we must prepare for a financial and economic deluge which will come early next year.

We Tories would be wanting in gratitude were we not to admit that this Attlee Government is resurrecting our fortunes. I will give you one instance. In Bournemouth,[59] without any great effort on our part, the Tory Association has trebled its membership in the space of twelve months, and in comparison with our past balance-sheets we now have loads of money. In this respect Bournemouth is not exceptional. I understand that all over the country many middle-class people are joining the Tory Party because of the losses they have incurred through the nationalization of railway, electricity and other shares.

Though I am not over optimistic about the Tory Party's fortunes, I feel that if Attlee continues to lead the country nothing can stop a Tory revival, save some act of folly on our part, such as an attempt to produce a policy which will compete with 'Let us face the future'.[60]

(Sgd) Yours ever,
Brendan.

---

58 Lord North's Government of 1770–1782 was mainly notable for the loss of the American Colonies.
59 Bracken's parliamentary constituency, 1945–51.
60 The Labour Party's manifesto for the 1945 General Election.

13 August 1947 (Telegram)   *Toiling under the yoke*   73

Beaverbrook to Bracken
13 August 1947 (Telegram)

Brendan Bracken,
Carlton Hotel,
Johannesburg.

Andrew Duncan[61] tells Trevor Evans[62] there will be a general election this year with small Labour majority and coalition under Bevin stop Duncan implied he could have a post in Government stop He said quote a few of us have indicated our readiness to serve under Bevin unquote stop Duncan says he has seen Morrison and there will not be any general or partial nationalization of steel before the General Election.[63]   Max.

In 1945 Bracken had become Chairman of Union Corporation, created by his close friend and co-partner in The Economist Sir Henry Strakosch who died in 1943. The Union Corporation had extensive mining interests in South Africa and it was for the purpose of visiting the company's interests there that Bracken visited South Africa several times a year during the late 1940s and early 1950s. His time was divided between Union Corporation's headquarters in Johannesburg and its mines in Western Transvaal and the Orange Free State.

Bracken was active in South Africa at a time of dramatic and controversial change in the country. In 1948 General Smuts was defeated in a general election and the Nationalist Government that took over started institutionalising the apartheid system that lasts to this day. Bracken was an acute and informed observer of the scene and his letters to Beaverbrook from South Africa offer an excellent impression of the forces at work in South Africa at that time and the very different forces of nationalism and socialism blowing through the rest of the continent of Africa.

61 Sir Andrew Duncan (1884–1952). Industrialist. M.P. (National) 1940–50. Chairman of the Executive Committee of British Iron and Steel Federation 1945–52.
62 Industrial Correspondent of the *Daily Express*.
63 The new British Steel Corporation eventually came into being during Attlee's second administration, on 15 February 1951. See Kathleen Burk, *The First Privatisation* (London: Historians' Press, 1988) for an account of Duncan's part in the nationalisation and denationalisation of steel.

Bracken to Beaverbrook Carlton Hotel,
31 August 1947 Johannesburg, S.A.

My dear Max,

Long & dull was the journey from London to this City. We spent thirty four hours in the air & three on the ground.

This must be one of the noisiest cities in the world. Everyone, save the natives of Africa, seems to have a large & sleek American motor car.

The shops are full of trashy but very expensive goods. The Americans seem to have collared the market for imported clothes & shoes. I am told that there has been an increase in imports from Britain. Alas! Our goods are not well displayed or advertised.

This country is roaringly prosperous. It abounds in exotic & small producing industries. They will suffer greatly when a slump comes. The owners, most of whom crossed the Red Sea with dry feet, have taken the precaution of placing blocks of their shares with the trusting British investors. I grieve for them.

Johannesburg is acclaimed or condemned for its vivid way of life. It is, in fact, less lively than Dundee. There is no night life. Nor is there a good restaurant in this large City. Most of the population live in expensive suburbs where they, I am told, give large & very genteel dinner parties. After 8 p.m. the City is almost empty.

The newspaper set-up in Johannesburg will give inspiration to monopolists. There is but one morning & evening paper. Both are modelled on the Daily Telegraph. Their respectability is oppressive. They have the merit of being sympathetic to our country in its grievous ordeal. They are also very critical of the Socialists.

The principal shareholders in both papers are the mining houses. If a man with fire in his belly started a paper here he would indeed become rich & powerful.

There are no good magazines in this country & the radio is infinitely duller than the B.B.C.

I had a long talk with the old gentleman who used to sit opposite us in No. 10. By comparison with him you and I are moderate critics of the Attlee Govt. He is also very critical of the Yanks & holds that terms of their loan are deeply injurious to the British

15 November 1947   *Toiling under the yoke*   75

Empire.[64]

Bracken to Beaverbrook   8, Lord North Street,
15 November 1947   Westminster.
My dear Max,

The result of the Municipal elections alarmed the Socialists and astonished the Tories.[65]

There was a great increase in the Socialist vote. But the enormous rise in the Tory poll was an overwhelming compensation for the new votes given by the grateful beneficiaries of Socialist spending.

Our new organizers of victory were Shinwell, Strachey, Cripps and Woolton.

At long last the public is showing resistance to controls, austerity, insolence and incompetence in high places.

Public anger will increase. Our white Ghandi,[66] now the Minister of Economic Affairs is enforcing a crack-pot plan to empty the shops at home in order to provide for shrinking, not to say, mythical markets abroad. His export targets are cock-eyed and must lead to profound disillusionment and great unemployment in Britain.

Cripps is mounted on a very high horse. He is Attlee's champion against Bevin, Morrison and Bevan.[67] They are out to unsaddle him. But they will not have to over-strain themselves. The jockey is a fanatic in a panic and will soon say or do something which will lose him the not over enthusiastic support he gets from Socialist back benchers in the H. of C.

Some prophets hold that the Socialist bosses, who know the consequences of the mess they have created and foresee the economic storms of 1948, will seek an election when the Lords throw

---

64 The American loan of December 1945 had stipulated that Sterling should become convertible on 15 July 1947. This had led to a massive outflow of capital from the country, of such magnitude that the Government was forced to suspend convertibility on 17 August, a decision ratified by the American Government on 20 August.

65 The municipal elections were held at the beginning of November, and whilst the Conservatives won 636 sets, Labour lost 687.

66 Sir Stafford Cripps.

67 Aneurin Bevan (1897–1960). Celebrated left-wing Labour politician. Minister of Health 1945–50, Minister of Labour and National Service 1951. Resigned from the Government over health charges in 1951.

out their amendments to the Parliament Act. This prophecy is based on the theory that the Socialists expect defeat by a small margin of votes.

I am sure that far-seeing Socialists would now welcome an electoral defeat which would enable them to escape responsibility for riding an economic storm. In Opposition they could harry the Tories and re-unite their party.

The snag in this prophecy is that most of the so-called far-seeing Socialists are not in office. The really forceful Ministers like Bevin and Morrison are ageing and ailing and therefore desire to enjoy the time left to them in the seats (and motor cars) of the mighty. They will fight to keep the Socialist party in office until 1950. I shall be greatly surprised if they do not glue their colleagues to the Treasury bench.

The Tories have been given a wonderful tonic. The critics of Churchill in our Party are suddenly discovering his great qualities. They now deem him the only man to save the country. They clamour for his immediate installation in No. 10. Who can doubt that their new found loyalty will abide if W. has places to give them!

Politics is a business of endless surprises and so the Socialists may yet find a way of placating the middle class people who rushed to vote Tory at the Municipal elections. But the odds are heavily against them. Britain's economy is visibly faltering and the only remedy proposed by the Government is more controls and stricter regimentation of masters and workers. Food rations are being reduced, potatoes have been rationed, clothes and household equipment will be scarcer and more expensive. In such conditions miracle workers cannot save the comrades....

Mountbatten (the Earl, not the Bridegroom)[68] has done much mischief by his foolish letter to the Maharajah of Kashmir. It was in effect a declaration of war on Pakistan. How touched the Maharajah must have been by Mountbatten's appeal to him to save the honour of his State![69] The former 'Mr A' is in a funk

---

[68] Earl Mountbatten of Burma (1900–79). Supreme Allied Commander, S.E. Asia 1943–46. The last Viceroy of India 1947, Governor-General of India 1947–48. First Sea Lord 1955–59. His nephew was Prince Philip (later the Duke of Edinburgh), due to marry Princes Elizabeth on 20 November 1947.

[69] On October 24, the Princely State of Kashmir was invaded by Pathan

15 November 1947   *Toiling under the yoke*   77

hole outside Kashmir and without a comforter from Piccadilly.[70] Supremo's[71] admirers are dwindling rapidly. Mieville[72] has given up his job at Delhi and Ismay[73] comes home for good next month. His account of conditions in India is heart-rending.

My chances of enjoying your company in Jamaica are slender. Having spent 3 1/2 months out of England in 1947 my dear Constituents and my business impatiently require attention. And I have also been landed with the job of running the opposition to the Bill to nationalize the gas industry. A bleak project.

Yours affectionately,
Brendan

Bracken to Beaverbrook   8, Lord North Street,
15 November 1947   Westminster
My dear Max,
The Dalton affair is another heavy blow against the dwindling prestige of the Socialists.[74]

H.D. is an ebullient and indiscreet man. He is also greatly

---

tribesmen, aided and abetted by Pakistan which entertained hopes of absorbing Kashmir and its large Muslim Community. Before Mountbatten, in his capacity as Governor-General of India, would commit Indian troops to come to the aid of the Maharajah of Kashmir, he wrote an oft-criticised letter to the Maharajah insisting that Indian troops would only be used for the defence of Kashmir *if* Kashmir immediately renounced its independent status and acceded to the new State of India. The panic-stricken Maharajah accepted on 26 October and a military airlift to the capital at Srinagar began at once. This antagonised the large Muslim community in Kashmir as well as Pakistan. For a time it looked as if India and Pakistan would come to blows over the issue of Kashmir.

70 Perhaps F.M. Sir Claude Auchinleck (1884–1981). Commander-in-Chief in India, 1943–47. He had pleaded with Mountbatten to send British troops to protect British citizens in and around Srinagar some days earlier, but Mountbatten had preferred to stick to his own plan.
71 Mountbatten.
72 Sir Eric Mieville (1896–1971). Principal Secretary to the Viceroy, 1947.
73 General the Lord Hastings 'Pug' Ismay (1887–1965). Chief of Staff to Churchill 1940–45, Chief of Staff to Mountbatten in India, March–November 1947.
74 On 12 November 1947 Hugh Dalton, the Chancellor of the Exchequer, resigned, having told a journalist, a few minutes before he started speaking, the main items of the budget that he was presenting to the House of Commons that afternoon.

liked by the T.U.C. bosses who are the ringmasters of the Socialist party and by most of the Government's supporters in the House of Commons.

Dalton's financial policies were altogether harmful to Britain. And enormously popular with the majority of Socialists!

On public grounds I am glad Dalton has left the Treasury. But I am sorry for him. He has paid too harsh a penalty. If he had not criticised Attlee's leadership our meagre Prime Minister would have kept him. Attlee behaved like a Pontus Pilate in a panic. His position is infinitely more precarious with the arrival of Cripps at No. 11 Downing St.[75]

Cripps will soon create a Cabinet and a party crisis which will make him or Bevin Prime Minister or will send Attlee scurrying to the country. I do not believe that the socialists could win an election with Attlee as leader. Neither do the Comrades!

As Cripps has not an atom of common-sense he must soon run foul of the Trade Union bosses and their creatures in Parliament. The Socialists will never accept a policy of deflation and they are sick of the austerity prescribed by Cripps. If that gentleman becomes Prime Minister he would wreck his Party within a few months.

Bevin's Russian policy has lost him much prestige with the Left. Moloteff(sic)[76] comes to London next week and may unwittingly convert some of Bevin's critics. If M. breaks up the meeting of Foreign Ministers and Bevin shows more sorrow than anger, many of our left wingers will become temporarily reconciled to his policies.[77]

During the past month Socialist stock has had a catastrophic fall. Potato rationing, direction of labour, the Dalton affair and the Allingham-Walkden (sic) scandal[78] have enraged or disillusioned

---

[75] Sir Stafford Cripps succeeded Dalton as Chancellor.
[76] V. M. Molotov (1890–1986). Soviet Diplomat. People's Commissar for Foreign Affairs 1939–46; Foreign Minister 1946–49, 1953–56.
[77] The 5th Council of Foreign Ministers (attended by Bevin, Molotov, Marshall and Bidault) was held in London from 25 November to 15 December.
[78] Two Labour MPs, Evelyn Walkeden and Gary Allingham, were found guilty by the Parliamentary Committee of Privileges of passing on secrets of Parliamentary Committees for money to newspapers. In October 1947 Allingham was expelled from the House of Commons.

15 November 1947   Toiling under the yoke   79

millions of electors. Many supporters of the Government have an uneasy feeling that Ministers are thoroughly incompetent. The crusading spirit that animated Socialist workers in the back streets is crushed. Meanwhile the Tories are recovering confidence and are out for blood.

Woolton[79] is more confident of winning Greenwich. If we can beat the Socialists there and in Camlachie, the face of British politics will be changed beyond recognition.[80]

The best thing that could happen would be a faltering attempt by Socialists to hold on to office for another year. By that time widespread unemployment and mounting grievances about food, clothes, fuel and housing would sweep the comrades out of office.

When the Tories return to power we must expect the battle between the Parties to be transferred to the Production line. That is one of the many problems to daunt aspiring Tories. Lots of courage and energy will be needed to cope with Britain's home and overseas problems. But the prospect of office makes heroes out of timid politicians in opposition.

In our present mood of exaltation we perhaps forget the changeability of public opinion and the fervour in battle that the socialists will show when defending their jobs and seats.

Halifax[81] intends to oppose Salisbury's policy of rejecting the amendments to the Parliament Act.[82] I am sure the Lords will not be influenced over-much by Halifax, even though he has converted Sam Hoare. What a pair of trimming ritualists!

Yours affly
Brendan

79 Lord Woolton (1883–1964). Conservative politician. Minister of Food 1940–43, Minister of Reconstruction 1943–45, Chairman of the Conservative Party 1946–55, Lord President of the Council 1951–52, Chancellor of the Duchy of Lancaster 1952–55.
80 The Conservatives gained Camlachie from Labour in January 1948. This was very much a freak Tory gain on a low poll in a very working-class district.
81 1st Earl of Halifax (1881–1959). Conservative politician. Viceroy of India 1926–31, Lord Privy Seal 1935–37, Foreign Secretary 1938–40, British Ambassador to Washington 1941–46.
82 Salisbury was responsible for leading the Conservative attack on Labour's proposals to curtail the delaying powers of the House of Lords. The Parliament Act was eventually passed against the will of the Lords in December 1949.

Bracken to Beaverbrook   Princes House,
19 November 1947   95, Gresham Street,
                                                            London, E.C.2.

My dear Max,

....Poor Winant.[83] The last days of his life must, indeed, have been gloomy. He was running out of money and he was greatly in love. He was much too old to have married the girl and would have had no means of supporting her. A very strange man was he. But a courageous and splendid friend to Britain in times of great trouble.

Woolton's hopes of winning the Gravesend Election are rising. After the Allingham scandal, Transport House[84] decided that they must produce a candidate of high integrity for Gravesend. Acland[85] fitted that description because he gave (or appeared to give) most of his money away and they also hoped that he would pick up a goodly part of the Liberal vote. On paper it looked a cunning choice. In fact, Acland is a crackpot and his bookmanite (sic)[86] orations in Gravesend are not going down well. Some of the Tory organisers assert that we shall get a 5,000 majority. The main issues at Gravesend are potatoes, the basic petrol ration and direction of Labour. All splendid issues from the Tory point of view.

The 'Daily Herald'[87] has gone to town with Truman's[88] proposal to restore controls in the United States. I believe that Truman has stuck his head into the most vicious of hornets nests. Unless the Yanks have changed completely during the last few months, I cannot be persuaded that they will accept the re-imposition of

---

83 John Winant (1889–3 November 1947). United States Ambassador to Britain, 1941–47. He committed suicide.
84 The headquarters of the Labour Party.
85 Sir Richard Acland (1906–). A hereditary baronet, he served as Liberal M.P. for Barnstaple, 1935–45. Co-founder of the wartime Commonwealth Party, he served as Labour M.P. for Gravesend, 1947–55. Consistent with his views on wealth, he gave away the family estate in Devon only retaining a cottage for his own use.
86 Buchmanite; member of a movement founded at Oxford by Frank Buchman (1878–1961), and otherwise known as Moral Rearmament.
87 The official paper of the Labour Party.
88 Harry S. Truman (1884–1972). President of the United States of America 1945–53.

Controls. And even if they were to do so Controls could not be effective in the United States in peace-time. They would set up a Black Market which would dwarf all the Black Markets of the World put together. Truman seems anxious to add to the Republican vote!

Lewis Douglas has been offered the job of Administrator of the Marshall Plan.[89] He is inclined to accept it. If he does he is taking on a thankless job that may easily diminish his chances of becoming Senator for Arizona.

Cripps has made his first speech as Chancellor of the Exchequer. To the surprise of some innocent Tories who believe that he is a great Statesman, he announces his strong support of food subsidies and ultra cheap money. The mugs now call him Sir Hugh Cripps. I am not the least surprised by Cripps' decision to continue Dalton's policies. For he is a fanatic with limitless ambitions and his main object in life is to move into No. 10. Attlee's treatment of Dalton has driven some more nails in his coffin. The booming Doctor is furious with him. And so are many Labour Back-Benchers, who already resent the dismissal of poor old Arthur Greenwood.[90]

Little Max has completely recovered and works hard at his Sunday Express.

Yours affly, Brendan

Bracken to Beaverbrook
25 November 1947

Princes House,
95, Gresham Street,
London E.C.2.

My dear Max,

.... That baubling old John Anderson[91] has given the Socialist Party plenty of ammunition to use against us in the Gravesend by-election. A few months ago he made a speech advocating

89 Lewis Douglas (1894–1974); American financier. During the war he held a number of minor posts in Roosevelt's administration and from 1947 to 1950 served as Ambassador to Britain.
90 Arthur Greenwood was dropped from the Cabinet in a reshuffle at the end of September 1947.
91 Sir John Anderson (1882–1958). Civil Servant and subsequently Conservative politician. M.P. for Scottish Universities 1938–50. Home Secretary 1939–40, Lord President of the Council 1940–43, Chancellor of the Exchequer 1943–45. A neighbour of Bracken, who nicknamed him 'Pomposo'.

the cutting down and eventual abolition of food subsidies. The Socialists made good use of this gift from Pomposo. A week ago he felt obliged to try to explain his speech away and the explanation was worse than the speech.

Our people are getting cold feet about the result of Gravesend. They are abandoning their notion of a 3000 majority and now think that they will only scrape in.[92]

Master Barry[93] has been pushed out of the News Chronicle by the dithering Lord Layton. His Lordship came to lunch with me yesterday to discuss the question of filling a vacancy on the Board of the Economist. He talked interminably. That, of course, is habitual. But he took my breath away by suggesting that we should appoint his son to the Board. I was so startled by this proposition that I turned it down with elephantine flatness![94]

You cannot imagine how I miss your company. I often think of you and deplore the fact that our evening gossips are no more.

Winston is going to Morocco for Christmas. He also has a vague plan to visit the United States.

(Sgd) Yours affectionately,
Brendan

Bracken to Beaverbrook
5 December 1947
My dear Max,

.... Robbie has doubtless sent you a little cutting from today's 'News Chronicle', about Cripps' Press Conference at the Ministry of Food. Whitehall's Poobah grows in self-esteem every day. His powers are so tremendous and his judgement so erratic that his uncontrolled decisions may easily land this country into an even deeper mess. *I enclose another cutting on Cripp's Press Conference from the F. Times.*

The Epsom Election result was very good.[95] It would have been better if the Tories had more petrol for their transport and if the Polling Day had not been cursed by atrocious weather.

[92] Labour won the Gravesend by-election with a small majority.
[93] Gerald Barry (1898–1968). Editor of the *News Chronicle* 1936–47, Director-General of the Festival of Britain 1948–51.
[94] Bracken was a co-proprietor of the *Economist*.
[95] The Conservatives held Epsom on 4 December, with an increased share of the vote.

Some of the Left-Wing newspapers have been publishing stories that Lord Mountbatten, who will soon be a displaced person, is to be the next British Ambassador to Washington. If there be any truth in these rumours, our Embassy in Washington will be a second home to Hollywood and to scribblers like Walter Winchell.[96]

.... The dispossessed Lord Lieutenant of Sutherland[97] tells me that he is going to eat his Christmas dinner with you. Another aristocrat is about to go to Jamaica — my predecessor — Lord Lyle.[98] Your island of Jamaica seems to be magnate (sic) for the noble and the rich. Two centuries ago the English made a lot of money in Jamaica and returned to be enrolled. Now the aristocrats are taking much softer money to Jamaica. We live in a mutable world!

Do the Jamaicans realise that Napoleon wrought more harm to their prosperity than all the Free Traders in Downing Street? Not long ago I read a very interesting account of his economic warfare against the West Indies. He himself issued orders to all his officials to grow sugar beet in France and in the territories he conquered in Europe. Those officials were told that the richest part of the British Empire was the West Indies, and that Sugar was the foundation of their prosperity. If you destroy the West Indian pre-eminence in sugar, said Napoleon, you will have done irrevocable harm to those prosperous islands and you will have inflicted sharp losses upon British traders.

There is the probability of a by-election at Stoke Newington. As you no doubt know, the present Member has been sentenced to a year in jail. If his appeal fails, a by-election must follow.[99] I am told that Stoke Newington is one of the most anti-semitic spots in London and that Mosley[100] is thinking of running a candidate.

---

96 Walter Winchell (1897–1972); American newspaper columnist.
97 Probably Sir Archibald Sinclair, leader of the Liberal Party 1935–45 and M.P. for Caithness and Sunderland — the largest constituency in Britain — until beaten in the 1945 general election.
98 Lord Lyle of Westbourne (1882–1954). President of Tate and Lyle Ltd, purveyors of sugar cubes to the British nation.
99 The Labour M.P. for Stoke Newington, Mr. Weitzman, was found guilty on a minor technicality under the Defence Regulations on October 30, 1939. However his conviction was quashed in March 1948, so there was no need of a by-election.
100 Sir Oswald Mosley (1896–1980). Leader of the British Union of Fas-

If he should do so, we may expect one of the most ferocious Elections London has ever known.

(Sgd) Yours aff.

Brendan

P.S. — Your fine ham arrived from Canada this morning. My cook think (sic) you are a saint and she now can easily be converted to Presbyterianism. Many thanks.

Bracken to Beaverbrook   Princes House,
18 December 1947   95, Gresham Street,
London E.C.2.

My dear Max,

We had a great schenozzle in the House of Commons last night, and were it not for the fact that the Tory Party turned up in strength, the Government would have been beaten on the financial proposals they fathered for the benefit of Princess Elizabeth and her spouse.[101] The background of this row is interesting. Maurice Webb[102] assumed the leadership of the Opposition to provide Princess Elizabeth with £40,000 a year and the Duke of Edinburgh with £10,000. A Party meeting was held yesterday morning and Webb and his friends carried a vote against Attlee. This was an intensely embarrassing development for the Government and so they hit on the cowardly compromise of taking off the Whips and letting the Comrades vote as they liked. This was Heaven for the Socialists. More than half the Party voted against the Government and more than a hundred abstained. Many Ministers did not vote.

Attlee was greatly upset by the speeches he had to listen to in the House and by the conduct of his Party. He sat on the Treasury Bench looking like a hen-pecked Bank clerk about to be arrested for embezzlement.

The Socialist Parliamentarians are not in the least bit repentant. They now want an investigation to be made into all the allowances made to the Royal Family and they may succeed in their endeavours.

cists 1932–39. He was active in Right-wing politics after the war.
101 Princess Elizabeth (later Queen Elizabeth II) and Lieutenant Philip Mountbatten (later the Duke of Edinburgh) married on 20 November 1947.
102 Maurice Webb (1904–56). Journalist and Labour politician.

18 December 1947   *Toiling under the yoke*

Doctor Davies has nearly succeeded in polishing me off this mortal coil. I have had a touch of Tonsilitus (sic) and so he prescribed injections. What do you think they consisted of? Pencillin! I assure you that I have gone through most of the pangs of being burned alive. Having spent a completely sleepless week I am now getting out of my troubles.

Doubtless Robbie has told you that a fellow named Harold Drayton,[103] who is the son of the late Lord St. David's partner in his investment Trust Companies, has now moved into the newspaper business. Drayton is Chairman of the British Electric Traction Company and had millions of pounds invested in road transport. The Government have, of course, taken over most of that business. He is also a Director of many South American Railways. Mr. Peron[104] has taken over most of that business. And so Drayton has lots of money to put into newspapers. He has bought Akermann out of the Argus Press and he has bought Grotrian's shares in United Newspapers, together with a large block held by Lloyds Bank.

Drayton was a Liberal candidate at the last Election but is, I think, veering towards Toryism. He is a coarse, bumptious man, a hell of a bore, but has plenty of aggressive ability.

I am told that he intends to make an offer for the News Chronicle. The giggling Cadbury[105] is anxious to get out. He does not fancy the future of the newspaper business. And he is bitterly jealous of Layton's Peerage.[106] Cadbury thinks that the owner of the News Chronicle should have gone to the Lords and not the Manager. It is said that Cadbury requires a price of £3,000,000. Drayton will be a damn fool if he pays such a sum for the News Chronicle.

I am sending you a cutting from today's Daily Mirror. Are you

---

103 Harold Drayton (1901–66). Financier. He took over as head of the British Electric Traction Company in 1947. He did not buy the *News Chronicle*, but became Chairman of United Newspapers.
104 President Peron of Argentina (1895–1974). President 1946–55, 1973–74.
105 Laurence Cadbury (1889–1983). The *News Chronicle* was owned by the chocolate-making Cadbury family; Laurence was Managing Director of Cadbury Bros. Ltd 1919–54.
106 Sir Walter Layton, the editor-in-chief of the *News Chronicle*, had accepted a peerage earlier in the year.

not pleased to have such swell friends![107]

(Sgd) Yours affctly,
Brendan

Bracken to Beaverbrook
9 January 1948

Princes House,
95, Gresham Street,
London E.C.2.

My dear Max,

Don't be alarmed by news of Winston's illness. He has had a touch of bronchitis but Moran[108] is satisfied that he has got out of his troubles.

During the last few weeks the Governments stock has improved a little. The public, accustomed to a succession of jolts or discomforts from Whitehall, are encouraged by the fact that no new dismal controls have been slammed upon them during the last fortnight.

The Government is raising a tremendous amount of ballyhoo about the success of their appeal to coal miners, the B.B.C. and many newspapers are saluting them as production heroes. They would not, of course, have reached the target were it not for the fact that Gaitskell's[109] officials hit on the bright idea of inventing a year of fifty-three weeks. Much of the improvement in coal production is due to opencast operations. Consumers are screaming with rage against the quality of the 'coal'. It is an odd mixture of grit, slates and tombstones.

Our people are living in a synthetic paradise. British warehouses are full of goods that cannot be exported to overseas markets. The Government calls them 'frustrated exports'. Cripps, in order to keep up his export figures, is now supplying countries like Egypt and India with great quantities of British goods. The Egyptians are, of course, not paying anything for these goods. They merely chalk off a little of the inflated war debt we owe them. You will remember that this Government declared that it intended to scale down our vast inflated war debts to countries

---

107 The cutting shows Earl and Countess Mountbatten, he in full-dress uniform, going to a ceremonial Durbar. Beaverbrook's aversion to the royal Admiral was legendary.

108 Lord Moran (1882–1977). Churchill's physician and close friend.

109 Hugh Gaitskell (1906–63). Labour politician. Minister of Fuel and Power 1947–50, Chancellor of the Exchequer 1950–51, Leader of the Labour Party 1955–63.

like India and Egypt. This, like many other promises, has proved to be worthless, and I think the time has passed now that we can hope to secure a proper adjustment of these debts. I have always feared that dilatoriness and lack of firmness in standing up to our creditors in India and Egypt would encourage those countries to behave like Shylock.

Cripps has just treated the Press to a long dose of gloomy prophecies. He declares that without Marshall aid[110] our meagre standard of living must be severely slashed. He has also been lecturing the Trade Unions on the evil of increases in wages. This will be grist for Pollitt's mill.

Lord Burnham,[111] who was an intimate of Barrington-Ward's,[112] tells me that he doubts if he will return to active work as the editor of The Times. He has gone off to Africa to try to restore his health.

The Royal Commission on the Press is settling down to its job. It has now made an arrangement with its landlord to lease his office until 1950!

....I envy you basking in the sun and enjoying the fascinating conversation of Lord Rothermere.

(Sgd) Yours affly,
Brendan.

*A. G. Millar (for Beaverbrook)
to Bracken*

Dear Mr. Bracken,
Lord Beaverbrook asks me to send you this small package of Blue Mountain Coffee from Jamaica, with his regards.

Lord Beaverbrook asks you please not to bother to acknowledge it, but to let me know if it is in good condition, and if it is any good or not.

Yours sincerely, [A. G. Millar]

---

110 The American aid to Britain and Europe which started in 1947 was named after Secretary of State Marshall.
111 Lord Burnham (1890–1963). Managing Director of the *Daily Telegraph* 1945–61.
112 Robert Barrington-Ward (1891–1948). Assistant Editor of *The Times* 1927–41, Editor 1941–48. He died 29 February 1948 on the sea voyage out to South Africa.

Bracken to Millar (for Beaver-   Princes House,
brook)   95, Gresham Street,
5 February 1948   London E.C.2.

Dear Millar

Many thanks for sending me such a good package of Blue Mountain Coffee from Jamaica.

I shall be writing to Lord Beaverbrook to thank him.

Airmail communications with Jamaica do not seem to be worthy of the great talents of Lord Nathan.[113] I had a note from Lord Beaverbrook the other day saying he was hoping for a letter from me. He has had five!

           Yours sincerely,
           (sgd) Brendan Bracken

Bracken to Beaverbrook   Princes House,
5 February 1948   95, Gresham Street,
           London, E.C.2.

My dear Max

If you haven't heard from me for a long time the blame must rest with your noble colleague, Lord Nathan, for I have sent you four or five letters. I should have liked to have sent you a lot more were it not for the fact that for the first time in my life I have really had to sit down to hard jobs of work.

The Union Corporation is full of business and those financial newspapers of ours are blossoming out. We have just bought ourselves a good interest in a group of Trade Papers. This investment should help to cope with the difficulties of what you rightly call 'a feast or famine business.'

I regret to have to tell you that this Government's stock has gone up a bit. I believe if Mr. Strachey fed the British public on arsenic, many of our fellow citizens would declare that it was entirely due to a dollar shortage and not to any fault of His Majesty's Government.

The doctors, under that strange character, Hill,[114] have done

---

113 Lord Nathan (1889–1963); Labour Peer, Minister of Civil Aviation 1946–48.
114 Dr Charles Hill (1904–). Secretary to the British Medical Association (1944–50) and as such a leading opponent of Bevan's plans for the National Health Service. He later occupied a number of junior posts in

a marvellous job of propaganda. I believe they will throw out Bevan's National Health Service. Great credit should be given to Hill for the way he has run this campaign. He has managed to get the younger doctors to join with the citadel in Harley Street in refusing to accept Aneurin Bevan's dictatorship. Hardly any day passes without impressive accounts of meetings of doctors all over the country who place themselves on record as being willing to sacrifice the considerable bribes offered by Bevan rather than sign away their liberties. If the Tories had as good a propagandist as Hill we might make some progress against the Comrades.

Miss Maxton won us the Camlachie seat. That constituency is, as you know, a collection of suppurating slums. It is an encouragement to the Tory Party that our candidate polled over eleven thousand vote *in such a place*.

Our gold and Dollar reserves are steadily seeping. Representative industrialists are now beginning to air in public their doubts about the future of our export trade. France, Italy, Chile and Brazil are following Dr. Schact's example in setting up double-faced currencies. I think that they are wise. At any rate, they have no other way of getting out of their present troubles.

Winston has written two volumes of his war memoirs. He hopes to write another quarter-of-a-million words before the year ends.

Your Lordship's House is having an hell of a tussle about reforming itself. Morrison and Salisbury have been playing the toughest of games of poker. It looks as if Salisbury will win out. I cannot understand why the Government are willing even to discuss House of Lords Reform. The Lords' bogey has always been useful electoral ammunition. I cannot believe that such a cunning politician as Morrison has opened up the vista of a reform of the Lords without having planted a trap-door somewhere for our dear Tory Party.

Eddie Derby[115] died today. Death has been merciful unto him.

Churchill's government and became Lord Privy seal under Macmillan, with special responsibility for propaganda. He was Chairman of the Independent Television Authority 1963–67 and Chairman of Governors of the BBC, 1967–72.

115 Edward Stanley, 17th Earl of Derby (1865–1948). A prominent Conservative politician and large hereditary landowner at Knowsley in Lancashire.

He was, as you know much better than I, a man who greatly enjoyed and made good use of his position and wealth. He liked the company of pretty women and they greatly enjoyed his gaiety and benevolence. The war ended all his fun. He had to spend the remainder of his life cooped up at Knowsley with some very fractious domestics. His successors will never know the happiness that he inherited.

Linlithgow[116] has recently delivered a speech to the Midland Bank shareholders, which might have been written by Michael Foot!

When are you coming back to us?

I am flying out to South Africa on May 23rd to be present at the celebrations of the Fiftieth Anniversary of the Union Corporation. I hope to be back within a week or ten days.

Bracken to Beaverbrook Princes House,
7 May 1948 95, Gresham Street,
London, E.C.2.

My dear Max

Here is a nice die-hard speech for you to read.[117] Its only merit is that it is short.

You will notice that the hard-bitten Tory who runs the Financial Times has handed over his nice fat fee arranged by his predecessor, Lord Camrose,[118] to the staff in order that they may have a Pension Fund. I am now beginning to regret this decision!

(Signed) Yrs affly
Brendan

Beaverbrook to Bracken Fredericton, New Brunswick
11 May 1948

My dear Brendan,

I have read your 'die-hard' speech and I think it is very fine. The Tory party would do well to read it, heed it and take the advice it gives about the taxing of reserves.

116 3rd Marquess of Linlithgow (1887–1952). Viceroy of India 1936–43 and Chairman of the Midland Bank 1944–52.
117 A summary at the end of the next letter. It was given to the shareholders of the *Financial Times*.
118 Lord Camrose had sold the *Financial Times* to Bracken in 1945.

I have also read the speech of the poor Socialist who says he must remain silent while Brendan Bracken abuses him and hurls epithets at him. That shows successful opposition.

Make them squeal. Hit them where it hurts. Tell them about the big salaries paid to the bosses of the new bureaucratic machinery — £5,000 a year. Their Comrades get £5 a week. The £5 Comrades don't like it.

Here we are having an election. My friend John McNair is standing as a Liberal and my friend Hugh Mackay on the Tory side.[119] A nobleman has a vote.

I have a telegram this morning from Mackenzie King[120] There are signs that St Laurent[121] is being treated the same way Churchill treats Eden.

I have been reading the story of Eden's resignation in Churchill's memoirs. I have been told differently. The same applies to Sir Duff Cooper.[122]

This is the place for free enterprise and no nonsense. It is the home of liberty.

I am hoping for a letter from you giving all the news. I can send plenty from this side of the Atlantic but you would not be interested. Sometimes I think I am not interested either.

Yours ever, (unsigned).

Summary of Mr Bracken's Speech
(Attached to letter)

Hoped to establish branches overseas where opportunities exist. Policy of the Financial Times is reaffirmed as the support of free

---

119 Both were duly elected.
120 W.C. Mackenzie King (1874–1950). Prime Minister of Canada 1921–30, 1935–48.
121 Louis Stephen St-Laurent (1882–1970). Prime Minister of Canada 1948–57.
122 The account of Eden's resignation from the Foreign Office in February 1938 can be found in *The Gathering Storm*, Volume I of Churchill's war memoirs. This account does indeed omit a crucial element in the story, namely Eden's anger at Chamberlain's off-hand rejection of President Roosevelt's offer to intervene and begin a process of consultation amongst the democracies to alleviate the deteriorating European situation. A fuller account of Eden's resignation can be found in Robert Rhodes James, *Anthony Eden* (Weidenfeld and Nicolson, 1986) pp. 187–195.

enterprise. Mr Bracken attacks the planners, calls them 'power misers'. He does not suggest that free enterprise will produce immediate abundance. Points out that many economic troubles are old and deep-seated. All political parties must be censured for failure to understand policies like taxing company reserves have brought industrial obsolescence. This year more than £250,000 will be paid away in income tax and profits tax. Chairman has given up his 6 per cent to donate to a pension fund.

Beaverbrook to Bracken
13 February 1948
(Telegram)
With increasing loneliness I send you a birthday message and I mean to join you soon in the land of make believe where the Government liquidates our only remaining asset the British Empire — Max

Bracken to Beaverbrook   Princes House,
25 February 1948   95, Gresham Street,
                                                                       London, E.C.2.

My dear Millar,

Thank you for your letter, telling me that Lord Beaverbrook is sending me a ham.

I shall certainly acknowledge that gift. In the times in which we live it is better than a present of a Cullinan diamond.

                                                                               Yours sincerely,
                                                                  (Sgd) Brendan Bracken.

Bracken to Beaverbrook   Durban Club,
28 May 1948   Durban (South Africa)

My dear Max,

When I landed here two days before polling date, representatives of the Government and the Opposition were sure that Smuts[123] would have a working majority.

They too quickly forgot Churchill's experience in 1945.

And now Smuts' party are busily blaming their defeat on a

---

[123] Jan Christian Smuts (1870–1950). South Africa Statesman, Prime Minister 1939–48. In the General Election of 1948 Smuts was unexpectedly defeated, even in his own constituency.

28 May 1948   *Toiling under the yoke*   93

number of men. The most abused is Hofymr[124] (sic) (the Deputy Prime Minister and altogether unconnected with the newspaper business!).

H. has for long advocated a more liberal treatment of the coloured people. The colour issue brought the Nationalists to power under Hertzog.[125] It is political dynamite here. I daresay it played a part in Smuts' defeat.

A big part was played by the soldiers. They have been waiting to punish the almighty Prime Minister and like all warriors they have plenty of personal grievances.

Smuts' recognition of Israel was an electoral error. Johannesburg is full of Jews. They would have voted for Smuts without his gesture to Israel. But many thousands of people who disliked the gentlemen who crossed the Jordan with dry feet were stung to fury and to voting.

Controls also damaged Smuts. Bad in themselves, they are administered by young Nationalists civil servants, who enjoyed goading the public as they knew that Smuts would suffer.

The preachers here also useful to Smuts' enemies. They are as powerful as the priests in Ireland.

The new Prime Minister[126] is a former preacher — or 'predikant', as the office is called here. His critics admit that as Minister of the Interior, he was the best in the Union's history. Old John Gretton[127] was a liberal by comparison with Malan.

If, as the newspapers predict, he appoints Havenga[128] to be Minister of Finance, Montagu Norman[129] will probably be asked

---

124 Jan Hofmeyr (1894–1948). Smuts's able lieutenant, Minister of Finance and Education 1938–48, Deputy Prime Minister 1948. Hofmeyr died suddenly in December 1948.
125 James Hertzog (1866–1942); founder of the South African National Party and life-long political rival of Smuts. As Prime Minister 1924–29, he was largely responsible for institutionalising racial segregation in South Africa.
126 Daniel Malan (1874–1959). Leader of the National Party and Prime Minister of South Africa 1948–54.
127 Colonel John Gretton (1867–1947) Chairman of Bass, Ratcliffe and Gretton, brewers; Conservative M.P. 1895–1943.
128 Nicholas Havenga (1883–1953). Minister of Finance, Union of South Africa, 1924–39 and 1948–54.
129 Montagu Norman, Governor of the Bank of England 1920–44 and a champion of financial orthodoxy.

to come here as his adviser! Havenga is a crusader for hard money and fought to the end against S. Africa's departure from the gold standard and thus nearly ruined the gold mines.[130]

I am flying back to England next week. The journey is infinitely boring. One is dazed by the infinity of the deserts. May the Lord help Britain if she sinks what is left of her free resources in Africa.

Yours affly
Brendan.

Bracken to Beaverbrook Princes House,
8 June 1948 95, Gresham Street,
London, E.C.2.

My dear Max

I returned to London yesterday after my visit to South Africa. I feel rather tired having spent sixty-four hours in the air. This is perhaps too much flying put into thirteen days.

The Government Bosses here are at each other throats. Bevan is bitterly abusing Shinwell; Dalton attacks Cripps; Morrison is highly critical of almost all his colleagues. The sound is going out of old Ernie Bevin. Attlee is the only really perky Minister; so long as his colleagues are fighting each other he is certain to maintain his leadership.

I am told that when the results of the Coal Board's financial year are published, enormous losses will be shown.Meanwhile production is steadily falling.

I have a friend in the Transport Commission who tells me that they too are piling up immense losses. And when our old friend, Lord Citrine,[131] produces his accounts they too will disclose heavy losses. The terms of trade are getting much worse from our point of view. We are now beginning to pay the price of our fatuous bulk purchasers. These ignorant and presumptuous men boasted of their success in avoiding market higgling. They regarded hedging as a bad form of gambling. And now they are at the mercy of suppliers like Colonel Peron who will take much more than a pound of flesh off John Bull.

130 Hertzog took South Africa off the Gold Standard in December 1932.
131 Lord Citrine (1887–1983). General Secretary of the Trades Union Congress 1926–46, Chairman of the Central Electricity Authority 1947 to 1952.

8 June 1948 *Toiling under the yoke* 95

Morrison and his moderates now realise the necessity for some sort of clean-up in the nationalised industries. They fear that their nationalization follies will further diminish middle-class support and so they are making soothing speeches about the hardships of professional people and small rentiers.

The Tories have now got the Socialists up against the ropes and we should be bashing them with all our might. Alas, this is the moment chosen by Butler and that semi-Socialist Eccles[132] to publish pamphlets calling for further instalments of planning from Whitehall. I have always held the view that the public will revenge themselves upon planners and controllers at the next General Election. But if we are associated with those tribes of starry-eyed power-misers we shall lose many of our electoral advantages.

Sweet reason will, for a time, mark all the actions of the new Ministers in South Africa. The Prime Minister is seventy-four years of age. He has made four speeches since he took office. In all of them he expressed his surprise, not to say bewilderment, that the Nats.[133] did so well. He also announced that the Election had disturbed his plan to go into hospital for a month's check-up. His health is very bad and I do not think he will last long.

Dr Malan is a retired Predicant. He loathes the British, the Blacks and the Jews. Many of his principal Ministers wanted South Africa to make a separate peace. One of the most important of all declared that Hitler's victory would be good for South Africa.

My fellows in South Africa tell me that the Government will be more considerate to the Gold Industry than was Smuts'. I shall not be surprised if this proves to be true. The Gold Industry pays about 80% of the taxes of the country and is finding the burden too heavy. It would be quite a popular move to lift a little of the heavy taxes the industry is now bearing. I do not believe in any immediate increase in the price of gold. It would add to our problems in South Africa. The unions are very restive and would demand great increases in pay. And the Government which ought to reduce the taxation of the Gold Mines would probably mark

---

132 David Eccles (1904–). Conservative politician. Served in a number of Government posts from 1951 to 1973.
133 The National Party.

an increase in the price of gold by taking further rakes off the industry.

My views are not fashionable in Johannesburg. I gave them at some length to the shareholders of the Union Corporation at their Jubilee Meeting. I also expressed some doubts about the miraculous Orange Free State. I was amused to see in the newspapers this morning a declaration from Sir Ernest Oppenheimer[134] that the Orange Free State was much better than the Promised Land.

Will you be here early in July? I miss you and am greatly looking forward to a reunion.

(Sgd) Yours affly
Brendan

Bracken to Beaverbrook Princes House,
16 June, 1948. 95, Gresham Street,
London, E.C.2.

My dear Max

I send you a cutting from the Financial Times criticising a silly pamphlet issued by Mr Eccles, M.P. who, in the intervals of criticising Churchill, says some very uncharitable things about you. He ought long since to have joined the Socialist party. But as he regards himself as an aristocrat because of his marriage with the daughter of that old undertaker's friend, Lord Dawson,[135] he cannot contaminate himself by joining a low-born Party like the Socialists!

Herbert Morrison has just made a damn fool of himself. He attacked Churchill for drawing his salary as Leader of the Opposition and failing to attend regularly at the House of Commons. For reasons you well know Churchill would, indeed, be silly to draw his salary as leader of the Opposition. It would all dissolve in income tax. Morrison has now been forced to apologise and as he is not very popular in his Party he cannot afford the sort of snub that Churchill has given him.

I dined with Lew Douglas[136] last night. Smuts was the other

---

134 Sir Ernest Oppenheimer (1880–1957). Founder and Chairman of the Anglo-American Corporation of S. Africa Ltd., South Africa's biggest mining concern.
135 Eccles had married Sybil, eldest daughter of the celebrated physician Viscount Dawson of Penn, in 1928.
136 The American Ambassador.

guest. The old man declared that looking back on a long life of politics dating from 1895 when he was Minister of Justice in Kruger's[137] Government he regarded the defeat of Churchill in 1945 as one of the great landslides in human history. Douglas argued that it was better for Churchill that he was deprived of office after the war. He would have been confronted by a series of General Strikes, Coal Strikes and every other sort of strike. Smuts replied that Churchill could have coped with such developments and they were of little account when weighed against the fact that the present Government have destroyed a large part of the British Empire *and Churchill would have saved it*.

Yours affly

Bracken to Beaverbrook   8, Lord North Street,
Tuesday (July 1948)   Westminster.

My dear Max

They that say a prophet is not without honour, save in his own country are often wrong.

I honour your gift of prophecy. For your fine case of Scotch arrived before Cripps' new tax on whisky.

I shall not see its like again. For all the chosen, the fabulous football pool promoters and the new national monopolies are now cornering the little good Scotch that remains to Britons. They are indeed incited to buy by Cripps. And I could not compete with those rich men.

I am deeply grateful to you for helping me to drown my sorrows.

Yours affly
Brendan

---

137 Stephen Kruger (1825–1904); President of the Transvaal Republic 1882 to 1900. Smuts became State Attorney of the Republic in 1898.

My Dear Max (undated: 1948)

Bracken to Beaverbrook
(undated: 1948)

Princes House,
95, Gresham Street,
London, E.C.2.

My dear Max

Let me first of all thank you for all your hospitality.

I never enjoyed anything more than the performance of Bonnie Prince Eddie.[138] His constant complaints that the public never appreciated his generosity in paying for half his father's tombstone were an entertainment of the highest order. And when he said in the presence of Churchill that Chief Justice Hughes[139] and old Elihu Root[140] were the great orators of this century, he ended what was, indeed, a memorable appreciation of oratorical genius!

Your house is, indeed, one of the most attractive places in the world and altogether worthy of your Lordship.

(Sgd) Yours affly
Brendan

Bracken to Beaverbrook
18 November 1948

Princes House,
95, Gresham Street,
London, E.C.2.

My dear Max

Our Socialists got a real knock at Edmonton[141] and we Tories are naturally jubilant at the great increase in our vote. The only explanation I can give for this is that working-class women are fed up with Strachey and Bevan.

Rather less than 250 houses have been built in Edmonton since the war ended. More than 6000 people, now huddled together in rooms, have been waiting for homes and I imagine they voted against the Government.

The Second Reading of the Steel Bill ended last night. On

---

138 The Duke of Windsor, formerly Edward VIII.
139 Charles Evans Hughes (1862–1948). Chief Justice of the United States 1930–41.
140 Elihu Root (died 1937). American lawyer and Senator, Nobel Prize winner 1912.
141 Although Labour held Edmonton at a by-election on 13 November 1948, there was a swing to the Conservatives of 16.2%.

this occasion the Opposition had much the best of the argument. Andrew[142] gave a superb speech. His great knowledge of steel, plus a sort of effortless superiority, made the Socialists listen to him for nearly an hour without a single interruption.

I doubt if there is much public interest in the Steel Bill. Considering people are, of course, appalled by the prospect of the Government's obtaining control of hundreds of trades and industries that are subsidiaries of Iron and Steel Companies. But the result of an election is not settled by considering or even intelligent people.

I imagine that Socialist tactics at the next election will be to offer more food to the public, reduce taxation on beer and cigarettes and to offer all sorts of other bribes to their followers. Many millions of people in Britain have now a vested interest in socialism.

The Comrades will make use of another very powerful electoral weapon. They will say that Socialism has eliminated unemployment and that the quickest way of depriving millions of people of their jobs is to return the Tories.

Britain's dollar-financed nationalization schemes must in the end do much to encourage the growth of Socialism in the United States of America. I doubt if many Americans realise this truth. Bernie Baruch sent me a letter the other day, saying that he and some of his friends were getting fed up with the American policy of financing our Socialists in order that they may vivisect British industry. I think Baruch forgets that the real reason for American aid to British Socialists is that they hope that this country will play a useful part in stopping Stalin. Surely Attlee and his colleagues owe more to Uncle Joe than they do to George Marshall. His wondrous plan was hatched as an answer to the bosses in the Kremlin.

How are you feeling? We have had a wave of influenza in England. I have had the damned disease twice and I now feel like a damp rag.....

You probably have been told by your London Office that Kemsley published a long and involved article in the Sunday Times, suggesting that Winston should become nominal leader of the Tory Party and hand over most of his functions to Eden. I don't

142 Sir Andrew Duncan (1884–1952). M.P. and Chairman of British Iron and Steel Federation 1935–40. A close friend of Beaverbrook's from the war.

think the result will do much beyond providing comfort for the Daily Herald and other papers supporting the Government. Kemsley gets out of his depth when he writes or talks politics. I imagine that during the next few months that nobleman will have less time to give to political affairs. I don't think he is very much looking forward to the prospect of getting more paper nor to the freeing of sales.[143]

I am looking forward to your return. But I may not see you this side of Christmas. I am planning to fly out to Africa on the 13 December and I don't expect to be back much before Parliament re-assembles. Morrison thinks that that will be about January 20.

(sgd) Yours affectionately
Brendan

Bracken to Beaverbrook   Carlton Hotel,
19 December 1948   Johannesburg, S.A.
My dear Max

Oh! to be with you at Cherkley instead of spending Christmas in this noisy, steaming city. It is undergoing the worst heat wave in its brief and lurid history.

Britain's political problems are mild by comparison with South Africa's. The Government headed by an ancient and ailing parson who know not what to do in handling urgent and complex financial and economic problems. And so they seek and find a popular diversion of chasing after the coloured people who are the chief labour force in this country. Racial warfare is a good starter, but the worst of finishers.

The Government are advantaged by the weakness of the Opposition. Hofmeyr, Smuts' deputy leader and a man of rare gifts of courage and speech died in his prime a few weeks ago. Four of Smuts' principal helpers followed him to the grave in the course of a few days.

There is a famous passage in Donne's writings that runs in words like these 'No man is an island, entire of itselfe'.[144]

Smuts is. Approaching his eightieth year he must now travel all over this vast sub-continent in order to give heart and hope to his

143 Bracken was anticipating the end of newsprint rationing that had been in force since 1939.
144 'No man is an Island, entire of it self; every man is a piece of the continent, a part of the main...' Donne, *Meditations* XVII.

unhappy and divided party. He must also shoulder Hofymyr's (sic) burden of parliamentary duties. Hofmeyr was a most gifted Parliamentarian. Smuts is not. But he must shoulder the burden as no one else in his Party can meet Ministers in debate.

And he must tackle all these tasks while he is afflicted by sharp domestic sorrows. His eldest son has recently died and the Smuts house (a converted army hut with a few simple additions) is overcrowded by young Smuts' widow and five small children.

The old gentleman's cup of sorrow is almost bottomless. His wife has been very ill. He must soon leave for the Cape where Parliament meets. A thousand miles will divide him from his stricken home.

What an end to the life of an octogenarian whose life has hitherto been rewarded by almost all the most glittering of earthly honours! But he has not lost courage faith and hardness. I greatly admire the old boy in his days of savage adversity.

I hope you will be in England when I return on January 17.

Yours affcly
Brendan

Bracken to Beaverbrook
28 January 1949

Princes House,
95, Gresham Street,
London, E.C.2.

My dear Max,

I was grieved beyond all telling to have missed you. As every year passes I feel what a great chunk is taken out of my life by the fact that we are separated by so much salt water. I am optimistic enough to hope that you will get bored by the Caribbeans and the Canadians and will establish yourself in your lovely house in the South of France[145] and in your battered Cherkley. The price you pay in boredom by spending so much time in North America is, indeed, too high...

The performance of Central Office in announcing that you were no longer a subscriber to the Epsom Tory Association[146] passes all understanding. If I had been in England at the time, I would have stuck in our column an invitation to Woolton to give us a list of the many Tories who are in our shadow Cabinet or in both houses of

---

145 La Capponcina at Cap D'Ail.
146 Beaverbrook did not renew his subscription, but continued to send £100 a year to the Ashton-under-Lyme branch.

Parliament, who have ceased to send cheques to Central Office. What fools Central Office are to go out of their way to offend some one who can be of incomparable value to the Party at the next General Election.

South Africa is in a rare mess. Smuts has little hope of ever returning to power. More than 67% of the population now speak Afrikaans and I imagine most of them agree with Malan's policies for segregating the coloured people. Many of Smuts' followers share that belief. I don't. South Africa is suffering from a chronic labour shortage. If whites would take the trouble to make better use of black labour, they could solve many of their present problems.

The financial and economic problems of South Africa are very grave. But the Government is not the least bit interested in economics or, indeed, in finance. They are always hoping something will turn up to relieve their situation. Meanwhile, they can make good use of all the funk money sent by London to South Africa. Some of our great merchant banking houses in London who put their reserves there, are now anxiously attempting to recover them. They labour in vain. The Afrikaaners who have been brought up by Presbyterian Ministers during the most of the last century are not lacking in the shrewdness that belongs to the Caledonians....

I derived great amusement from the town we are establishing in the middle of the Bush in the Orange Free State.[147] When I saw it last it consisted of three houses. It has now twenty-two streets of well built houses and a school building that the University of New Brunswick might envy. It is a strange experience to have lived in the greatest comfort in a town that is only a year and a half old. I was given the most delicious food and some very good wine. In fact, I greatly enjoyed myself. All I wanted was your company. And so I hope you are returning here soon.

(Sgd) Yours affectionately
Brendan

[147] Welkon.

Beaverbrook to Bracken
17 February 1949

Cromarty,
Montego Bay,
Jamaica, BWI

My Dear Brendan
I was very glad to get your letter of January 28. There is no mail here. Either all correspondents have deserted me, or I am out on an island where mail is seldom delivered. Sometimes air-mail letters take between ten and fifteen days to reach me.

There are three newspaper proprietors on this island. The other two are Lord Camrose and Bertie McCormick.[148] To my surprise, Bertie has said in an interview with the Kingston 'Gleaner' that he met Lord Camrose at dinner in London. I don't believe it.

Camrose's party is having a tough time. Margaret,[149] Lady Birkenhead, gave an admirable account of the journey, lapsing now and then into mimicry of her companions. I saw Freddie[150] on the pier yesterday. He was walking just like his father, with his head forward, and the demeanour of a man carrying a great weight on his shoulders.

He tells me Elsie Kipling has objected to the publication of his life of her father. I gather he means to force it. I did not go into details as I expect I will hear Elsie's side of it before long.[151] And that controversy can be neither strengthened or weakened by the interference of an old man now nearing seventy.[152]

I have had some tough telegrams from Churchill. He is angry

148 Robert McCormick (1880–1955). American newspaper proprietor, publisher of the *Chicago Tribune*, reputed Anglophobe.
149 Margaret, wife of F.E. Smith, 1st Earl of Birkenhead (1872–1930).
150 Frederick Winston Smith, 2nd Earl of Birkenhead (1907–75). Only son of F.E. Smith, who had been a close political colleague of Churchill and Beaverbrook.
151 Rudyard Kipling's surviving daughter, Elsie (Mrs Bainbridge), had agreed terms with Birkenhead in 1945 to write a life of her father. However, when he submitted a first draft of his book to Elsie in 1948, she refused to allow it to be published during her lifetime, as she was, in fact, entitled to do under the terms of her agreement with Birkenhead. He was compensated for his labours by Elsie, and the book was eventually published in 1978 after the death of both Birkenhead in 1975 and Elsie in 1976. For a full account of this curious episode, see the introduction to *Rudyard Kipling* by Lord Birkenhead (Weidenfeld and Nicolson, 1978).
152 Beaverbrook was 70 on 25 May 1949.

with the Evening Standard because of a leader.[153] I have since read it and can't see anything wrong with it. But don't tell him. Before I read it, I said I deplored it. I said that because I had hurt his feelings.

The lords and ladies are scattered all over the front. They are met outside by day, and inside by night. Young Lord Lambton[154] is a character growing in interest. He has considerable powers of caricature in his account of imaginary conversations. He builds up good stories, and without any regard for the reputation of any man... or woman. I think he will make a success of his Parliamentary career on back bench lines.

Clare has been staying with me. And Harry.[155] She goes to Mass every morning, taking my motor car. You never know how long Mass will last. Sometimes it will be quite late in the morning. I miss my motor car. Harry goes to Mass with her when required.

I am told by my nurse that he knows all the answers. But his pride in his heritage from the Manse will, I think, keep him at the admiring stage. Father Sheean will get nothing on Harry.

Clare knows nothing about the Roman Catholic Church, and nothing about the Immaculate Conception. She can't grasp the difference between the Roman Catholic Church and the orthodox church. But she does talk when she develops her own line. Clare at the dinner table reminds me of Ernie Bevin's in Churchill's Cabinet.

I have another visitor here, a friend of Clare's. He is the Prime Minister of New Brunswick.[156] He is going to take Clare on a fishing expedition in his Province. He means to give her a guard of honour. (There are no elections there for three more years !)

---

153 An *Evening Standard* leader of 11 February 1949 had argued that the Liberal Party should run more candidates during a string of impending by-elections. Churchill, as leader of the Conservatives, had despatched an angry telegram to Beaverbrook alleging that the leader was 'so obviously designed to injure Tory chances'. Beaverbrook had neither instigated it, nor even seen the leader, and telegraphed to Churchill to 'deplore' it. But encouraging the Liberals was an old ploy of Beaverbrook's and he personally found nothing objectionable in this leader. (See Taylor, *Beaverbrook*, p. 592).
154 Lord Lambton (1922–). His parliamentary career did indeed flourish until cut short by scandal in 1973.
155 Clare and Harold Luce.
156 Hugh John Flemming.

I saw Mrs Randolph Churchill not long since. Randolph is thin and sober.[157] She has some of the attributes of Clemmie, and she might even reform that sinner.
This is enough.

Bracken to Beaverbrook
3rd March 1949

Princes House,
95, Gresham
Street, London, E.C.2.

My dear Max

Many thanks for your letter and for your Birthday present. That wine you sent me is the best of Hocks and we shall not see its like again.

Some of the Tories are greatly excited about the loss of Hammersmith.[158] I could never see that we had any great chance of winning it. The constituency is rather like North Paddington. Between the wars more than 65% of the electorate of North Paddington had moved away. Houses that contained one family were turned into slums that contained three or four.

Some of the more chicken-livered Tories are now in a state of great nervous excitement. They declare that we must have a policy to defeat the Socialists. It will be very difficult for the Tories to scratch up the sort of policy they want. Attlee and company have hit on a very good vote — getting policy which is to bear gifts to the public. And so long as the Yanks continue to finance dollar-Socialism I see no reason why Mr Attlee should not do quite well at by-elections. The Comrades are preparing their programme for the next election. It will, I am told, include such items as free clothes for school children.

Mr Bevan has published a new Housing Bill which will enable Local Authorities to build houses costing up to £5000. The exchequer will pay 50% of the cost. He is also authorising Local Authorities to open restaurants in building estates, to sell furniture, to start laundries and to do many other things that should bring votes to the Socialists.

157 Randolph Churchill (1911–68). His first marriage to Pamela Digby was dissolved in 1946, and he married June Osborne in 1948. This marriage was dissolved in 1961.
158 Labour held South Hammersmith in a by-election on 24 February with a decreased majority.

These are but a few instalments of the sort of election prospectus that the Socialists will put out. I am inclined to the view that they will probably have their election this year.[159] The much vaulted (sic) export drive is faltering. Pat Hennessy[160] tells me that the British Ford Company's biggest export is to the United States. He says that many of their cars are now placed in warehouses in New York but are included in the export figures given to the House of Commons by Mr Harold Wilson.[161]

I have no doubt whatsoever that we are drifting into a slump and I am quite certain that the Yanks will also have to cope with what they call a 'recession'. How they deal with it I do not know. They may either cut Marshall Aid or add to it. I think that the latter policy may prevail. They can get rid of quite a lot of their glut of commodities by giving it away to Europe. And both you and I know well that sooner or later they will dump motor-cars, refrigerators, wireless-sets and all sorts of other consumer goods in export markets from which we now derive some prosperity.

Some of our colleagues who were formerly enthusiastic about the American loan are now beginning to ascribe the Tory Party's misfortunes to that loan!

I imagine that Cripps will have to budget for an expenditure in excess of three-thousand-hundred million pounds (sic) in the next year. Most of the new Social Services must automatically increase. And so the outlook for the people who are not friends of the Socialists is bleak indeed.

Meanwhile most of the important businesses in this country no longer possess the cash necessary to replace machinery worn out by over-work since 1939. You know much better than I do how obsolete plant can increase the selling costs of goods. But the majority of the electors are not interested in these matters. Their appetite for gifts grows steadily. The latest joke is that the electors will bite the hand of the politician who does not feed them.

More than two million people are now employed by the government and the Local Authorities. Most of them have wives and so you can see how a pretty little Socialist vested interest is created. For most of these Civil Servants or Municipal Servants

---

159 The election took place in February 1950.
160 Sir Patrick Hennessy (1898–1981); Chairman Ford Motor Co., 1956–68.
161 Harold Wilson (1916–); Labour Politician. President of the Board of Trade 1947–51. Resigned 1951. Prime Minister 1964–70, 1974–76.

4 May, 1949   *Toiling under the yoke*   107

believe that if the Tories come into Office they will prune jobs and salaries.

I am glad to get the good news that you will be here on 7th April. You are greatly missed.

(Sgd) Yours affectionately
Brendan

Bracken to Beaverbrook 8, Lord North Street,
3rd May 1949 Westminster

My dear Max

I am pleased beyond all telling by your gift of Alsation (sic) Wine.

Let me say that for a son of the Manse you follow too closely the example of the Pope in not dining out. It is about time you honoured this humble house with your presence and so I hope you will dine with me soon. I shall ask Winston and David Margesson[162] so that we may have a real gossip about politics.

(Signed) Yours aff
Brendan

Bracken to Beaverbrook Princes House,
4 May, 1949 95, Gresham Street,
London, E.C.2.

My dear Max

Do Presbyterians ever burn heretics at the Stake? If they do I recommend that you send some faggots from Cherkeley (sic) to burn the Moderator of the Presbyterian Church in Great Britain.

John Knox believed in private property and in making profits. You will see from the Moderator's speech that he despises profits and believes in a Socialist planned Society.[163] You gave £25,000 to re-house this ordained trimmer.

162 Capt. David Margesson (1890–1965). Government Chief Whip 1931–40, Secretary of State for War 1940–42.
163 The Moderator of the General Assembly of the Presbyterian Church of England, The Rt. Rev. Herbert Stephenson addressed the General Assembly of the Presbyterian Church at Manchester on 2 May 1949. During his discourse, Herbert Stephenson declared that 'the idea of a planned society ... is the inevitable outcome of centuries of struggle, economics, industrial, social and religious. The planned society has come to stay and to form a permanent feature of community life'.

Ask for your money back.

(Sgd) Yours aff
Brendan

Ask Robertson to show you the balance sheet of Outrams, the very *respectable* owners of the Glasgow Herald. Their auditors have inserted a note complaining that the directors have sold properties in which they were personally interested to the Company at a price above the fair market value.
Another Presbyterian outrage!

Bracken to Beaverbrook   Princes House,
8 December 1949   95, Gresham Street,
London, E.C.2.

My dear Max
Many thanks for a magnificent ham.

No words of mine can describe the vacum created by your absence. Your companionship is very precious to me and no day passes without my thinking of you and hoping that you will return soon.

All the pollsters here declare and pronounce that the Tory Party will win the next election.[164] I hope they are right. But the Socialists, under Herbert Morrison's competent management, will give us the toughest electoral battle we have ever known. They will be greatly advantaged by their slogan 'Under Labour Britain has no Unemployment'. In cities like Liverpool, Manchester and Glasgow that slogan will be a great vote-getter.

A great asset of the Tory Party is that that large section of the middle-class who voted Socialist at the last election have been put on the rack by the Comrades. They greatly resent Ministers like Strachey.

Angry housewives are most formidable enemies of the Socialists so we must do everything in our power to increase their fury.

Churchill in a very firm and polite way has washed away all Butler Charters and now rightly declares that devaluation has created a situation that does not allow us to commit ourselves to any policies that involve large expenditure of public money.

Little Max and Mike Wardell[165] gave a dinner to the Duke of

---

[164] The general election was held on 23 February 1950.
[165] Mike Wardell; described by A. J. P. Taylor (*Beaverbrook*, p. 235) as

10 January 1950   *Toiling under the yoke*   109

Windsor on Tuesday night. There was no damned austerity about that repast. It was worthy of the high standards of Cherkley and Arlington House![166]

(sgd) Yours affly
Brendan

Bracken to Beaverbrook   Princes House,
10 January 1950   95, Gresham Street,
London E.C.2

My dear Max

In a very short space of time most of the politicians will be on the hustings and will be busily engaged in lacing promises with abuse.

I doubt if any considering person is willing to prophesy the result of the election. In great industrial centres such as Manchester, Liverpool, Newcastle, Leeds, Bradford and Glasgow a large part of the voters has a vested interest in Socialism. Their pay packets are the biggest they have ever known. If you tell them that England is in a desperate economic crisis, they will reply 'long may it continue; we have never been better off'.

The Socialists are fairly cockey and our old friend, Woolton, is confident of a Tory majority of between 50 and 150. A wide margin this![167]

Stafford Cripps opened the Government's campaign during the weekend. On Sunday he preached in St Paul's Cathedral and staked out a claim that he was a man set apart and peculiar to God. On Monday he held a vast Press Conference in which he claimed that everything was good in John Bull's garden. He conveniently forgot to make any reference to Marshall Aid, without which a lot of our factories would have to close down for lack of raw materials. Uriah Heep would have envied Cripps' capacity of disingenuousness.

Randolph Churchill has been adopted as Tory candidate against

a 'man of high social connections who entered Beaverbrook's circle and employment in 1926'.
166 Beaverbrook leased a flat in Arlington House, St James's Street, during the post-war years, Stornaway House having been rendered uninhabitable by bomb damage.
167 Bracken was right to be sceptical; for although the Conservatives won 43.5% of the vote, Labour took 46.1% and was returned with an overall majority of five seats.

Michael Foot. Hot, indeed, will be the contest at Devonport.[168]

Winston is painting in Madeira. I spent a day with him before he left. He was in high spirits and seemed to be in remarkable physical health. He ardently hopes to be back in Downing Street at the beginning of Spring. He says if we lose the election he will promptly retire and spend the rest of his life in enjoying himself!

Are you enjoying yourself in Jamaica? I should have loved to spend a week in your company. Alas, I am committed to making speeches all over the place and I must give up a good deal of time to wooing the electors of Bournemouth.

(Sgd) Yours affly
Brendan Bracken

Bracken to Beaverbrook
24 April 1950

Princes House,
95, Gresham Street,
London E.C.2.

My dear Max

.... A truly wonderful position is arising in the present Parliament. A very large minority of the Tory Party want to throw the Government out. The charter-mongers and the irresolute want to keep them in, in the hope that some issue will turn up that will rebound to the disadvantage of the Socialist Party.

I sometimes look at politics through the eyes of our opponents who are certainly not lacking in shrewdness. If Herbert Morrison deemed it harmful to Socialist prospects to hold office, the Government would long since have cleared out. They are obviously benefitted by the power of manoeuvre inherent in the Prime Minister's right to ask for a dissolution when it suits him. Some politicians who pour (sic) over Erskine May and Dicey maintain that if Attlee were to ask the King for a dissolution, he would not get one. I cannot bring myself to believe that the present monarch will do anything to upset the comrades. Messrs Morrison and Attlee know this.

The English who take the view that the future of Britain lies in developing Africa ought to visit that large continent. A sort of Bush Telegraph is now operating between the borders of Uganda and the Cape. The message it carries is — 'The Indians have thrown the Whites out of their country, let the Africans follow their good example'. In places like the Gold Coast, Tanganyika

---

[168] Michael Foot won the contest.

and Kenya, and to a lesser extent in Northern Rhodesia, there is a steadily rising opposition to British rule. This opposition has been created by Creech-Jones[169] through his crazy constitutions. It was his object to create an unofficial majority in the legislative councils. The meaning of that policy can be conveyed in a few words — to put the Governor and the principal officials on the defensive and to render them impotent.

There was an election in Nigeria the other day. The Party that is opposed to British rule in Nigeria won a majority even though its leaders were in jail.[170]

Attlee will occupy a considerable niche in history. He has got the British out of India and he may succeed in getting them out of Africa.....

David Margesson has been very ill. One of his doctors declares that he has thrombosis. Another physician from Vienna declares that all he has is 'influenza of the heart' — whatever that may mean.

(Sgd) Yours affly
Brendan

Beaverbrook to Bracken
25 June 1950
My dear Brendan,

I have been reading your column[171] this Monday morning in the Financial Times on Houldsworth, the Coal Commissioner and Chairman of the Coal Board and others.

I must say that the column is so vigorous that I would like to employ you for the Daily Express, and I offer you £20,000 a year. But in depreciated £'s.

Yours ever,

On 25 June 1950 North Korean forces crossed the 28th parallel into South Korea, thus beginning the Korean War. Within a week America and Britain had committed armed forces under the aegis of the United Nations to the South Koreans, to resist the Communist aggression.

169 Arthur Creech-Jones (1891–1964). Labour politician and an expert on colonial affairs, Colonial Secretary 1946–50.
170 This election was indirectly to lead on to the Macpherson Constitution of 1951, designed to give a large measure of self-rule to the Nigerians.
171 The Men and Matters column.

Bracken to Beaverbrook Princes House,
30 June 1950 95 Gresham Street,
London E.C.2.

My dear Max

.... Why don't you come home? I miss you very much.

You had better take a last look at London before the storm breaks. If your old friend, Uncle Joe,[172] gets really tough I imagine that he will try out some of his charming new weapons[173] on London and the great American air bases in East Anglia.[174] What a wonderful thought it is that President Truman can ring a bell and give an order that American aircraft can load their bombs and fly from London to Moscow! The interest of their visit will not be returned on Washington, it will be returned on poor old London. All this talk about giving up national sovereignty doesn't mean much when the President of the United States of America can use England as an aircraft carrier without the knowledge of the Ship's Company.

Yours aff
Brendan

Bracken to Beaverbrook Princes House,
10 July 1950 95 Gresham Street,
London, E.C.2.

Max

.... I wish I could stay with you in Capponcina. I cannot because I have lots of commitments and also the climate in the South of France in the summer always makes me feel ill. I wish I were as tough as you.

In the preliminary rounds the North Koreans are certainly giving our American friends a pasting.[175] I grieve for the G.I.s with

---

[172] Beaverbrook had always been more sympathetic to Soviet Russia than most of his friends and was particularly associated with Stalin in the public eye after his celebrated mission to Moscow in October 1941 to offer Stalin British aid.

[173] The Russians exploded their first atomic bomb in September 1949.

[174] Since the Berlin airlift crisis of 1948, American bombers had been, and remain, stationed at air bases in East Anglia. These bombers had a nuclear capacity.

[175] United States forces landed in the Korean peninsula at the beginning

little training and with no tank support who are being knocked about by trained Russian troops.

I am told that the Americans have only a total of five effective combat Divisions. My informant is an accurate man. One of Churchill's informants declares that the Russians have two-hundred-and-fifty well trained divisions and enormous reserves which can be quickly mobilised.

The Russian tanks used in Korea are far better than anything the Yanks have been able to bring into action. As we know that the Russians have the strongest Air Force in the world and possess quite a formidable submarine fleet; we had better quickly look to our own defences. If war started in Europe tomorrow I greatly doubt if we could put one effective Brigade into action. At the time of Munich Chamberlain had four reasonably trained Divisions.

Many wiseacres have declared that Russia does not want to start another World War. They are entitled to their opinion but this Korean affair is as desperate as holding a fire-work display in a dynamite factory.

Socialist management of our defence affairs is just about as skilful as Bevin's management of the Foreign Office. We certainly do not suffer from the fact that we have an absentee Foreign Secretary. If the old gentleman were about he would probably be making explosive speeches.[176]

Yours affly,
Brendan

Bracken to Beaverbrook
24th November 1950

Princes House,
95, Gresham Street,
London, E.C.2.

My dear Max

I think this Government of ours is sitting on a volcano that will erupt soon. The cost of living and the lack of houses plus the adherence of many Liberal voters to the Tories is, of course, the

---

of July, and immediately found themselves being driven back by Communist forces from North Korea.

176 Ernest Bevin was confined to hospital in the early summer, and by the first week of July was only able to read Foreign Office papers in his hospital bed. He was 69 at the time.

real reason for our by-election successes.[177] There is a good deal of strife within the Cabinet. Bevan and his adherents wish to ride for a fall. They hold that if the Tories are in office they will have to put up with the effects of the rising cost of living and it will surely rise more as we have not yet felt the full consequences of devaluation. If the Socialists were in opposition Bevan would obviously eclipse Attlee and Morrison and his prospects of becoming leader of the Party might be improved. If that were to come to pass it would be greatly advantageous to the Tories as most of the Liberals and what are called the middle of the road voters would prefer to vote for the Tories rather than a Party led by the vermin extinguisher.[178]

The Tories smelling blood of office are now 100% behind Churchill. It would be a great thing for you and for me if Winston were back in Downing Street, more especially as neither of us have any intention of ever sitting in that damned Cabinet Room again.

I should have like to have written you a good long gossipy letter but I have been ill for weeks with a combination of antrum poisoning and tonsillitis. There is no bloodier combination. I cannot eat and find it an awful business to swallow two cups of Bovril or soup a day. Gill Carey[179] thinks I am getting better. I have been given a thorough x-ray examination and it looks as if the whole trouble may re-start again if I get a cold, as I have a structural defect in the nose and bones above the eyes. And there is no effective method of dealing with it save to be born again. Can you imagine anything worse than a re-birth!

Yours ever,
Brendan

[177] During the autumn of 1950 the Conservatives enjoyed a series of promising by-election results, with a swing of 5.6% to the Conservative candidate in the Birmingham Handsworth by-election on 16 November. Nonetheless, the Conservatives had only gained one seat from Labour in a by-election since the 1945 election.

[178] At a speech in Manchester on 4 July 1948, Nye Bevan had famously said of the Conservatives: 'So far as I am concerned, they are lower than vermin.'

[179] Godfrey Fraser Carey, Bracken's surgeon.

Beaverbrook to Bracken
25 November 1950
(Telegram)
Brendan Bracken, M.P., 8 North Street, London, S.W.I., England. Try Terramycin STOP I had marvellous results STOP Also Sir James. Dunn[180] and Sulzberger[181] STOP With affectionate good wishes and praise of Nassau where the hot weather helps.

Max.

Bracken to Beaverbrook Princes House,
11 December, 1950 95, Gresham Street,
London,E.C.2.

My dear Max

Would you have any objection to Copland having a look at the property called Butleigh Court which is not far away from Cricket Malherbie? The Churchill Trustees are anxious to buy land and this property has been recommended to them. I cannot think of a better adviser than Copland. He is a shrewd, hard bitten gentleman who knows a good deal about the snags of landed property. If you do approve, will you ask your secretary to tell Copland.

I have but little news to give you as I have been laid up about a month. I am getting better and I hope to spend a couple of weeks in the country at Christmas. I can do a lot of walking which is good for me and the house I am staying at has not got a telephone.

I don't think there is any sense in the newspaper speculations about forming a Coalition in the present Parliament. A large number of Socialist M.P.s are at heart pacifists and they will do their very best to defeat any Government that contained Tories. They would also do their best to cut down expenditure on defence. In any case we would be damned fools to join a Coalition. What we want is an Election as soon as possible.

The Comrades in Parliament are becoming more and more anti-American. If Shinwell was extremely foolish in criticising Mac-

---

180 Sir James Dunn (1875–1956). Businessman and boyhood friend of Beaverbrook.
181 Arthur Sulzberger (1891–1968). Publisher of the *New York Times* 1935–61.

Arthur[182] and thereby flatly contradicting Bevin's statement that he had not exceeded the powers given him by the United Nations, what can be said for Stokes who, in a public speech, defended the Chinese who are killing British and American soldiers.[183]

The economic muddle here grows apace. Our bulk buyers have once again misjudged the commodity markets. They expected a fall before the end of the year so most industries are short of zinc and other base metals. There may be a big hold-up in production in places like Birmingham as a result of their follies.

I wish you a very happy Christmas and I am grieved beyond all telling to see so little of my beloved comrade.

Yrs affly
Brendan

Beaverbrook to Bracken
13 December 1950

Montego Bay,
Jamaica,
B.W.I.

My dear Brendan,

I was indeed happy to receive your letter dated December 11.

I have advised Copland to look at the property called Butleigh Court. I have warned him that he must not pass it unless it is agricultural land. There is a great deal of property these days passing for agricultural land which is nothing of the sort.

Unless you buy in the fertile centres in Britain, you will lose money in the end.

If you buy in the Yeovil Valley or in the Vale of Taunton or in North or South Petherton you will not go wrong.

I am so sorry to hear that you have been laid up. I do wish I could persuade you out this way, where sunshine has influence even if you do not take direct advantage of it.

---

182 General Douglas MacArthur (1880–1964). U.S. Military Commander. C-in-C Allied Forces, S.W. Pacific 1942; C-in-C Allied Forces, Far East Command 1942–51; C-in-C United Nations Forces, Korea 1951.

183 On 29 November, the first day of a two-day debate in the House of Commons on the Korean War, Bevin had assured the House that MacArthur was acting within the agreed policy parameters of the United Nations. This statement was somewhat undermined the next day when reports reached London from Washington that MacArthur was considering the use of the atomic bomb against the Communist Chinese and North Koreans. This led to strong protests from several M.P.s, including Shinwell, the Minister of Defence.

10 January, 1951   *Toiling under the yoke*   117

I am surprised at the suggestions about a Coalition. It would be foolish indeed.

The whole country is anti-American. There is more sympathy for the Chinese than for the U.S.A. It is shocking, and foolish, and futile.

Just the same, the people elect Tom Driberg.[184] So what can you do about it?

I have given Churchill plenty of bad advice. But I once gave him very good advice which he did not make full use of. It was the occasion of the Edinburgh speech, when he mentioned direct negotiations with Stalin.[185]

Why can't he now take up those lines? And particularly keep off the speeches about the use of the atomic bombs. These will be used any way.

If only that great man could persuade the public that he will lead them out of war, which I am sure is the fact, he will carry everything before him.

How I long to be in England, now that war is here.

Yours affectionately,

Bracken to Beaverbrook   Princes House,
10 January, 1951   95, Gresham Street,
     London,E.C.2.

My dear Max

I wish I could have accepted your invitation to go to Jamaica. Alas, I was so enfeebled by poisoning and incapacity to eat that I went off to the Lakes where the climate is mild and had a complete rest. I cut myself off from letters, newspapers and the radio; this treatment has yielded good results.

The darkness deepens here. At the beginning of the present parliamentary session Attlee told the House that our raw material position was satisfactory. Last week the Ministry of Supply issued

184 Tom Driberg (1905–76). A Beaverbrook journalist — during which time he founded the 'William Hickey' column on the *Daily Express* — and Labour M.P., 1942–74. Driberg enjoyed and Beaverbrook endured a love-hate relationship, crowned by Driberg's waspish biography of his former employer *Beaverbrook: A Study in Power and Frustration*, published in 1956.
185 In a speech at Edinburgh on 14 February 1950, Churchill had called for a summit meeting with Stalin, arguing for a 'supreme effort to bridge the gulf between the two worlds.'

a series of panicky orders, rationing most of the essential raw materials required for industry. Our reserves of raw materials are lower than they have ever been. As a result of the folly of our bulk purchasers many small traders will be ruined and many important industrial companies cannot hope to work more than a four-day week. This Government has never been enthusiastic about a re-armament programme. They have now unconsciously made it impossible quickly to create the arms we need.

Churchill has been given some hair-raising information about the R.A.F. and the Army. We are in a very much worse position now than we were in 1939 when Chamberlain was bitterly attacked for his failure to send more than four reasonably equipped Divisions to Europe. If war were to take place now Britain could not send one fully equipped Brigade!

Hundreds of thousands of our youngsters who have been conscribed (sic) by the Armed Forces know the appalling state of our defences and have doubtless communicated this knowledge to their parents and friends. But this information from reasonably experienced persons has no affect on the public. Nothing can apparently disturb the passivity of Britons. They will now put up with anything.

We have temporarily staved off a worse fuel crisis than that we experienced in 1947 by importing American coal at £7 a ton. The shedding of electricity has created manifold hardships. The most of towns in Britain now must put up with cuts that last for two hours which deprive their homes and factories of lighting and often of heating. The meat ration is lower than it has ever been and in many places fish is scarce and very dear. The cost of goods essential to the housewife inexorably rise. It is probable that if an election came soon the Government would be turned out. Meanwhile the pubic are apparently willing to put up with many new and avoidable hardships without making any effective protest.

This strange acceptance of Government orders and patience with Government follies is indeed a strange development. English history is marked by a continuous strain of what one might call political rambunctiousness. For nearly a thousand years the English have been prepared to pull down the arrogant or the mighty from their seats and until this century they have always striven to limit the authority of their political masters. As we enter the second half of the twentieth century one notices a creeping fatalism. The younger generation have no belief in the almost mechanical progress that was the lot of their forbears. Very large numbers of people are quite willing to trade liberty for the mirage of security. Perhaps this change in the national character is due to loss of faith in what the Victorians describe as Britain's Mission, plus a sense of bewilderment when people hear or read about the immensity and variety of the ugly problems that are constantly thrust upon them.

When Henry Adams was here during the Civil War he wrote a discerning though rather gloomy analysis of Britain's problems for the benefit of his prophetic brother, Brooks Adams.[186] At the height of mid-Victorian prosperity he declared that the English economy was based on the most fragile foundations and that the remedy for this evil lay in economic unity between Britain and her wide flung possessions beyond the seas. The immense prestige of Britain in Victorian days might have given us this blessed economic unity. Is it too much to hope that hardship and suffering may in the end persuade the countries that are left in the Empire to understand that their best hope lies in creating a Commonwealth or Empire with the same measure of free trade within its borders that is enjoyed by the United States and the Union of Soviet Republics. Before this century ends the terms of trade are bound to turn against most of the members of the British Commonwealth when they are in competition with great raw-material countries like the United States and Russia. Awareness of this fact may yet lead the Commonwealth to build itself upon more solid economic foundations. We may not live to see this but it is our best hope.

Churchill is in Marrakesh. When he returns I shall show him your letter. Of your charity you left out an important fact. When

---

[186] Henry Adams (1838–1918) was the elder brother of Brooks Adams (1848–1927). They were both historians and scions of the celebrated American political family which has spawned two Presidents and a host of lesser worthies. Their father was U.S. Ambassador to London during the period of the American Civil War, staying from 1861 to 1868. During his time in England, Henry Adams took the opportunity to write various articles on Britain's economic position, which found echoes in his brother's later work *The New Empire* (Macmillan and Co., 1902) which celebrated the new hegemony of American financial power.

Roosevelt was at Changrila he was overbusy with his stamp collection which is a sure sign that he was disaffected by our Lord and Master.[187]

Yours affly
Brendan

Bracken to Beaverbrook Princes House,
11 January, 1951 95, Gresham Street,
London,E.C.2.

My dear Max

I have been living on the ham and the noble cheese you sent me. I ascribe my recovery to those gifts rather than to the abundance of medicines given me by the doctors.

Walter Monckton stormed the Tory fortress of West Bristol and his success greatly upset the Tory ex-Ministers and other so-called Party stalwarts who had hoped for nomination.[188]

B.

Beaverbrook to Bracken Montego Bay,
16 January, 1951. Jamaica,
B.W.I.

My dear Brendan,

I am so sorry you will not come out here. It would be the making of you. You would have a year of good health, peace and tranquility if you spent a month with me. One month of boredom is a small price to pay for eleven months of good health.

I have had Baxter here with me.[189] There is a great difference between Baxter and Wardell. When Baxter is sober he is great

187 Shangri-la was President Roosevelt's retreat in the hills of Maryland — later renamed Camp David. During the war, Churchill spent a weekend at Shangri-la as a guest of the President in 1943; stamp collecting was the President's favourite hobby.

188 Sir Walter Monckton (1891–1965). Lawyer and Conservative politician, who rose to prominence through his handling of King Edward VIII's legal affairs during the Abdication crisis. He served under Bracken at the Ministry of Information during the War. In January 1951, Monckton was persuaded by Churchill to stand for the constituency of West Bristol in the by-election following the death of Oliver Stanley. He was duly elected and served in Churchill's Cabinet as Minister of Labour, 1951–55 and in Eden's Cabinet as Minister of Defence, 1955–56. He resigned over Suez.

189 Beverley Baxter (1891–1964). A Canadian who was the Managing Director and Editor-in-Chief of various Beaverbrook publications dur-

good fun. When he gets drunk, he is quarrelsome. When Wardell is sober he is somewhat gloomy; when he gets drunk he is a splendid companion.

So I am going to arrange things in future so that I have Baxter when he is sober and Wardell when he is drunk.

I am looking forward to getting back to the South of France where I will spend part of March and April.

The young Squire has been here, and he has left again with his bride on his arm.[190] She is a charming young girl, quite simple, and the young Heir is going to teach her a lot about life.

My Grand-daughter teaches in the Convent for two hours every morning.[191] She is a formidable young woman, and if she ever goes to work she will live to do a great deal of mischief.

I think the Walter Monckton story is good fun. I see that Hore-Belisha was right there on a photo-finish.[192] I expect it is his Press Agent who calls it a photo-finish.

And with affectionate good wishes,

I am, Yours ever,

Beaverbrook to Bracken
9 February, 1951

My dear Brendan,

I have been reading your speech. It is great fun. When you told the member who asked you what your plan was for getting more coal, you get a high mark.[193]

I cannot give you any information about English politics, and I do not know anything about English politicians except the visitors

ing the 1920s and 1930s. He served as a Conservative M.P. from 1935 until his death.
190 Beaverbrook's son Max Aitken (1910–86) was married for the second time at a Presbyterian Church in Jamaica.
191 Probably Lady Jean Campbell, Beaverbrook's favourite grandchild. She was the daughter of his daughter Janet and her first husband Ian Campbell, later Duke of Argyll.
192 Hore-Belisha stood against Monckton, but finished well down in the poll.
193 On 1 February 1951, Bracken had savaged the government over the poor coal production figures. At one point, asked by a Labour M.P. what he would do about the coal shortage, Bracken had replied that he would 'change the Government'. See Hansard, Vol. 483, Cols 1092–1194 for this debate.

to these West Indian islands.....

Cooper, the Socialist Member, has disturbed Jamaica.[194] He wants to bring to an end the democratic system set up by Oliver Stanley, the Tory Minister.[195] He is right. For the Parliamentary institution in Jamaica is like the French constitution under the Martyred King — 'the constitution won't march'.

Lord Kemsley and bride occupy their house on the hillside. I went there to dinner. She is thinner.

His Lordship tells me he is thinking of advancing the price of his 'Sketch' to $1^1/_2$d. Then he thinks he must consider the wage claims of his workers.

He will also consider the case of the wholesalers.

He does not suggest acting independently of the other proprietors. But he does think they will have to jog along with him.

He is not quite so cocky about the libel action. If the defendants will pay some damages, he will consider his wounded feelings well healed.

He says Lord Camrose sat next to Bevan, who said to Lord Camrose, 'You take me to the House of Lords.' Camrose said it was his brother. 'All the same thing,' said Bevan. 'Different,' said Camrose.

I am longing to go to England. The 3rd March is my sailing day.

With affectionate good wishes.

Yours ever,

---

[194] John Cooper (1908–); Labour M.P. 1950–51, PPS to Secretary of State for Commonwealth Relations.
[195] Oliver Stanley (1896–1950); Conservative Politician, Colonial Secretary 1942–45.

Bracken to Beaverbrook Princes House,
14 February, 1951 95, Gresham Street,
London,E.C.2.

My dear Max

I much enjoyed your letter and I am delighted by the news that you will be here early in March.

You will arrive in time to see the political cauldron boil up. Though Herbert Morrison is full of wiles and may be described as a Socialist Mark Hanna I do not think he can rely very much longer on the votes of the fellow-travellers and pacifists who call themselves his supporters. His strong card is of course that he can always tell Socialist M.P.s that if they press the Government too hard an election will follow and many Socialists will lose their seats. There is no way of uniting the Socialist Party save perhaps for Mr. Attlee to declare war on the United States.

Our little friend, Herbert, has established his right of succession to the Foreign Office, but there is some doubt whether he wishes to go there.[196] If he does not I think that Attlee will appoint an unwashed yes-man called Gordon-Walker.[197] Our wonderful Prime Minister says that he is the easiest Minister he has found to work with and that he would never make any difficulty in carrying out Attlee's instructions in matters of foreign policy.

The newspaper reports that Hartley Shawcross[198] contemplates retiring from politics are true. Hector McNeill[199] tells me that great efforts are being made to persuade him to stay in his place but that Shawcross is not susceptible to blandishments. I had a talk with that eminent lawyer the other night and he told me that there never was such drudgery as politics. He declares that he has no private life and wonders how civilised men can stay in office. He may of course, be forced to change his mind, for his decision

---

[196] Herbert Morrison succeeded the ailing Bevin as Foreign Secretary in mid-March. Bevin died on 14 April.
[197] Patrick Gordon-Walker (1907–80); Labour politician, Under Secretary of State at Commonwealth Relations Office 1947–51, Secretary of State for Foreign Affairs 1964–65.
[198] Hartley Shawcross (1902–); Attorney-General 1945–51. Known by Churchill as 'Sir Shortly Floorcross'.
[199] Sir Hector McNeill (1906–1955); Labour Politician. Minister of State at the Foreign Office 1946–50. Secretary of State for Scotland 1950–51.

to arrest some of the dockers' leaders has led those gentlemen to declare that he is much better in causing labour unrest than they could ever be.[200]

The Tories have belatedly decided that clubs are better than Charters in the battle against the Socialists. Hard hitting is now the order of the day. And so Churchill has come into his own.

Yours aff.
Brendan

Thank you very much for your gift of noble wine.

Bracken to Beaverbrook 8, Lord North Street,
4 April 1951 Westminster.

My dear Max,

After 4 months of what a hymn writer called toil of breath Clemmie,[201] the Prof[202] and I found a tidy property consisting of seven good farms in West Lothian. The price was £38 an acre.

We were to sign the contract tomorrow. Alas, the only begetter of our funds read a paragraph in the Evening Standard (reproduced from The Scotsman) relating to this sensible transaction. To him this paragraph seemed manna to Socialists and a hatcher of trouble to Tory fortunes in a fierce Parliament.

Every effort I made to persuade him that he was magnifying a small and transient matter was not answered by peerless invective. The reply was worse. 'Do you want to drag my (sic) down in my last year?'

While I sometimes think that I am more careful of his interest than even he is; I, to adapt words of Gibbon, sighed as a Trustee but obeyed as a friend.... [203]

Master W., absolved from his real estate woes is Hell bent on an election. He is right. Fiercer Parliamentary tactics of forays

200 Shawcross had started legal proceedings against 3 Communist dockers who had allegedly stirred up trouble during the June-July 1949 London dock strike. Shawcross also prosecuted 10 workers involved in a strike by North Thames Gas Board Workers in November 1951.
201 Clementine Churchill (1895–1977), wife of Sir Winston.
202 Professor Lindemann, Lord Cherwell (1886–1957). Nicknamed 'The Prof' he was a close personal friend of Churchill and the Prime Minister's scientific adviser during the war.
203 '...I sighed as a lover, I obeyed as a son...', from Gibbon's *Autobiography* (Routledge Kegan and Paul, 1970), p.55.

have been proposed by him to the manifest discomfort of his charter-knitting colleagues. I think they would be happier or at any rate more easy under the comparatively gentle leadership of Guy Fawkes.

That gentleman prescribed euthanasia for Members of Parliament. W. favours the rack.

When are you coming back to us?

Yrs affly
Brendan

W. is flying to and from Philadelphia. I had hoped Sir Charles[204] would have opposed. How remarkable it is that he should develop a good bedside manner when dealing with his solitary patient!

Bracken to Beaverbrook
Wednesday (Early September 1951)

8 Lord North Street, Westminster.

My dear Max

St. Paul says that it is a test of a Christian that he should be given to hospitality.

Judged by this test, who can doubt that the gates of Heaven will be opened wide for you? Is Heaven a better place than your La Capponcina? I doubt it & so I hope that a wisely judging God will leave you as his legate in France & make me the guardian of your halo.

Yours gratefully
Brendan

---

[204] Sir Charles Wilson, Lord Moran. Churchill's physician.

7
WINSTON'S RETURN
1951 – 1955

On September 20 1951 Prime Minister Attlee had declared his intention to go to the country to seek a new mandate. The election campaign was unremarkable, enlivened only by the Daily Mirror's scare-mongering tactics of portraying Churchill as a warmonger by printing a large picture of a man with a cigar in close half-profile, with the caption 'whose finger on the trigger?'. Churchill immediately brought a legal action against the paper and extracted a full apology.

Polling day was on 25 October 1951. When the result was declared, the Conservatives won 321 seats, as against 295 seats for Labour. However, more votes were cast for Labour (13,948,605) than the Conservatives (13,717,538). The eclipse of the Liberals was confirmed: they polled only 730,556, winning just 6 seats.

Within hours of kissing hands as the new Prime Minister, Churchill got down to the serious business of cabinet making. Amongst the many survivors of his wartime Government who were pressed back into service were Field Marshal Alexander, Lord Leathers, Lord 'Pug' Ismay, and Lord Cherwell; John Colville was recalled as Churchill's Principal Private Secretary.

Amongst this gallery of old faces, two were conspicuous by their absence — Beaverbrook and Bracken. There is no evidence that Beaverbrook was ever offered a post in the new Government, probably because Churchill was warned that this would be a deeply unpopular move with the bulk of the Conservative Party, who still held him responsible for the 1945 débâcle. Some have speculated that Beaverbrook was hurt by this neglect, and having spent the election period in England he returned to Canada soon after the result was declared. Bracken, however, was pressed by Churchill to join the new Government. On hearing that

Bracken had declined the Colonial Office, a distressed Churchill tried to woo him with offers of less exacting Ministries, but the answer remained 'no' to all of Churchill's blandishments. Ill-health certainly played a part in Bracken's decision; he was already aware of his declining powers and knew that he would no longer be able to survive the burdens of office. Bracken was also aware that he was profoundly out of sympathy with the general tenor of Conservative Party policy, and although he might prosper under Churchill he would be dangerously exposed when Churchill retired, as he was widely expected to do within a year or two of his election victory. Bracken gave his own account of his reasons for refusing office to Lewis Douglas in a letter of 7 November 1951:

> Winston pressed me hard to join his government and I could hardly have refused to do so were it not for the fact that before the election I had an acute attack from my old enemy — sinusitis....
>
> I have not been able to leave North Street since the election (except to go over to the House of Commons to vote for the new Speaker) and to add to my troubles I have developed tonsillitis. The latter disease is, of course, consequential. Last year I was laid up on four separate occasions with bad attacks of sinus and I have no reason to believe that I shall have any better experience during the next year. I think it wrong in the public interest to have a Cabinet Minister who is away from his office for long periods during the year.
>
> The argument that most swayed me, however, was that the Colonial Secretary, if he is to do his duty, must fly to Malaya, Hong Kong and our many troubled colonies in Africa. My health makes it impossible to do this.[1]

He contested the general election and was returned with an increased majority for Bournemouth and Christchurch. However, in November Bracken took his final step out of politics by resigning his seat in the House of Commons. In the 1952 New Year's Honours he was elevated to the peerage as Viscount Bracken of Christchurch, a decision that later caused him some regret. He never took his seat in the House of Lords.

Bracken to Beaverbrook	8 Lord North Street,
19 December 1951	Westminster

My Dear Max

Many thanks for your letter. I wish I could accept your invitation. Alas the climate of the Bahamas is too hot for me. I am going to the highlands of Kenya for a few months. When I come back Gil

---

[1] Lysaght, p. 290

Carey can deal with my sinus and cut out my tonsils.

Some of our new Ministers can be best described as political Buchmanites. Thorneycroft[2] after a few days in Office rushed down to the House to announce the supreme difficulty of re-opening the Liverpool Cotton Exchange. Lloyd[3] turned all four cheeks to the mining Members who heckled him on coal. The old lady who is Minister of Education[4] waited until the House adjourned to issue a White Paper on education which has infuriated many Tories & all the Liberals.

Poor Gomer Berry is in great distress. His Daily Graphic is losing at the rate of £300,000 a year & he has other losers in his stable. He can find no buyers for the Graphic & holds that his 'prestige' will greatly suffer if he has to end its life. I am very sorry for Gomer; he is ageing rapidly & is much disillusioned about the worth & power of his newspaper empire.

When Cadbury[5] returns from Australia he will have to drink something stronger than his own cocoa to fortify him in totting up the losses of his paper.

Samuel[6] is retiring from the Liberal leadership in the Lords & Archie Sinclair[7] will succeed him. Archie is greatly pleased by the prospect of leaving his cold hermitage in Caithness for the rhetorical delights of Westminster.

Thank you for sending me such fine ham. I shall have a good Christmas dinner.

Yours affectionately
Brendan

---

2 Peter Thorneycroft (1909–). Conservative politician. President of the Board of Trade 1951–57, Chancellor of the Exchequer 1957–58, Minister of Aviation 1960–62, Minister of Defence 1962–64. Chairman of the Conservative Party 1975–81.
3 Geoffrey Lloyd (1902–84). Conservative politician. Minister of Fuel and Power 1951–55, Minister of Education 1957–59.
4 Frances Horsburgh (1889–1969) who was the first woman to sit in a Conservative Cabinet.
5 Laurence Cadbury, proprietor of the *News Chronicle*
6 1st Viscount Samuel (1870–1963). Liberal politician. Home Secretary 1916, 1931–32. Leader of the Liberal Party 1931–35, after which he was leader of the Party in the House of Lords.
7 Sinclair was created Viscount Thurso in 1952, but was unable to succeed Samuel in the House of Lords due to illness.

Bracken to Beaverbrook 8 Lord North Street,
15 January 1952 Westminster

My dear Max

Many thanks for your letter.

Translation to the morgue is a curious experience.[8]

Our Mr Butler[9] has a stronger digestion than the toughest of ostriches. He has evacuated his charters with no sign of a blockage & is now preparing to slaughter the do gooders & easy spenders in Government service. He talks like Hicks-Beach:[10] may he wield his axe as vigorously!

He is, I think, converted to the policy of freeing the pound & may soon create machinery for an exchange equalisation fund which is, of course, the best way of restoring a wide measure of convertibility.

The Government's first installment of deflation has created more wailers around London Wall than Jerusalem ever knew. The next installment may induce the City to erect a statue to Dr Dalton.

The Socialists are starting a great witch hunt after Miss Horsburgh.[11] Clem Davies & his Liberals must support them. To become shining saviours of education is a first rate part for Attlee Morrison & Co. The next Session will be a fierce business for the Government.

I fly to Africa on Friday where I hope to get a long rest in the highlands of Kenya.

Sir John Anderson is turning himself into Lord Waverley — a romantic name for a prosaic man. He is still furious about C's offer of the Duchy of Lancaster which he considers an outrage to his dignity & worth.

Yours ever
Brendan

---

8 On 8 January 1952, Bracken had been raised to the peerage.
9 R. A. Butler had become Chancellor of the Exchequer in Churchill's new Government.
10 Michael Hicks-Beach (1837–1916). Conservative politician, Chancellor of the Exchequer 1885–86, 1895–1902.
11 Florence Horsburgh was Secretary of State for Education in the new Government.

Bracken to Beaverbrook 8 Lord North Street,
28 April 1952 Westminster

My dear Max

Thank you very much for your treat of Caviare & also for Jesse Jones' book.[12] He has led a two-fisted life & has grasped as well as punched.

Here is a piece of news for your private edification. 'The Times' are thinking of offering Haley[13] (the B.B.C. boss) the editorship.

Astor[14] toyed with the notion of appointing Oliver Franks[15] but gave way to the criticism that amateurs are hardly the best editors. Franks leaves Washington at the end of this year. The F.O. is striving hard to fill his place with what the Yanks call a career diplomat.

Churchill may have other ideas for filling this boring & almost inconsequential job. I know Harold Macmillan wd like it but he must stick to his hod.

Come home soon.

Yrs affly
Brendan

Bracken to Beaverbrook Princes House,
8 August 1952 95, Gresham Street,
London, E.C.2.

My dear Max

....I suppose it is right to use the platitude 'it is better for him that he is dead' about George McCullagh.[16] This world must be a terrible place for a man with melancholia akin to madness. Still, I grieve greatly for George. Sometimes his grasp on the obvious

---

12 Probably Jesse Holman Jones, *Fifty Billion Dollars, My 13 Years with the R.F.C., 1932–1945* (New York: Macmillan, 1953), of which Beaverbrook might have obtained an advance copy.
13 Sir William Haley (1908–88). Director-General of the BBC, 1944–52; Editor of *The Times* 1952–66.
14 John Jacob Astor (1886–1971). Co-chief proprietor of *The Times* 1922–66. M.P. for Dover 1922–45. The full story of Haley's elevation to the editorial Chair of *The Times* can be found in Iverach McDonald, *The History of the Times*, Vol V, pp. 200–202.
15 Oliver Franks (1905–). Academic and diplomat, Ambassador to Washington 1948–52.
16 George McCullagh (1905–52). Canadian Newspaper proprietor.

made one wince, but this counts as nothing when compared to his manifold good qualities. George was a lusty life-giving fellow full of combativeness curiosity, and a steady persevering friend.

Our country's friends are not increasing in Canada and so on national grounds one can say that George's death is a considerable misfortune. Looking back on those grim war years, I don't know anyone who was a more steadfast friend of Britain. We owe him a lot.

I wish I could stay with you in the South of France, but your weather is, I think, too hot for me. What is it like now? I miss your company very much and as you will be away all the winter and most of the spring I think I should, if necessary, go to the Sahara to see you.

Clemmie came back yesterday and though her health is improved she cannot get rid of this low blood pressure condition which must at times be intensely depressing. She is, as you know much affected by political affairs and there is little comfort to be derived from the Government's present position. Our Ministers have inherited great misfortunes and I am afraid that most of them have not enough daring to weather the storms that will break upon Britain before many months pass.

I followed your advice and took a house 16 miles from a village and without a telephone. The newspapers only came once a week and so I was very much out of touch with happenings in London. I am told that those tar-brushed American Hebrews whom you are honoured to have as enemies have been attacking the "Express".

Our Men and Matters column has unfortunately folded up for a month or so.[17] Had it been going I should have written a piece about the Press Council[18] and suggested that if it were in existence it might have done something to defend the rights of old Jim Garvin who made the 'Observer' and was turned out by his ungrateful bosses.[19] Garvin's account of the way he was plagued

17 Bracken's column in the *Financial Times*.
18 The Press Council was set up in the wake of the Royal Commission on the Press, 1947–49, to monitor the activities of the press.
19 J.L. Garvin (1868–1949). Celebrated and autocratic editor of the *Observer*, and early patron of Bracken. The paper was owned by Lord Astor, husband of Lady Nancy Astor; Lord Astor refused to renew Garvin's contract as editor in 1942 after political disagreements over the merits of Churchill's Government.

by her Ladyship to get a Government job from Winston for her dessicated spouse is one of the most squalid stories known to a hard-bitten old man such as I am.

When are you thinking of coming back to England?

(Sgd) Yours Affly
Brendan

P.S. The figures you gave me about Gomer's[20] papers make depressing reading. I think the 'Manchester Daily Dispatch' has seen its best days. Before the 'Express' led the invasion of Manchester the 'Dispatch' could claim to be first with the news in the intensely populated country of Lancashire. In those days it had no real competition as the 'Manchester Guardian' and the 'Liverpool Post' never have and never will appeal to the populace. Poor Gomer has a lot of trouble on his plate.

Bracken to Beaverbrook　　　　　　　　　　　　Princes House,
11 September 1952　　　　　　　　　　　　95, Gresham Street,
　　　　　　　　　　　　　　　　　　　　　London, E.C.2.

My dear Max

Here is an advance proof of Young's 'Baldwin'.[21]

It contains some devastating criticisms of Baldwin's indolence and levity in the management of great affairs.

There is nothing very new in his account of the Abdication. Baldwin is, however, reported as saying on Page 241 'Only time I was frightened. I thought he might change his mind. But I need not have been. He had given his word and that was enough.' How oddly this sentence compares with Baldwin's claim that he laboured with all his might to persuade King Edward VIII to remain on the throne!

There are, of course, many references to you in the book. You will notice on Page 30 Baldwin declares that you and he 'had fought for the soul of Bonar Law'. This was followed up by some sort of crack which Young has blacked out.

(Sgd) Yours ever
Brendan

---

20 Gomer Berry, 1st Viscount Kemsley
21 G.M. Young (1882–1959). Oxford historian who wrote the first posthumous life of Baldwin.

Bracken to Beaverbrook   Princes House,
7 January 1953   95, Gresham Street,
                                                                 London, E.C.2.

Many thanks for your letter and the cutting you sent me about the former Colonial developer. Unlike the corporation he ruled, that gentleman's fortunes seem to have increased.

I had a cable from Churchill this morning — he says he is enjoying himself immensely in New York.[22] Walter Bagehot[23] once described the Englishman as an 'enjoying man'; an infusion of American blood turns him into a rip-roaring man. You and I derive great pleasure from the fact that the old boy is back in office which he revels in, and that what may be the last lustre of his life should be spent in place and power, which is heaven to him.

His Government is doing well at the moment. Bevan is doing a better job of work for the Tories than Woolton could ever do. I think, however, that Ministers will have to face a lot of trouble with some of the Unions in the course of the present year. The miners are particularly rambunctious. One expects that the Scottish and Welsh miners should give trouble, for their bosses are Communists. Up to the present the most solid and moderate of the mining communities has been Yorkshire under the leadership of Hall. Now the Yorkshire miners are in the van of the agitation to secure an immediate wage increase of 30/- a week. If they don't get it, I think we may easily get strikes and an extension of the ca'canny which has already reduced output in the coal fields.

The Coal Board can't possibly pay this increase which would probably cost them about £50 million a year. At the present time the Board is losing large sums of money and is once again pressing for power to increase prices. Ministers can't be blamed for this unrest in the coal fields, but they are open to much criticism for their failure to do something to clean up the mess inside the Coal Board. To you who know all about the importance of management in industry, the Coal Board must seem a crazy contraption. The Chairman is a pleasant second rate lawyer with Left Wing

---

22 Churchill's second trip to the United States as Prime Minister lasted 5 January to 9 January, after which he flew to Jamaica, lunching with Beaverbrook on 11 January.
23 Walter Bagehot (1826–77). Economist and journalist.

affiliations.[24] He has never had any experience of business, nor has he any force of character. Two of his principal colleagues are ex Trade Union officials, basking in their free motor cars and their £5,000 a year salaries. They are utterly useless as controllers.

Geoffrey Lloyd[25], who is a human rabbit, is terrified of making any changes at the Coal Board lest it would get him into trouble with the Miners' Union. It certainly would, but if something isn't done to provide a sensible organization at the top plus a great deal of devolution in the provinces, we shall probably live to see the day when English coal is as costly as South African diamonds.

While both Sandys[26] and Lennox-Boyd[27] have shown considerable capacity in the House of Commons, neither can be rated as a good departmental minister. Sandys' new constitution for the steel industry is much more rigid and bureaucratic than the one set up by the Socialists. Hundreds of firms who where excluded from the terrors of nationalised steel are now being dragged in under State control by a Tory Minister. What a spectacle! I think Sandys will find that when Parliament meets he will have to drop some of the worst excrescences of his Bill.

Lennox-Boyd spends most of his time defending the Transport Commission's monopoly services between the northern cities and London. It is indeed scandalous that the Tories should buttress up this wicked monopoly. The British Electric Company, which is a holding company for bus services, will take a passenger from Edinburgh to London for £3; the railways and the State buses require about £6.10.0. If the Coal Board is a rotten organisation, all that one can say of the Transport Commission is that it is worse. The old Chairman is a retired Civil Servant who has never been given to work and his two principal colleagues are pensioners of the N.U.R.[28] These fellows couldn't run a successful bus service

[24] Sir Hubert Houldsworth (1889–1956). Chairman of the Coal Board 1951–56.
[25] The Minister of Fuel and Power.
[26] Duncan Sandys (1908–). Conservative politician, son-in-law of Churchill. Minister of Supply 1951–54, Minister of Housing 1954–57, Minister of Defence 1957–59, Minister of Aviation 1959–60, Secretary of State for Commonwealth Relations 1960–64.
[27] Alan Lennox-Boyd (1904–83). Conservative politician. Minister of State for Colonial Affairs 1951–52, Minister of Transport 1951–54, Secretary of State for Colonies 1954–59.
[28] The Chairman of the British Transport Commission from 1947 to 1953

from Leatherhead to Epsom. Will Lennox-Boyd touch a hair of the heads of these duds in charge of transport? The answer is 'no'.

The railways are once again going to raise fares and freight charges, even though they know this leads to a diminishment of traffic. I can understand Ministers being unwilling to denationalise Coal and Transport, but I cannot see any sense in their policy of tolerating organisations that can only solve their problems by putting up their charges to the public.

Taking them all in all I should think that Monckton and McMillan (sic) are the most successful Ministers.[29] Monckton is, of course, all things to all men, but that is a most desirable quality in a Minister of Labour. McMillan is desperately anxious to get out of the Ministry of Housing, but I don't think Churchill will let him go to his spiritual home, which is the Foreign Office. Alone among the press the Times newspaper has pointed out that when the Socialists bolted they left behind them no less than 216,000 unfinished houses. It wasn't difficult, therefore, to induce good housing returns during the first year of a Tory Government. Conditions will be very different this year and so Master Harold is right to try to find alternative employment. It must, of course, be said that McMillan has shown a great deal of good sense in his dealings with the public. Small touches, such as his arriving on the scene after the floods in Devonshire, are very much applauded by the public, and rightly so.[30]

I tried some propaganda on Winston about cutting out some of these ridiculous departments which are a burden to the community. It is really ridiculous that we should have a Ministry of Raw Materials and that we do not amalgamate the Ministry of Pensions with the Ministry of National Insurance. But my missionary efforts were of no avail; Churchill doesn't want to change anything

   was Sir C. Hurcomb.
29 Sir Walter Monckton was Minister of Labour, 1951–55. Harold Macmillan was Minister of Housing, 1951–55.
30 'In August 1952, a violent storm dumped nine inches of rain on Exmoor, leading to a devastating flood that swept away much of the pretty Devonshire Coast of Lynmouth, drowning many people...The damage to housing was enormous. MacMillan was promptly on the scene, wearing a rustic cloth cap and declaring that the havoc reminded him of 'Wipers'(Ypres)'. Alastair Horne, *Macmillan 1894–1956* (Macmillan, 1988) p. 338.

in his Government and one cannot blame him for taking this line which is one that has been taken by most of his predecessors.

The budget this year will be like Jack Price's balance sheet when business was in trouble. As you know, I have always held that Butler's estimates were grotesquely optimistic. Despite a lot of window dressing they are down by nearly £600,000 after nine months of the financial year have passed. He will, of course, collect big sums of money in the next three months, but his expenditure is also increasing rapidly. We shall have to find about 200 million dollars a year to pay for the maintenance of our army in Germany, and most of the civilian departments have also exceeded their estimated expenditure. There is a vague hope in the Treasury that the Americans may do something to relieve us of our financial difficulties. I don't think they will and I think it thoroughly harmful to Britain to take any more money from the Americans, whether it be for the purpose of meeting current commitments or backing a convertible £.

While I share your view about the desirability of convertibility, I can see no prospect of it being achieved for a long time. Our gold and hard currency reserves are still pitifully small and there are all sorts of loopholes in our financial system which would enable currency speculators to grab them in a month or two.

Sir George Bolton, who is a director of the Bank of England and our chief Exchange Controller, told me a curious story the other day. He avers that five-sixths of Keynes's fortune was made between 1940 and 1946. Bolton ought to know as he was in daily contact with Master Keynes.

I wish I could accept your invitation to go to Jamaica, but I see no prospect of being able to do so. I am, however, half-thinking of going to the United States for about three weeks. I don't expect to enjoy this visit, but I have obligations there which ought to be fulfilled. The Union Corporation still earns millions of dollars for John Bull through the metal markets in New York.

I sometimes selfishly wish that the Caribbeans would emulate the Mau Mau[31] for the purpose of driving all the whites back to Britain, for I cannot tell you how much I miss you. There are very few people in this town whom I would wish to spend much time

---

31 The Mau Mau were engaged in a terrorist campaign to eject the British from Kenya.

with. Most of the politicians are boring propagandists and the City of London is mildewed.

How odd it is that London should look upon itself as one of the financial centres of the world even though we are running out of our small reserves of capital. The Treasury now admits that Britain is no longer a country of savers; we actually spent last year more than the savings anticipated by our wonderful planners. What the position will be like in the next financial year is beyond my comprehension, for E.P.L.[32] will be in full operation with the result that the most of British businesses will have to hand over about 73% of their earnings to the Treasury. And, as you know, E.P.L. is only one of a trinity of Taxes on industry. The ordinary British company has to hand out 9/- in the £ of all its earnings; we then have the swingeing Profits Tax and on top of that E.P.L. The position wasn't put badly in the Financial Times on Monday, from which I enclose a cutting.

I had a cable yesterday from Lord Brownlow,[33] offering me his house in Jamaica, but there is only one house in that part of the world I should wish to go to and, alas, that is not within my power. I was greatly grieved by his Kitty's death. Doctors often say that long life is due to the strength of ones ancestors. When you remember the length of days given to the father and mother of Jean and Kitty, one realises how hollow this generalization is.

Kemsley was wise and indeed lucky to get Rothermere to take over his Graphic. Rothermere tells me that he intends to run it as a 'family newspaper'. If that be his ambition it was an odd choice of partners to bring in the News of the World. From a circulation point of view Rothermere's two most successful papers are the Sunday Dispatch and the Overseas (and over-sexed) Daily Mail. I shall be very surprised if the Sketch doesn't in the end become as fruity a paper as the Daily Mirror.

Here is a piece of private news for you. Kemsley has been told by Camrose that the Telegraph cannot continue its self-denying ordinance not to publish a Sunday paper. This has greatly disturbed Gomer as he knows well that the Sunday Times may suffer

32 Excess Profits Levy.
33 Lord Brownlow (1899– 1978). Parliamentary Private Secretary to Beaverbrook at the Ministry of Aircraft Production, 1940. He owned a house called Roaring River in Jamaica. His wife, Katherine, died in 1952.

grievously from the competition of a Sunday Telegraph.[34] Kemsley was also much irritated by Camrose's telling him that the decision to publish a Sunday Telegraph was taken by his family who will be in charge of the paper in years to come, rather than by him. It is for this reason that he wants to start a Sunday edition as soon as possible!

What a disgraceful piece of notepaper you wrote on! I have a good mind to ask that benefactor of the newspapers, Sir Eric Bowater, to send you some good paper instead of the flimsy rubbish you write on.[35] He can well afford to do so in view of what he is still taking out of the newspapers.

The Financial Times people tell me that Stanley Bell[36] holds that all the newspapers can expect by way of a reduction in newsprint price is £4 a ton. The truth is, of course, that paper ought to be reduced at once by at least £10. According to the manager of the Financial Times, Bowater is pressing the Board of Trade hard to resist any really adequate reduction in price. I don't know what the Board of Trade has got to do with fixing the price of paper; I think Ministers will be very stupid if they once again succumb to the blandishments of the handsome and honest Sir Eric.

When you have some spare time write me a letter and I will send you a reply as long and as boring as the one you have just finished reading.

Yours affly
Brendan

---

[34] Gomer Berry, Viscount Kemsley, was proprietor of the *Sunday Times* and brother of Lord Camrose, proprietor of the *Daily Telegraph*. The *Sunday Telegraph* was started in 1960.

[35] Sir Eric Bowater (1895–1962). Chairman, Bowater Paper Corporation Ltd., 1927–62.

[36] Stanley Bell (1899–1979). Industrialist, chairman of the Astley Trust.

Beaverbrook to Bracken   'Cromarty'
15 January 1953   Montego Bay,
                                                                                    Jamaica

I went to see Churchill on Sunday. He is tired and disappointed over his American journey.

Soames is very good to him.[37] He is not worrying him at all, like some of the others. He says the right thing and at the right time. I was warmly received by Clemmie, and was gratified.

The Reynolds lot were here last night. They are on both sides of the struggle for power in the U.S.A. One branch is for the Republicans and the other working with the Democrats. (The Democratic branch expect to capture Congress in eighteen months.)

Both groups took the conventional view of Churchill and his mission. And they did not show any restraint in their conversation, even though they were under attack.

The Republican branch of the Reynolds group declare that the President[38] will set things to right. That he will quickly deal with Persia, protecting Middle East oil against Communist infiltration. He will not permit Venezuela to degenerate into chaos. In fact, he may do to Venezuela what Teddy Roosevelt did to Columbia — that was the actual statement.

The Americans are without restraint in their foreign relationships. They say they are doing to the world what England has perpetrated for the last two hundred years. And that ends that. Take it or leave it. But the English cannot alter it.

There is no use in looking back. For the future I am glad that Churchill is not returning again to America in March.

Three U.S.A. firms including one with a Canadian Charter control bauxite.... The industry will not give Jamaicans any measure of prosperity or employment. The Reynolds' farms employ more men than their bauxite mining operations.

The Americans are on the way to complete control of the island. They are about to invest thirty-five million pounds, mostly in the development of agriculture. Their military bases, now vacant, give them a dominating position. In the day of trouble, the American army is sure to come back again. When they open up their American market for Jamaican agricultural produce, the

---

37 Christopher Soames (1920–87). Churchill's P.P.S and son-in-law.
38 Eisenhower.

British connection will come to an end.

It is such a sad situation. For the people are intensely loyal to the British tradition. They do not show any desire to relinquish their Empire associations.

We have a big British colony here. The sterling currency brings them. But we have had nothing but rain for long. The ex-Member Everard Gates said: 'Oh, to be in Jamaica, now that England's here'.

Churchill demands that I shall attend at Government House at Kingston on Saturday, following him throughout the functions — with two luncheons, one dinner and a cocktail party, a visit to the University and two processions through the streets.....

Beaverbrook to Bracken   'Cromarty'
30 January 1953   Montego Bay,
                                                                                   Jamaica.

My dear Brendan

....This lovely climate is no guarantee against illness. I have been laid up for eight days, and am just now getting my balance again. It was a painful interlude, and it disturbed me a good bit, although there are no after-consequences. When you are seventy-three years of age, the heart muscle does not take kindly to a high temperature.

The last days of Churchill's visit turned out to be wonderfully satisfying to him. There were crowds everywhere. He had a happy time. His health was good. He wanted to swim, and he did not even need to take off his wet bathing suit.

He was accompanied everywhere by Foot and his wife.[39] Foot insisted on being in every picture and always sat on the same seat with the Prime Minister. He never allowed an opportunity for publicity pass.

Foot's wife is, I should think, a Jewess and possibly a radical. Perhaps an extreme radical. She is on the best of terms with every section of the community and has an easy and pleasing way of dealing with the black population. I think there is a considerable capacity for mischief. I mean, of course, political mischief.

She did not judge Churchill quite rightly, although I think he liked her very much. There is a swimming place called Doc-

---

[39] Sir Hugh Foot (1907–). Governor-General of Jamaica 1951–57.

tor's Cave. I would have taken him there because the British and American visitors would get a chance to welcome him. And he would have liked it. But her Ladyship opposed it. And in no time at all, the black police advised against it.

I was delighted with Soames. He seldom talks nonsense. His views are sound, although he has not yet developed to the full his political philosophy. He never wanders from Mary's side.

On the whole, I feel that Churchill will never want to come back to Jamaica.

I see that Lady Mountbatten has gone to visit Nehru.[40] Lady Cripps is there already. Before you can say 'Sir Stafford Cripps' Nehru and her Ladyship will visit Mau-mau. I understand Nehru has expressed understanding with that movement, if not sympathy with it.....

We have got many distinguished visitors in this island. They think the climate is lovely. I think it is bloody. But then, I have had a temperature!

Noel Coward is in his cottage. Lady Rothermere is with her doxy. Errol Flynn is giving a party and Edward Molyneux[41] is laying the corner-stone of a new house.

Here in Montego Bay, the Reynolds family (Bauxite) dominate the hillside, and the Dupres rule in the valley.

I hear of the impending arrival of Arthur Sulzberger[42] and of his principal columnist. O'Donnell[43] of the 'News' has just gone home. And Charlie Knickerbocker[44] cannot be far behind.

I am wishing for Capponcina. If I could get news of warm weather there, I would be on my way.

I have the 'Manchester Guardian' enclosure. I had already seen Parkinson's address. It is, of course, the policy of the Government. It is intended to develop sales to the U.S.A. to the extent that Canada will be independent of Great Britain. It cannot be done.

The Government in Canada is fighting for existence. Many persons think the ministry will be defeated.

---

40 Jawaharlal Nehru (1889–1964). 1st Prime Minister of India, 1947–64.
41 Edward Molyneux (1894–1974). Fashion designer, who sold Beaverbrook La Capponcina at Cap d'Ail.
42 Arthur Sulzberger (1891 – 1968). Publisher of the *New York Times*.
43 O'Donnell (1896-1961). Journalist.
44 Charles Knickerbocker; Columnist.

142   *My Dear Max*   30 *January 1953*

I am sending you a life of Mackenzie King.⁴⁵ It is fun. Much of it you may ignore. In fact, if I had the book here I would mark the passages you should read. On reflection, I will send the book through the office, and it will be marked.

Our British Government is not in close touch with the present Canadian Government.

P.S. I see a headline in the 'Daily Gleaner' this morning — 'Governor a remarkable man' — I expected it. And he is a remarkable man, but he has no facility for expressing himself like his brother, Michael.⁴⁶ However, the others will say it for him.

Bracken to Beaverbrook   Princes House,
11 February 1953   95, Gresham Street,
                                                         London, E.C.2.

My dear Max

Many thanks for your letter.

I was greatly grieved by the news of your illness, but I am reassured by the liveliness of your letter which prove that there are no after-consequences. You were wrong to link age with illness; years are often a yoke, but to you they are but a spur. Some people are old at 40; others renew life at 70.

You are quite right in thinking that Master C. will see Jamaica no more. He would have been excruciatingly bored were it not for your sophisticated company.⁴⁷

Whitehall is already mourning the departure of Truman and Acheson. The preposterous Dulles has upset many people here, but that, of course, causes him no distress.⁴⁸ Dollar diplomacy is now the order of the day and we are being told in the crudest, not to say the rudest, way that we must conform to American policies

---

45 The 'Life' of W.L. Mackenzie King (Prime Minister of Canada 1921–30, 1935–48) in question is probably *Mackenzie King, The incredible Canadian* (1953), by Bruce Hutchinson.
46 Michael Foot, the Beaverbrook journalist and Labour politician, was the younger brother of Sir Hugh Foot.
47 Churchill stayed on the island from 9 to 29 January. It was indeed his last visit to Jamaica.
48 President Truman and Secretary of State Dean Acheson, defeated in the 1952 Presidential election, left the White House on 20 January 1953. The new President, Dwight D. Eisenhower (1880–1969) chose John Foster Dulles (1888–1959) as his new Secretary of State.

if we are to receive more doles from Uncle Sam.

I am altogether opposed to asking the Yanks for another cent and even if I were not I am quite sure that an economy-minded Congress will slice our dole. Unless John Bull is financially independent he can play no worthy part in the world. For this reason I deplore Butler's visit to Washington. He has a bright scheme for partial convertibility which will require American support. The idea is that the International Monetary Fund should provide support for some select brands of sterling.[49]

The Yanks, of course, control the I.M.F.[50] which was the brain child of Keynes and that very dubious character, Harry White.[51] I don't think the Yanks will agree, but if they do they will attach all sorts of conditions to their concurrence.

Last night I spent a few hours reading the American papers. I notice that our friend Mr. Luce continues to welcome the elimination of British imperialism. The 'U.S. News' which is under the patronage of Eisenhower, lectures John Bull as if he were a fraudulent bankrupt. Pravda is a rather more friendly paper!....

Yours affly
Brendan

Beaverbrook to Bracken Aitken's House,
19 February 1953 Nassau,
Bahamas

My dear Brendan,

Thank you for your letter. I am in Nassau, and fighting against the medicine given me by the doctors. They cured my lungs and ruined my stomach and bowels.

I have been reading your column on Clare Luce. I quite agree with what you have written, although it might be considered an over statement by some persons. Certainly not by Harry Luce, for his magazine 'Time' has made a statement about Clare. According

---

49 This plan, canvassed at the Commonwealth Economic Conference in Nov.–Dec. 1952, was a watered-down version of Operation Robot, a scheme devised in Whitehall during 1952 for sterling to become convertible. Robot was named after its three chief protagonists, Sir Leslie Rowan, Sir George Bolton and Otto Clarke.
50 International Monetary Fund.
51 Harry Dexter White (1895–1948), the chief American negotiator at the Bretton Woods Conference on post-war financial and commercial affairs.

to this account, she is (1) clever (2) wise (3) has good judgment (4) witty (5) cultured (6) a brilliant writer (7) next to Mrs. Roosevelt, the best-liked woman in the U.S.A. (8) a great speaker (9) possesses statesmanship of the first order (10) beautiful.

You know, of course, that she is likeable. But she is hostile to the English and to Duff Cooper.[52]

I wish you would persuade Butler not only to ask nothing of the Americans, but to take nothing.....

There is little news I can tell you of Nassau.....

Lady Bailley (sic)[53] is here with a party of nine, including herself. I mean to go and see her in a few days. She is a lovely woman.

How I wish you could come out here!

And with affectionate good wishes,

I am,
Yours ever,

Bracken to Beaverbrook Chequers
Sunday (March 1953) Butler's Cross,
Aylesbury,
Bucks

My dear Max

Many thanks for giving me such an appropriate birthday present. Alsatian wine is good for the old-growing.

Your former Under Secretary[54] Harold Macmillan is here; he ascribes his remarkable performance in housing to his apprenticeship to you. He is indeed right. Enlisting men from industry with fire in their bellies & looting the Treasury are good Maxian doctrines for a Minister required to fulfil exceptional tasks.

Success has turned Harold into a healthy heretic & has shed his defensive armour of respectability. He is now chock-full of fun & is looking for new fields to conquer. Agriculture is beginning to attract him — I can't think of a better man to stir up that moss

---

52 Alfred Duff Cooper (1890–1954). Diplomat and Conservative politician. Secretary of State for War 1935–37, First Lord of the Admiralty 1937–38. Resigned from the Government over Munich. Husband of Lady Diana Cooper.
53 Probably Lady Baillie (1900–1975). American heiress, owner and restorer of Leeds Castle in Kent.
54 Macmillan had been parliamentary secretary to the Ministry of Supply during Beaverbrook's brief tenure at the Ministry.

grown department & to create hell in its appendage the Farmers Union. Under him more food wd be grown & so too wd budget deficits. In any event we shall get the latter & so it's a sound idea to cultivate every acre of these islands.

Clemmie & Mary were very taken by your Jean.

Yours aye
Brendan

The Russians have just sent £90,000 to the fund for aiding victims of the great gale. W. rightly wishes to treat this as a gesture of friendship & so Gromyko[55] has been invited to Downing Street tomorrow to receive the thanks of Government & to be photographed with the boss. Sensible & imaginative is this invitation.

Bracken to Beaverbrook Princes House,
18 March 1953 95, Gresham Street,
London, E.C.2.

My dear Max

.... The Spring is here again and so it is time you came back to this island. *Mount Allison's choices are also good.*

I am also sending you a cutting from today's Financial Times. Our Toronto correspondent avers that a great base metal find has been made near the town of Bathurst which I saw with you when you were home on the range and we were the guests of the local boy who had made good, Sir James Dunn.

Our stay with the local boy was indeed eventful. Many were the miles we travelled on what he described as his private road and I remember every time he told you how much he had spent to keep it in good repair, you, recovering from bumps on the head caused by deep ruts, mechanically replied 'Your contractors must have cost you a lot of money, Jimmy'.

The high-light of our visit to the Dunn abode was when the hot water system gave out at 8 o/clock in the morning. Jimmy was so enraged that his boyhood friend, Max, could not have a bath that he stalked up and down outside his house, brandishing his revolver and threatening to commit suicide. Apart from this small point of a hot water shortage, Jimmy was a princely host and no man ever strove harder to give happiness to his guests.

---

55 Andrei Gromyko (1909–89). Soviet Ambassador to London 1952–53, Minister of Foreign Affairs 1957–58.

You ought to tell Jimmy to stake a claim near his birthplace.

This New Brunswick discovery, tho' a low grade proposition, may be a very rewarding affair for the Province. If it shows signs of really satisfactory exploration results you should spend some of your Trust's money on a chair of mining in the U of New B.[56]

Yours affly
Brendan

Enclosure from the Financial Times

NEW BRUNSWICK MINERALS
Magnitude of Recent Find
From our Own Correspondent

TORONTO, March 16. The base metal find at Austin Creek, 16 miles south of Bathurst, was 'of tremendous magnitude,' Mr. C.S. Clements, director of Mines of New Brunswick, told the Prospectors and Developers Association.

He said that drilling has gone to a vertical depth of 805 ft and the ore-body as explored so far is 1,500 ft long, with an average width of 182 ft. The tonnage to a depth of 1,000 ft is in the order of 30m. tons. Average grade is 5.2 per cent, zinc, 1.6 per cent, lead, 1.92 ozs of silver per ton and about one-half of 1 per cent, copper.

'This ore-body.' he said, ' is comparable in size and value of metals with deposits like those of Noranda, Quebec and Flin Flon, Manitoba.'

Of other mineral bodies in the region, Mr. Clements said: 'Taking the Austin Brook ore-body as a centre, the new Calumet Orvan Brook deposit is 35 miles to the North-West; the Keymet mine is 32 miles to the North and the M.J. O'Brien and Noranda mines' lead-zinc-copper properties are 16 miles to the North.

From a geological concept the existence of a great diversity of minerals in New Brunswick is possible. Staking is going on in 13 out of 15 of the province's counties, he said, and so far 25,000 to 30,000 claims have been recorded.'

On Tuesday 23 June 1953, Churchill sustained a massive stroke while dining with the Italian Prime Minister De Gasperi, at Downing Street. Despite sitting through Cabinet the following day, his condition rapidly

---

[56] University of New Brunswick.

deteriorated until Lord Moran feared that the Prime Minister might not last the weekend. Churchill was driven down to Chartwell, while Sir John Colville secretly made constitutional arrangements with Buckingham Palace to ensure the continuity of Government should Churchill die or have to resign; arrangements that were made all the more urgent by the fact that Churchill's acknowledged successor, Anthony Eden, was at that moment undergoing a series of operations in Boston and so was similarly incapacitated. However, Churchill insisted that the extent of his illness should be disguised, so a bland official announcement was made, merely stating that Churchill had 'had no respite for a long time from his very arduous duties and is in need of a complete rest'.

Bracken's letter to Beaverbrook published below (undated) was probably written on the 24th, when Churchill's immediate Downing Street entourage — Colville, Soames and Moran — were persuading him not to appear in public or in the Commons. What is certain is that despite the bland official medical bulletin, Colville was still worried that the news of the stroke might leak out, so he summoned Bracken, Beaverbrook and Camrose to Chartwell over the weekend in an attempt to 'gag' Fleet Street. The three newspaper proprietors rallied to their old friend's cause and succeeded in ensuring that no news of Churchill's stroke, and the serious constitutional crisis that it nearly provoked, reached the British public — or Parliament. On Saturday, June 27, Bracken brought a wheelchair down to Chartwell which he had purchased in London and on Sunday the 28th Beaverbrook was Churchill's main dinner guest.

The reference to Bermuda in the letter pertains to the summit meeting between the British, Americans and the French that was due to start at the end of June. Churchill saw it as a preliminary to a full-scale summit meeting between the West and the new leaders of Soviet Russia following the death of Stalin on 5 March 1953. His enthusiasm for an East-West Summit was not shared by the French or Americans — let alone the Foreign Office — but Churchill had staked his political future on such a summit in a famous speech in the House of Commons on 11 May, when he had argued that to take advantage of 'The change of attitude, and, as we all hope, of mood which has taken place in the Soviet domains and particularly in the Kremlin since the death of Stalin...a Conference on the highest level should take place between the leading Powers without delay.'

However, Churchill's stroke scuppered the conference and on 26 June Churchill called to Eisenhower postponing the conference on medical grounds. By the time the Bermuda Conference did take place, in December 1953, much of the momentum had gone out of Churchill's initiative and his much hoped for East-West summit never happened.

Despite Lord Moran's dire predictions, Churchill in fact made a remarkable recovery and by 18 August was chairing his first Cabinet since his stroke eight weeks earlier.

Bracken to Beaverbrook
(Handwritten note)

W. is better tonight but lacks confidence about appearing in public with hesitancy in speech & a lowered jaw.

His finest hour may be in front of him. Do answer the letter you've had by saying that in him lies the hope of a world more tortured by the fear of war than the universal ruin that would follow another.

Dear Max — you who are Winston's oldest friend possess the good fortune to have Colville,[57] who cares for you greatly, to put your views to our ailing friend.

Do write & tell him to go to Bermuda even if it means that
"The Saviour comes not home tonight
Himself he will not save."

Bracken to Beaverbrook   8 Lord North Street
14 August 1953   Westminster

My dear Max

Our gartered knight[58] is, as you know, generous in all things. But for some odd reason – modesty might be the explanation — he hoards his paintings.

Three times has he growlingly accepted the suggestion of a painting for A.H.S.[59] I shall have another go. When is the birthday? If one can fix a date for unhoarding S. may get his heart's desire. The touching plea in your letter suggesting that age must diminish the N.Y. Times pontiff's power of appreciation wd be a red rag to the bull in Downing Street.

Bless him. He now thinks that the fractional measure of moderation induced by illness has well-nigh renewed his youth. Retire-

---

57 Sir John Colville, (1915–1988). Private Secretary to Churchill 1940–41, 1943–45, 1951–55.
58 Churchill had recently been made a Knight of the Garter.
59 Arthur Hayes Sulzberger, publisher of The New York Times.

ment is not in his vocabulary. Such defeatist trash is not for him! He must be ready to act for Butler when his days of convalescence come. And Swinton[60] may need a rest. O.L.[61] must soon leave the Mau Mau and Malayans whom he has handled exceedingly well. Somerset House thus serves the Mau Mau.

If C. were to take over the Colonial Office for a brief spell the so-called United Nations could cause less mischief. There is, to use C's favourite and hallowed peroration, a 'plentiful abundance' of opportunities for an energetic Prime Minister.

Cheering beyond all telling is this marvellous recovery.

Beaverbrook to Bracken P O Box 1028,
3 December 1953 Nassau,
Bahamas.

My dear Brendan,
I have been reading 'Family and Colour in Jamaica'. It is good.

I have told Millar to send a copy to Professor Bailey of the University of New Brunswick, keeping the copy you sent to me for the Library at Montego Bay.

It is not much of a Library, but it is enriched by this book.

I heard last night a very depressing broadcast describing the arrival of Churchill.[62] I hope he didn't listen in. I feel sure he was tired after his long journey. For certain he would recover in a few hours and show all the drive and energy that he has displayed recently.

Lord Moran might have bucked him up before presenting him to the assembled correspondents of all the American papers.

Nobody in the U.S.A. believes in Bermuda. They all say that

60 Philip Cunliffe-Lister, 1st Earl of Swinton (1884–1972). Born Lloyd-Greame, changed his name to Cunliffe-Lister in 1924 on his wife's inheritance of the Swinton estate from her uncle, the third Baron Masham. Conservative politician. Served in numerous Government posts between the wars. Raised to the peerage 1935. Chancellor of the Duchy of Lancaster and Minister of Materials 1951–52. Secretary of State for Commonwealth Relations 1952–55.
61 Oliver Lyttleton (1893–1972). Conservative M.P. for Aldershot, 1940–54. Member of War Cabinet 1941–45. Secretary of State for Colonies 1951–54. In the early 1950s Britain was involved in guerilla wars against the communists in Malaya and the Mau-Mau in Kenya.
62 Churchill and his entourage arrived in Bermuda for the Conference with the French and Americans on 2 December. It lasted until 10 December.

Eisenhower is going there out of respect for the Old Man.

The late Sir John Macdonald,[63] who dominated politics in Canada throughout his life, was asked, as his Premiership was drawing to a close, who should be his successor. He answered, 'After me the Deluge.'

I am sure Churchill will not make such a comment on his own Premiership. But I think it would rightly describe the situation.

The weather here is lovely. The yacht is beautiful; the sea is warm; the flowers are in bloom; the flies are sleeping. And we are shortly to have a visit from Lord Lyle and Mrs. Wood.

But before they arrive we are to have Captain Wardell with his camera, Stanley Morison[64] with his prayer-book, and Max Aitken with his bride.

I feel very much out of touch with the news. The B.B.C. is bloody. And the American broadcasters take little interest in European affairs, save only when they have got something to say that is disparaging to Britain and impertinent to Churchill.

My companionship is limited. There are no winter visitors here yet. There is no use in talking to the residents about politics. And I certainly can't talk to Christie about murder.[65]

It's futile to ask you here, so I won't do it.

With affectionate good wishes for the New Year and every year, I am,

Bracken to Beaverbrook
9 December 1953

Princes House,
95, Gresham Street,
London, E.C.2.

My dear Max

Many thanks for your letter.

I am not surprised by your account of what American broadcasters and journalists have said about W.S.C. These gentlemen have little sensitivity of nature and most of their readers or listeners relish 'de-bunking' stuff. Moreover, a large section of the United States believes that Churchill has gone to Bermuda with tempting

---

63 Sir John McDonald (1815 – 1891). Chief architect of Canadian Confederation, first Prime Minister of the Dominion of Canada, 1867.
64 Stanley Morison (1889–1967). Writer, typographer and journalist on the Staff of *The Times* 1930–60.
65 John Christie was being tried in England for the murder of at least six women.

food for geese and are afraid that their prize goose will therefore eat out of his hand. I wish he would, but as you rightly say, the Americans have well ringed their goose.

A remarkable country is the United States. A proof of this is that Mr. C.D. Jackson[66] is special assistant to the President and brought to Bermuda not merely to write speeches, but also to explain to the British and French the workings of Mr. Malenkov's[67] mind, which he is so well qualified to do on account of his former connection with psychological warfare. If Churchill had known that Jackson was going he ought to have brought one of those old gipsy palm readers who pass through Leatherhead on their annual visit to the Derby!

I don't know much about United States affairs, but I don't think I am wrong in averring that so far the Republican government has only accomplished one substantial thing, which is to have improved greatly the prospects of the Democrats.

I can give you little political news. The Comrades here have patched up their differences in public, but I think their inner feuds increase. A Welsh friend of ours who used to drink a lot of champagne at Cherkley,[68] was dining with his doctor, Sir Dan,[69] the other night and his description of some of his more eminent colleagues well deserves a place in a new anthology of invective.

It was a very funny dinner. Our Welsh comrade brought his lively wife and to match them Dan produced the Duke of Windsor and his lady. I couldn't have gone there unless I had brought with me Lord Lyle and Mrs. Woods who were long engaged to dine with me. And so you can well imagine the interest of a party which contained Lord Cube, Bollinger and the Prince over the Water.

It was all great fun, more particularly when Bollinger and his doctor, intermittently aided by the Duke of Windsor, proceeded to sing Welsh songs and hymns. 'God Bless the Prince of Wales' called for an encore and then was sung at least four times!

---

66 Mr C.D. Jackson. Originally with Time Life Inc. Jackson was Special Assistant for Psychological Warfare to Eisenhower.
67 Georgi Malenkov (1901–84). Stalin's successor in the Soviet Union.
68 Nye Bevan, nicknamed 'the Bollinger Bolshevik' by Bracken. The feud in the Labour Party between the Bevanite Left and the Gaitskellite Right was then at its height.
69 Sir Daniel Davies, physician to Bevan and Bracken.

There is going to be quite a lot of excitement in the City about the Savoy Hotel's attempt to purge itself of the invading Israelites. The boss of the Savoy, Mr. Wontner,[70] has hit on a crazy method of resisting the onslaught of Mr Samuel[71] and the backfire of Mr Clore.[72] He proposes, in effect, to create what one might call Savoy syndicalism. The voting shares which he thinks will baulk the Jewish terrorist are to be voted by the trustees of his Staff Benevolent Fund. A fine idea this! It provides the Socialists with a solution to what their left wing call 'workers' control'.

I don't believe Mr. Wontner will get away with his scheme, but if he does, keeping order in the Savoy is going to be quite a business when the bell-hops have the right to call themselves proprietors. It is all great fun, but poor Mr. Wontner has, I feel, lost the battle.[73]

(Sgd) Yours affly
Brendan

P.S. I am afraid the Government missed the bus when they didn't deal with the Socialist obstructionists in the House of Commons by asking the public for a bigger majority. Neither in home nor in foreign affairs can they hope for much luck during 1954: the most of their energies will be occupied in coping with criticisms such as the cost of living, the appalling state of our roads and the many other sour legacies they inherited from the Socialists.

Bracken to Beaverbrook
30 December 1953

Princes House,
95, Gresham Street,
London E.C.2.

My dear Max

This letter is written to wish you a happy new year and to sermonise you on the dangers of celebrating Hogmany (sic) according to the fashion of the Scots who, even though they are unsteady on their legs, continue to first-foot.

70 Sir Hugh Wontner (1908–). Chairman of the Savoy Group.
71 Harold Samuel, later Lord Samuel of Lych Cross (1912–1987). Property developer, Chairman of the Land Securities Investments Trust Ltd.
72 Sir Charles Clore (1904–79). Businessman, President of Sears Holdings Ltd.
73 Bracken was to be proved wrong. The Savoy Hotel remains independent to this day.

30 December 1953 *Winston's return* 153

I have got an effective palliative for my sinus troubles: it is stuff called Neophryn, made by the German chemist Bayer. It is filthy stuff to take because when it trickles into one's stomach it creates nausea if one has taken anything containing sugar. And so neither chocolates, nor alcohol nor even marmalade can be taken unless one wants to feel sick. I gave up these luxuries a fortnight ago and I do not miss them. The relief of getting rid of sinus pain is worth all the luxuries on earth.

I am lunching with Winston today who is in good fettle, but is, of course, very worried by the possibility of a crop of strikes during the coming year. The victory of the railwaymen who threatened to hold up all traffic at Christmas time has encouraged all other Unions to consider making use of the strike weapon.[74]

The understandable relief of the public at being freed from the prospect of a railway strike at Christmas time makes them overlook the significance of the decision to throw over the tribunal set up at the behest of the railway unions some 20 years ago. Its Chairman, Sir John Foster (sic),[75] has earned a golden reputation for fairness, most of all in Trade Union quarters. Luke Fawcett,[76] who, as you know, is a most respected retired Trade Union boss, was equally acceptable to railwaymen.

But when the tribunal gave its decision, the Unions promptly repudiated their own creation.

Walter Monckton,[77] who has many great virtues, has more grace than strength of character, and his performance may be well described in Winston's fine sentence about General Munro at Gallipoli — 'He came, he saw and he capitulated'. A large number of Monckton's colleagues are alarmed lest he should give way to the engineers, the builders and the many other Trade Unionists who want sharp increases in pay. But I think having chucked over the railway wage tribunal the Government will find it very difficult to resist the claims of other workers.

The Government's heroic conduct in putting a bull-dozer through the jungle of Rent Restriction Acts and regulations was an

---

74 The threat of strike action by the railway workers was deflected after a promise of increased pay.
75 Sir John Forster (1888–1972).
76 Sir Luke Fawcett (1881–1960). Trade Unionist, General Secretary of the Amalgamated Union of Building Trade Workers 1941–52.
77 The Minister of Labour.

act of high political courage, but its electoral expedience is open to great doubt. Many millions of electors live in rent controlled houses at quite inadequate rents.[78]

When you first came to England the small man never touched the Stock Exchange and he was probably none the worse for that. He put his savings into buying his own house and a couple of houses next door to him. Today these houses are occupied by people who are far better off than their landlord and who often sublet a part of the house they rent at very fat profits to themselves, the landlord, meanwhile, being required to keep the house in good repair, which in the most of cases he cannot do. This is the reason why there are several thousand missing 'landlords' in Manchester, Liverpool and Glasgow.

The effect of the Government's Rent Restriction reform Bill in Glasgow will be politically disastrous, according to political pundits in that city. A very large number of Glasgow electors live in rent controlled houses and a number of them voted Tory at the last two elections. It is estimated that we will only hold two seats in Glasgow when the next election comes to pass. *We now hold seven*.

I fancy your friend Lord Mountbatten will be the next First Sea Lord and for the first time since the war Admiralty House will be kept up in proper, not to say vice-regal, style.[79]

As you know newsprint costs are going up again next week and we shall all have to put up with those dreary restrictions on the use of paper. I reckon if we could get some more paper for the Financial Times we could not only increase circulation, but we could probably increase our revenue by 25%.

Last year we carried a little more trade and prestige advertising than we did financial advertising and we certainly cannot complain about the supply of the latter as we had more meetings than we have ever known in the paper's history.

That shop-walker, Woolton,[80] means well, but is clay in the

---

78 The White Paper 'Houses — The Next Step' was published by the Government in November 1953. Its recommendations were embodied in the Housing Repairs and Rent Act, 1954, under which Landlords could claim a rent increase if the landlord had spent money on repairs and put the dwelling into a state of 'good and tenantable repair'.
79 Mountbatten was appointed First Sea Lord in October 1954.
80 Lord Woolton was Chairman of the Conservative Party and Chancel-

hands of Treasury officials and the pensioners of Messrs. Bowaters and Reeds who constitute the paper experts in that ridiculous Ministry of Raw Materials.[81]

Woolton will be greatly enraged when he reads the Honours List for he will discover that his political twin, Lord Leathers, is being turned into a viscount. For many a year in toil of breath has Master Woolton pursued that dubious honour and it will greatly displease him that it should be given to the quiet Leathers.

Leo Lyle tells me that he is going to stay with you next month. Poor Leo is not very well and I wonder whether he is wise to go to a hot climate.

He has now some political preoccupations which are giving him some anxiety. Cranborne[82] is immediately retiring from his Bournemouth seat and as Lyle is not only President of the Association, but the political god of Bournemouth, he will have a decisive say in appointing a successor. On this occasion Mr. Hore-Belisha will not appear because in a short space of time he will be covering his pudding-like figure in scarlet and ermine and donning a coronet which will make him look like one of his own beacons.[83] Keep the news about Cranborne to yourself.

I wish you would come home; the climate of this country is almost as warm as Nassau.

I was sorry to hear that Aitken's House had been burgled. It was a damn good thing for the thieves that the lord and master of the house was not in when they arrived. Fiercer than a mastiff is he!

(Sgd) Yours affly
Brendan

Postscript

I had a long yarn with our friend at lunch & continued at dinner time.

He intends to give up before June — in fact he thought of resigning before Parliament meets next month.

    lor of the Duchy of Lancaster, with a seat in the Cabinet.
81 Bowaters and Reeds were the large paper manufacturers.
82 Viscount Cranborne (1916–). M.P. for Bournemouth West 1950–54, succeeded his father as 6th Marquess of Salisbury in 1972.
83 Leslie Hore-Belisha, as Minister of Transport (1934–37), had been responsible for introducing flashing amber lights at pedestrian crossings, afterwards known as 'Belisha beacons'.

I think this decision is quite definite. Though his health is not worse & he gets through a lot of work, the desire for office has diminished rapidly. I shd think he will spend next winter in Bermuda. He plans to write another book and to polish up another, hurriedly put together before the war but still unpublished. This shd be a good earner.

This news is top secret as we used to say in the war.

Bracken to Beaverbrook Princes House,
27 *January 1954* 95, Gresham Street,
London E.C.2.

My dear Max

Millar sent me the account of Darval's (sic) speech at Fredericton sent to you by the Captain.[84]

I know this Darvel fairly well.[85] He was, I think, brought into the Ministry of Information by Lord Macmillan and may well be described as a sloppy, chatty, porous man who never seems to have attained adolescence. He has, however, sufficient sense to get himself a highly paid job as Director General of the English-Speaking Union.

I know you want this stuff for the Express and I hope you will use it soon. My reason for saying this is that the English-Speaking Union lives on covenants given them by many businesses in this country who swallow the tale that it exercises a beneficent influence on Anglo-American relations. It is, in fact, an over-housed body of self-important people who certainly do offer lots of hospitality to visiting Yanks and, accordingly, to themselves. If a summary of Darval's speech is published in the Express or the Standard I should think that many companies will not renew their covenants.

I agree with you that the British Information Services should

84 Colin Mackay (1920–). Beaverbrook's choice as President of the University of New Brunswick in 1953.
85 Frank Darvall; Director-General of the English-Speaking Union of the Commonwealth, 1949 to 1957. On his tour of Canada in the autumn of 1953, Darvall made a speech at Fredericton during the course of which he criticised Britain for being less aware of the 'threat of Communist espionage or subversion' than Canada. This was all grist to Beaverbrook's mill, as he had long been a prominent critic of such bodies as the English Speaking Union and the British Council; the *Daily Express* ran a notorious campaign against the latter institution.

be closed down, but this can only be done over the dead bodies of Messrs. Butler and Eden. I grant you if Eden has an opportunity of reading Darval's speech he may take a different view of the usefulness of B.I.S., but Butler is a great culture merchant. You will remember that he, on becoming Chancellor, accepted the Presidency of the society that was to buy and endow Bernard Shaw's hideous Victorian villa in Hertfordshire. They appealed for something like £40,000 and the total subscriptions were under £1,100! He is also President of the Royal Society of Literature, which is a pretentious body stuffed with bores and snobs.

Butler spent a great deal of time in Sydney lauding the Randall Committee and the consequences of their report.[86] In this he showed a great lack of judgement as it should be obvious to any sensible man that in a Congressional Election year this report would be torn to bits by the arch-Protectionists in the United States. I should imagine that as a result of the Randall Report most members of Congress will get back pledged to increased tariffs against foreign countries who pay wages lower than those obtaining in the land of the free and the home of the brave. Any man with a grain of common sense should also recognise that America is now in some sort of recession and fears that it will grow greater. Unemployment is steadily rising and the volatile American public will soon be screaming for more and more protection.

There are no lack of political developments here. Monckton holds that as so many strikes are slated for this year, we may well have to face the consequences of what isn't in name, but is in fact, a general strike.

The Government's modest attempt to deal with some of the anomalies of rent restriction will greatly advantage Socialists at the General Election. Its effects on Scotland may be disastrous for the Tory Party. In the land of your ancestors rates are always readjusted when rents are increased.

I had luncheon with poor Archie Sinclair the other day and though he is not the most effective of politicians, he often says wise things. He kept plugging the point that if Churchill is not

[86] The Commission on Foreign Economic Policy, chaired by Clarence B. Randall, reported to the American Government in January 1954. It recommended a lowering of American tariffs to stimulate international free trade.

available to lead the Tories at the next election, they are bound to be beaten. According to Archie the public look upon W. as the prince of peace and it was for this reasons that the Tories won their surprise by-election at Sunderland.[87]

The Socialists are playing a very clever game by suggesting that many Tories want to push out Churchill. If he does resign they will set up a lot of maundering wailings about the wickedness of the Tories in parting from such a great leader.

The Daily Mirror is running a tremendous campaign against Churchill: it is a skilful compound of hatred, malice and greasy pity. This, of course, is their method of replying to Churchill's writ and the rough ride he gave the Mirror during the war.[88] I don't know what effect this type of attack really has on the public. The most of the readers of the Mirror are either mentally adolescent or natural supporters of the Left.

The bosses of the Mirror are certainly a skilful lot. The amount of money they must be making out of their investment in Reeds is truly enormous and they have plenty of other good nest-eggs outside the newspaper business.

I don't think anything is going to happen at the Berlin conference.[89] Our new Ambassador to Moscow, who is a young and able fellow,[90] says there has been no real change in Russian foreign and military policies. All Malenkov aims for is to get a couple of years' breathing space in order to fulfil his promise to raise the standard of living in Russia and, above all, to halt military expenditure by Western countries.

The American and British diplomats who have gone to Berlin are all convinced that Molotov means to spin this conference out indefinitely and try to put the blame for its breakdown on American (sic) and Britain.

87 In May 1953 a by-election at Sunderland South, previously a safe Labour seat, had resulted in the return of the Conservative candidate by 175 votes.
88 In 1951 Churchill had sued the paper for its personal insults during the election campaign and in 1942 Churchill had tried, against the better judgement of the rest of the War Cabinet, to suppress the paper altogether.
89 The Berlin Conference of Foreign Ministers of Britain, the United States, France and the Soviet Union lasted from 25 January to 19 February 1954.
90 Sir W.G. Hayter K.C.M.G.

Mr. Dulles wants to put an end to the conference as soon as it becomes clear that Molotov will give no appreciable concessions to the Western point of view. He is, not unnaturally, always peering over his shoulders to gauge the effect of his lengthy speeches on a Congress wholly hostile to all things Russian. How odd it is that an able and cunning Corporation lawyer should so often indulge in endless ranting speeches.

(Sgd) Yours affly
Brendan

P.S. I read in this morning's newspaper that poor Leo Lyle is in hospital in New York suffering from pneumonia. As his heart is rather dicky he will, I am afraid, have to go through some anxious times before he gets out of the doctors' hands.

Beaverbrook bought the Bonar Law and Lloyd George Papers, which, together with his own papers, would later go on to form the nucleus of the Beaverbrook Library. Beaverbrook's last years were spent writing several books of history and biography. One of his uncompleted projects was a book to be entitled 'The Age of Baldwin'; it was as a result of the research for this book that Beaverbrook sent Bracken the following letter. A full account of Baldwin's succession to the premiership can be found in Kenneth Rose, King George V (Macmillan 1984) pp. 266–274 or Roy Jenkins, Baldwin (Collins 1987) pp. 59–63.

Beaverbrook to Bracken P O Box 1028,
4 February 1954 Nassau,
  Bahamas.

Here is an extraordinary story.

On the 20th May 1923 Lord Stamfordham[91] wrote a Minute to the King, telling him that he must choose the Prime Minister, as Bonar Law refused to make a recommendation.[92] There would be only two possible alternatives said Stamfordham — Mr. Stanley Baldwin and Lord Curzon.[93] Among the arguments in favour of Baldwin, which was recounted in the Minute, was that Lord Derby[94] would be willing, if necessary, to serve under Mr Baldwin but not under Lord Curzon.

On the 21st May Lord Salisbury[95] informed Lord Stamfordham that Bonar Law had told Salisbury that he would 'on the whole be disinclined to pass over Curzon.'

An application from Colonel Waterhouse[96] to Stamfordham to see Amery[97] and Bridgman[98] was rejected as their advice would not be helpful, for they were in favour of Mr Baldwin.

On the same day Salisbury wrote to Stamfordham, 'I think at your own suggestion.' Amery and Bridgman had just been to see him.

[91] Lord Stamfordham (1850–1931). Private Secretary to King George V.
[92] Bonar Law (1858–1923). Conservative Prime Minister 1922–23. On 19 May 1923 he was forced to resign through ill-health, thus precipitating a constitutional crisis as he had refused to nominate a successor.
[93] George Nathaniel, Marquess Curzon of Kedleston (1859–1925). Conservative politician. Viceroy of India 1894–1904, Member of Lloyd George's War Cabinet 1916–19, Foreign Secretary 1919–24, Lord President of the Council and Leader of the House of Lords 1924–25.
[94] Earl of Derby (1865–1948). A pillar of the Conservative Party, the 'King of Lancashire' served as Secretary of State for War 1916–18, 1922–24 and was Ambassador to Paris, 1918–20.
[95] 4th Marquess of Salisbury (1861–1947). Senior Conservative politician, at that time leader of the House of Lords.
[96] Lt. Colonel Sir Ronald Waterhouse (1878–1942). Principal Private Secretary to three Prime Ministers.
[97] Leo Amery (1873–1955). Conservative politician and stalwart of the British Empire. First Lord of the Admiralty 1922–24, Secretary of State for the Colonies 1924–29, Secretary of State for India 1940–45.
[98] W.C. Bridgeman (1864–1935). Home Secretary 1922–24. First Lord of the Admiralty 1924–29.

Stamfordham marked the passage, 'I think at your own suggestion' — 'Never'.

Stamfordham then saw Geoffrey Dawson,[99] who had come up from Oxford. He brought a Poll of all present at All Souls College. Mr Dawson and his colleagues favoured Lord Curzon. Stamfordham saw him again at 8 p.m. when Dawson informed Stamfordham that opinion in the 'Times' office was equally divided, the older men being in favour of Curzon.

On the 22nd May Salisbury wrote, offering to try and arrange an appointment for Stamfordham with Bonar Law.

On the same day May 22 Stamfordham replies to Salisbury that he has learnt, directly or indirectly, from Bonar Law's family that he would be in favour of Baldwin.

The King did not wish to disturb Bonar Law who had just had an operation.

Stamfordham then wrote in effect to Salisbury that there was no use in approaching Bonar Law, as they already knew his opinion.

Now comes the elucidation of that situation.

On Tuesday, 22nd May, Colonel Waterhouse went to see Stamfordham.

Colonel Waterhouse told Stamfordham:

(1) Bonar Law would advise the King to appoint Mr Baldwin.

(2) Bonar Law had told Colonel Waterhouse before leaving London for Aldershot on Sunday that if the King were to ask Colonel Waterhouse any questions relating to a successor, Bonar Law advised him to answer, 'On the whole I think I should advise Baldwin.'

(3) Colonel Waterhouse said that Sir Frederick Sykes[100] supported his opinion.

(4) Colonel Waterhouse had consulted Mary Law, who was a very close confidant of her brother, and she endorsed the opinion that Bonar Law would support the appointment of Mr Baldwin.

It was on this information that Stamfordham wrote the letter to Lord Salisbury.

Now, the facts are that Bonar Law saw Salisbury on Monday morning, and agreed with Salisbury's intention to recommend Curzon.

---

[99] Geoffrey Dawson (1874–1944). Editor of *The Times* 1912–19, 1923–41.
[100] Sir Frederick Sykes (?–1954). Bonar Law's son-in-law.

The Waterhouse statements were utterly unauthorised so far as I know, and I think, fictitious.

That's how Prime Ministers are made.

You can tell this to Winston, but don't use it, as I mean to make full play with the story in my work on Mr. Baldwin.

I needn't tell you the whole story; it comes from the papers of Lord Stamfordham to which I have had access.

The Lord of Withygrove[101] came to dinner last night. He was gay. He gestured freely as he made his points — if he did make them. Her Ladyship was a fountain of gaiety. She had been two or three weeks in New York and she had had a fine time.

He wants to sell Chandos House and also his house in Nassau. He says that he cannot any longer summon his family about him. They have informed him that they do not want Chandos House, that they will not take it over on any account. Therefore he is parting with it.

He is not living in his house here. He is staying at an hotel. The house is let.

I think something is going on there.

I shall be with you soon. And I am longing to see you to hear the news.

Bracken to Beaverbrook
10 February 1954

Princes House,
95, Gresham Street,
London, E.C.2.

My dear Max

You certainly sent me a very remarkable story about the succession to Bonar Law.

Waterhouse always struck me as being rather a busybody. He revelled in the opportunity that was created by the uncertainty of the succession of Bonar Law. The fact that he was in a confidential position in Downing Street naturally gave him access to old boys like Jim Salisbury, who looked upon themselves as rightful consulters of the monarchy.

Waterhouse was then welcomed in all high quarters as a bringer of news and as a man who could indirectly exercise influence upon great affairs.

There have been few parallels since the 18th century of the position created by the imminent retirement of Bonar Law. Old King

---

[101] Lord Kemsley.

George V's concern in appointing a Prime Minister was to get one who would be acceptable to the public. He was, in fact, a sort of Dr. Gallop.[102] The only information he could get as to what the public required was from a few old cronies in the Tory party. Some of these old gentlemen had certainly little contacts with the so-called public and many of them felt that they had been wrongfully excluded from their rightful places in government by the victory of Bonar Law over Austen Chamberlain[103] and Balfour.[104]

When the Monarch was put into the position of taking the pulse of the public a man like Waterhouse saw his chance. He could unburden himself to Stamfordham about the intimate conversations he had with leaders of opinion and with the relations of Bonar Law. To him it must have seemed that his interest would be promoted by the promotion of Baldwin.

If the Marquess had gone to No.10 Waterhouse would have been out. The Marquess was no believer in private secretaries who were West End figures and whose names too often appeared in the newspapers. He was for anonymous private secretaries chosen from the higher ranks of the Foreign Office and the Treasury. W's part in the Baldwin appointment may indeed have been a decisive one. For the Palace was naturally not anxious to intrude on Bonar Law and his circle during the course of a rapid and mortal illness. It had to depend on men who could give them news of what was in Bonar Law's mind. It was open to Waterhouse to assert that all the information given him in his Downing Street capacity and as a confidential man of affairs to Bonar Law led to the conclusion that Baldwin was the best choice for the Premiership. Men of small consequence sometimes can play a decisive part in great appointments.

A ridiculous little man named Sinclair, aided by Lulu (sic) Harcourt, who was then private secretary to his father, pulled Ros-

---

102 Of Gallup public opinion polls.
103 Sir Austen Chamberlain (1863–1937). Conservative politician. Served in numerous high offices of State; Secretary of State for Foreign Affairs, 1924–29. Chamberlain and Walter Long were competing for Conservative Party leadership in 1911. Bonar Law was brought in as a compromise candidate to avoid a damaging split in the party.
104 A. J. Balfour (1848–1930). Conservative politician. Prime Minister 1902–1905, Secretary of State for Foreign Affairs 1916–19. He was forced out of the Tory leadership in 1911.

berry off his perch.[105]

You rightly say that Prime Ministers are often chosen by queer means. Both you and I may live to see the time when a Socialist Prime Minister is actually chosen by a party caucus and will have to submit a list of ministers for their approval before he goes to Buckingham Palace. For many years this has been the usage in Australia and New Zealand.

I am delighted by the news that you are coming home on March 10th. I have missed you greatly and I believe that your presence here will be an encouragement to our old friend who inevitably passes through long periods of depression.

I saw the Lord of Withygrove before he started his journey to Nassau. He has a noisy mind and is apt to lay down the law on subjects in which he is completely out of his depth. He gave me a much-interrupted harangue about politics which confirmed my view that the greatest mistake he made in his life was to part from his brother Bill[106] who kept him in his proper department, which was the getting of advertising, and never would allow him loose in editorial matters. The position of his papers here, in Manchester and in Glasgow confirmed the wisdom of his elder brother's judgment.

(Sgd) Yours
affly
Brendan

---

[105] The 5th Earl of Rosebery (1847–1929) was Prime Minister of the Liberal Government, 1894 – 95. His unhappy premiership was fatally undermined by his running battle with Sir William Harcourt (1827–1904), who had himself entertained hopes of succeeding Gladstone as Prime Minister in 1894. Harcourt's greatest advocate in the party was his son, Lewis 'Loulou' Harcourt, whose machinations on behalf of his father's quest for the highest office poisoned relations within the Liberal Party for a decade afterwards. Wearied by his struggles with the Harcourts, Rosebery resigned the Liberal Party leadership in 1896. John Sinclair was a Liberal M.P. and staunch supporter of Harcourt, but his role in Rosebery's downfall is obscure. See Robert Rhodes James, *Rosebery* (Weidenfeld and Nicolson 1963), and David Brooks, ed., *The Destruction of Lord Rosebery* (London, Historians' Press, 1986).

[106] Lord Camrose.

Bracken to Beaverbrook
16 February 1954

Princes House,
95, Gresham Street,
London, E.C.2.

My dear Max

Many thanks for your cable.

My neighbour, little Max, celebrated his birthday by having his daughter baptised by a Minister of the Kirk of Scotland. Very little water was poured on the baby but lots of champagne was poured down the gullets of the guests!

The farmers are generating lots of troubles for the Government. According to to-day's 'Times' the average farmer in England gets £1,000 a year by way of subsidy. According to Sir James Turner[107] this is not enough and he also holds that the farmer has no guarantee that this Treasury contribution will continue. I think it will because both Tories and Socialists are eagerly angling for the agricultural vote.

The Government has also got itself into a lot of trouble with teachers. It is well deserved as the Treasury have been using superannuation funds, to which the teachers are contributors, in the same way as they used the funds provided by the petrol tax. They now want teachers to contribute a good deal more to this rifled superannuation fund which is, in fact, a cunning Treasury method of reducing their emoluments. The teachers are in high state of indignation and they have built up a most formidable Lobby. They have flooded members of Parliament with letters which are all hand-written, marked 'Personal', and all more or less convey in terms which lack delicacy that they will work with all their might to put their members out unless justice is done them. I have always regarded Mother Horsbrugh as a disastrous Minister of Education and the Tories will pay a very high price for her services. She is a good old girl who doesn't conceal her disbelief in education.

A gentleman named Mr. Jay has declared to the 'Daily Mail' and 'Manchester Guardian' that he has bought £1 1/4 millions' worth of Ordinary Shares in Kemsley's newspapers. If his statement is correct his Lordship has some reason for concern as he and his family's holding amounts to about 26%. I don't believe

---

[107] Sir James Turner, President of the National Farmers Union 1945–59, cr. Baron Netherthorpe 1959.

Mr. Jay has bought anything like the amount of shares he claims. He certainly hasn't bought them through the market. Nothing is known about him save that he recently put in a take-over bid for the Manx Steamship Company and later wriggled out of it. Nor can I see any profit in a take-over bid in the Kemsley Group whose prior charges are very high and whose position in Manchester and Glasgow is, to say the least of it, vulnerable.

March 10th is going to be a great day for me.

(Sgd) Yours affly
Brendan

Bracken to Beaverbrook
25 June 1954

Princes House,
95, Gresham Street,
London, E.C.2.

My dear Max

Having tasted your noble cheese all I can say to you is it's the best I have eaten since Mr. Hitler started his experiment in redrawing the map of Europe. You ought to be very proud of the success of your farming operations at Cricket which enable you to produce cheese like poetry.

I am very grateful to you.

(Sgd) Yrs
B.

Bracken to Beaverbrook
Sunday (May 1954)

8 Lord North Street
Westminster

My dear Max

Thank you very much for your Dickens present.

Like many others I made the mistake of reading Dickens when I was very young & could not appreciate the range & versatility that made him so remarkable & purposeful a writer.

Today I find Thackeray (whom I used to admire) both finicky & stilted & I get much pleasure from Dickens, Trollope & Surtees.

W. may yet delay departure from his high place. He alone has the capacity to hold on to excitable Uncle Sam's coat-tails. No man can foretell what U.S. may do in fulfilling his declared intention of going all lengths to prevent a Communist domination of Indo China which may quickly spread over all S.E. Asia.

Unless U.S.'s allies show wisdom & firmness the world may be involved in the worst of wars. The volubility of Dulles and the

31 August 1954 *Winston's return* 167

pugnacity of the U.S. Chiefs of Staff may destroy the possibility of an armistice in Indo-China. The Sino-Russian axis is far more formidable & ruthless than the alliance forged by Hitler.

Public opinion here may yet prevent any quick change in Government leadership.

O.L. is to depart from the C.O. at the end of May. L.B. is to be his successor. Keep this news strictly to yourself.[108]

I am flying to South Africa on Sunday, 16 May. I think the climate and dust of the mining areas in that country will renew my sinus troubles. But I must go.

Yours affly
Brendan

Bracken to Beaverbrook
31 August 1954

Princes House,
95, Gresham Street,
London, E.C.2.

My dear Max

Thank you for your letter.

I shall be delighted to dine with you at Arlington House on the 6th.

I expect you have had a letter from Harry Luce asking for your views on his new sporting magazine.[109] I got one and have replied by saying that his new paper is much more friendly to British athletes than other Luce publications are to British statesmen.

Luce's consistent hostility to Britain and to Churchill puzzles me. In the last issue of Time his London correspondent declares that Churchill horned in on the delicate French political situation by inviting Mendes-France[110] to visit him at Chartwell. This statement is altogether untrue. Mendes-France pressed Churchill to see him for a few hours at his 'country residence'.

Luce's man in London is thoroughly hostile to Britain and his source of information are inaccurate people like Mr. Alistair Forbes.[111]

(Sgd) Yours affly
Brendan

108 Oliver Lyttleton retired from politics and went to the House of Lords on 9 September 1954 as Viscount Chandos. He was succeeded at the Colonial Office by Alan Lennox-Boyd (1904–1983) on July 28.
109 *Sports Illustrated*.
110 Prime Minister of France.
111 Alistair Forbes, English journalist.

Beaverbrook to Bracken
7 December 1954
My dear Brendan,
 I hear that you will not come to Nassau.
 That is a very great disappointment to me. And I hope so much that you will be persuaded by pressure later on.
 There is so much that I want to talk with you. And I assure you the weather is not too warm here in the month of January
 I have been reading Tom Jones'[112] diary with extraordinary interest. It is a story which puts Walter Moncton (sic) in a curious light.
 At one point Baldwin praises Walter Moncton who is invaluable to him.
 Then again, his name is put forward for the Spenderclay seat, which fell vacant.
 I am so sorry about the Churchill row.[113] These Socialists are quick to criticise him when he makes a mistake. But you will remember the 'unconditional surrender' statement by Bevin. Churchill made no disturbance, though I gave him the material at the time. He could have blown Bevin's statement to bits.
 Once more, I renew my passionate hope that you will come to Nassau.
 With affectionate recollections,

I am,
Yours ever,

---

112 Dr Thomas Jones (1870–1955); Deputy Secretary of the Cabinet 1920–30.
113 On 23 November 1954, Churchill had made a speech on foreign affairs in his constituency of Woodford. During the course of this speech he referred to a telegram he had sent to Montgomery in 1945 requesting captured German weapons to be carefully stored 'so that they could easily be issued again to the German soldiers whom we should have to work with if the Soviet advance continued'. Churchill claimed that this telegram had been published in Vol. 6 of his war memoirs, but it had not. The Labour Party picked up on this to deride Churchill's peaceful intentions towards the Soviets; Churchill later told Lord Moran 'I made a goose of myself at Woodford'. See Martin Gilbert, *Never Despair: Winston Churchill 1945–1965* (Heineman 1988) pp. 1078–1080 for a full account of this episode.

Bracken to Beaverbrook
15 December 1954

Princes House,
95, Gresham Street,
London, E.C.2.

My dear Max

Nothing would have given me greater pleasure than to have been with you in the Bahamas, for a small reason which is that I am sick of the city, but for a larger one which is that I desperately miss your company. When I find myself amongst my old colleagues nowadays they are too busy on personal or political propaganda and there is little fun to be got out of them.

W. is in tearing spirits though a bit tired after all the jubilations.[114] He tells me they greatly pleased him but he doesn't want any more.

There is nothing to report from this country except that every business is making enormous paper profits. People are spending in a mad way and almost every big storekeeper is taking on someone from the Inland Revenue to help in someway to avoid taxation and whittle down death duties. This, I think, is a labour in vain as Somerset House[115] are far too skilful.

Mr Gaitskell told a colleague of mine the other day who is a most reliable witness, that if the Socialists get in they will restore E.P.T.,[116] following the good example set by the Tories; they will put Profits Tax up to 10%, and introduce a capital gains tax.

Gaitskell knows that he must go very much to the left if he is to cope with enemies like Bevan.

(Sgd) Yours affectionately
Brendan

Beaverbrook to Bracken
27 December 1954

My dear Brendan,

I hope your decision about the Bahamas is not final. You would like it here for a little while. The weather is quite cool to-day, and the nights are always cool here on the hill where I live; much better than by the seashore.

We hear something of American politics here. I have just been

---

[114] His 80th birthday celebrations.
[115] Headquarters of the Inland Revenue.
[116] Excess Profits Tax.

hearing praise of Anthony Nutting.[117] But of course he is bound to be praised as long as he sings out each day, 'God Bless America'.

The Canadians say he has made a better impression than Selwyn Lloyd[118], and they think he has the complete confidence of Anthony Eden.

The Americans are under the impression that Eden takes a dim view of their Formosa policy.[119] But that Churchill possibly turns a friendly face to their defence. Personally, I think they would be mad to give up the stronghold of Formosa at the present time.

It seems odd to me that the English would complain about Formosa and, at the same time, expect support for Cyprus.

I am deeply distressed about Lord Brownlow. He will have much misery and many wretched hours.

So do please come.

Yours ever,

Bracken to Beaverbrook   8 Lord North Street
17 January 1955   Westminster
My dear Max

Many thanks for your letters.

There is, alas, no prospect of my being able to go to the Bahamas. The newly appointed managing-director of the U.C. cracked his skull on his journey back from London and is still in doctors' hands — much to the detriment of Union Corporation affairs. We are about to open up a number of highly hopeful new mines and our engines & geologists are tossing all sorts of problems to London which could normally be dealt with by our South African mg-director.

I may soon have to go to S.Africa & stay there for some time.

117 Sir Anthony Nutting (1920–). Conservative politician. Parliamentary Under-Secretary of State for Foreign Affairs 1951–54, Minister of State for Foreign Affairs, 1954–56. Resigned form the Government over Suez.
118 Selwyn Lloyd (1902–84). Conservative politician. Minister of State at the Foreign Office 1951– 4, Foreign Secretary 1955–60, Chancellor of the Exchequer 1960–62, Lord Privy Seal 1963–64.
119 The Americans were pledged to defend the islands off the Chinese mainland, including Formosa (Taiwan), against any attempts by the Chinese Communists to seize them. It was a policy which worried Eden.

17 January 1955 *Winston's return* 171

There is a lot of political news which cannot easily be put down in writing. Our friend, under no pressure from Cl.[120] Eden or other ministers, intends to depart before July.[121] Naturally this news is in our bond of secrecy.

He says, without any sign of regret, that it is time he gave up. His only wish now is to find a small villa in the South of France where he can spend the winter months in the years which remain to him.

I am certain that he will not change his mind. All his plans are made and when he leaves No. 10 Jock Colville will resign from the Civil Service to take a job in the City early in July.[122]

I have no doubt that many foolish Tories will rejoice in the news. They may well be disillusioned by the result of the next General Election.

E.[123] may well find himself the target of a bitter minority in Parliament. The middle classes here are bitterly disillusioned. They are the victims of an ever increasing cost of living but they have none of the power of the T.U.C. or the F.B.I. to compensate themselves for the ravages of inflation.

There is a great row going on in the News-Chronicle. I had a call from Layton & Cadbury the other day to advise the latter about the wisdom of appointing Plummer[124] to the managing directorship. Plummer is no ideal choice but he is tough and was trained in an exacting stable. He also happens to be the only qualified man available.

Layton told me that Cadbury might be able to make up his mind in a few days. He has. Plummer is not, to him, a suitable colleague & Cadbury is quite willing to wait for a year or more to find a manager to suit him. As these are no times for rudderless newspapers, Cadbury may find his problem solved by having no newspapers or seeing them disappear in the greedy maw of the Mirror Group[125].

Before you return you may get the news that your printers are

---

120 Lady Clementine Churchill.
121 Churchill resigned on April 8.
122 Colville became a director of Hill, Samuel and Co.
123 Eden, Churchill's successor as Prime Minister.
124 Sir Leslie Plummer, an ex-Express journalist and Labour M.P. for Deptford, 1950–59.
125 The paper eventually closed in 1960.

much better paid than the professors at McGill or New Brunswick.

The Kirk of Scotland now needs about 430 Ministers & knows not where to find them. Inflation corrodes devotion.

I hear Mr. Driberg has written a book about you which is much more atrocious than Citizen Kane.[126] This cunning ingrate needs tough & skilful handling. He has many American contacts who care nothing for libel actions.

Yours affly
Brendan

Beaverbrook to Bracken
25 January 1955
My dear Brendan,
 So very many thanks for your letter, and for the news which I look upon as bad news.

Please tell Mr. Churchill that he may have possession of my house at any time he wishes it from the first day of December till the first day of April in each and every year. He can staff it himself, with the exception of the permanent members who stay there all through the year.

I told Walter Layton that I wold join him in buying the 'News Chronicle' at a reasonable price. He may direct the policy of the paper and take full credit for it. I will put in an editor and also Tom Blackburn to manage it.

I don't suppose Walter can persuade Mr. Cadbury to relinquish control.

I think Cadbury is right to reject Plummer. He is a loyal fellow, but he has been a long time out of newspapers and has spent several years in politics.

There is only one condition on which I would take him. That would be on the basis of resignation from the House of Commons.

Tom Driberg came out here with his manuscript,[127] expecting me to pass it for his publishers. I told him that I would have nothing to do with it, or even comment on it.

126 *Beaverbrook — A Study in Power and Frustration* was published, to Beaverbrook's considerable fury, later that year.
127 The draft of *Beaverbrook — A study in power and frustration*. Driberg had initially had Beaverbrook's blessing for the book — but this soon ceased. For a full account of Beaverbrook's protracted dealings with Driberg over this book, see A.J.P. Taylor, *Beaverbrook*, pp. 616–618.

I don't care if he prints it, but I will of course take damages out of the publishers if I can establish a claim.

Tom won't publish the book in the U.S.A. if he can't bring it out in London. For, of course, the author is responsible for libel as well as the publishers.

The book is not a 'Citizen Kane'. It is made up of much praise for me with a Jekyll and Hyde theme.

He claims that I am kindly to a degree and generous and open-handed with money. But subject to terrible fits of gloom and depression, when I castigate all those about me and drive them almost, you might say, to suicide.

He pictures my political policy as absurd and preposterous. He glorifies Baldwin in my contest with that statesman. And he defends the Earl Mountbatten against my attacks, which he says are based on a vendetta arising from some social conflict.

He says I have a vendetta against Mr. Antony Head. And, on these two cases, he declares that I am a man of vendettas.

He refers to £1,000 which I gave him on one occasion when he was in trouble with the police. But he does not tell the nature of the trouble; nor does he disclose his own name. He says that he asked me to lend him the money. But that, in fact, I overwhelmed him by giving him the sum he required for his defence; namely £1,000.

He gives many other instances of my generosity. He does everything possible to damage the 'Daily Express', dragging out absurd quotations from ridiculous newspapers condemning the paper.

That's about all. I really don't mind, but I would like to take a large sum out of the publisher and also to leave Tom my debtor once more.

The odd part of this story is that Tom got me to advance some £3,000 on the plea that he was about to go bankrupt. He said that he would have to leave Parliament in disgrace if I didn't give him the money. He declared that he would resign forthwith if he got it. Instead, he gave notice of intention not to stand again.

I also gave him $500 in American money when he wanted to go to New York to see a woman. I was so intrigued by the mission that I handed out the money.

So Tom is doing well. No doubt he got some money from the publishers. But the book in its present form will never be published in England or America either.

I am now giving the retired Ministers of the Presbyterian church in the Maritime Provinces and the widows of the Ministers $300 a year each. Would you believe that that trifling sum is an amount of money to which each and every one of them attach immense importance.

It appears to me that the complete failure of Christianity will come to pass because the Ministers now in the Church will die off swiftly of worry and new men will refuse to enter upon a career of poverty.

Without Ministers the Church must perish.

I have had a visit from Bob Boothby.[128] He really is a Tory in name only.

Stanley Morison is here writing an essay on Northcliffe, Wilson and Sir William Wiseman. I understand Northcliffe and Wilson, but I cannot grasp why he puts Sir William Wiseman[129] into this group. He thinks Wiseman was of importance in the British political sphere of 1917 and 1918.

I have just been to Jamaica. Manley,[130] I imagine, will develop an Indian attitude to the British empire. I should think the rich men give Bustamante[131] immense sums of money, but the population take the cast and vote the other way.

This community is also in a state of turmoil. I should think many will save the 'Bay Street' group at the next election, but the

---

128 Robert Boothby (1900–1986). P.P.S. to Churchill as Chancellor of the Exchequer, 1926–29. Charges of financial impropriety ruined a promising political career in 1940.
129 Morison's essay, 'Personality and Diplomacy in Anglo-American relations' appeared in *Essays presented to Sir Lewis Namier* (St. Martin's Press, 1956), ed. Richard Pares and A.J. P. Taylor. The essay deals with President Wilson's dealings with Northcliffe and other British emissaries to the United States during the first World War; Sir William Wiseman (1885–1962) was director of British intelligence services in the United States 1914–1918, and Chief Adviser on American affairs to the British delegation in Paris, 1918–19. He was a close associate of Col. E.M. House, President Woodrow Wilson's confidant.
130 Norman Washington Manley (1893–1969). Lawyer, Jamaican Nationalist leader and co-founder of the People's National Party in 1938. Chief Minister of Jamaica 1955–62.
131 Sir Alexander Bustamante (1884–1977). Founder of the Jamaican Labour Party in 1943; first Prime Minister of independent Jamaica, 1962–67.

triumph of the Left appears to me quite certain some time in the future.

I am going to England at the end of February, as I have already told you, and to Capponcina on the first of April.

I shall try and persuade you to come out there.

And with affectionate good wishes and apologies for this typewritten letter,

I am,
Yours ever,

Bracken to Beaverbrook
2 February 1955

Princes House,
95, Gresham Street,
London, E.C.2.

My dear Max

Many thanks for your letter.

I was just about to write to you to give you worse news, which is that our friend has decided to advance the date. I will give him your message about La Capponcina.

You are right in saying that Layton can't persuade Cadbury to relinquish control. Nowadays Cadbury is very brusque with the unfortunate Layton, and I imagine Walter will part from the News Chronicle before very long.[132]

Layton has many complaints to make against Cadbury including one of being far too long-winded and never being willing to make up his mind!

Cadbury has never forgiven Walter for extracting a peerage out of Morrison. The cocoa maker says that if there were any peerages knocking around for News Chronicle people he as the owner of the business should have been given one. Believe it or not, the old Quaker is most anxious to get a coronet.

When I was M.O.I.[133] he buttonholed me for a long time telling me that that was his dearest wish. If I had had the power I would have given him one merely to be burdened no longer with his company. But that is not a principal reason for shunting a man into the morgue.

If Mr Driberg had a little more political instinct and a less acidu-

---

132 Cadbury refused to let Layton conclude a deal with Beaverbrook. Layton resigned from the Daily News Board, the controlling company of the *News Chronicle*, in September 1957.
133 Minister of Information.

lous and gossipy pen, he would have realised that your efforts to get rid of old Baldwin might well have saved us from the last war to which Baldwin's inertia was a great contributor.

When the Duke of Wellington was pestered for money by one of his mistresses who declared she would publish his amorous letters to her unless he complied, he answered 'Publish and be damned'. On reflection I think you are right to take the same view.

Driberg's conduct and Randolph Churchill's are an example of the truth of the saying that 'those whom you help hate you most'.

Retired Ministers of the Presbyterian Church in the Maritime Provinces and the widows of those Ministers are right to look upon an additional income of $300 a year as a great benefaction, for it enables them in their old age to buy the little comforts they care for and which inflation has put beyond their means.

Your view of the decline and fall of the Presbyterian church through lack of good young Ministers is shared by the Vice-Chancellor of St. Andrew's University, Dr. Knox. He was dining with me on Friday night and he told me that St. Mary's College, the oldest in the University and one which is entirely given over to the teaching of theology, has now only about 30 students and most of them are of poor quality. This description also applies to the formerly great Presbyterian College in Edinburgh University and to the Universities of Aberdeen and Glasgow.

Stanley Morison is putting William Wiseman in good company. Stanley must have been looking at some of the letters he wrote to Dawson and other moguls in The Times. As you know he has always been a great letter-writer and moves with the same air of mystery cultivated by Sir Campbell Stuart.[134]

Wiseman would certainly be a wonderful man if he had succeeded in persuading us when he came to Stornoway House during the last war and told us that the only way we could further our cause in America would be for the Treasury to put $6 millions in his bank at New York with the stipulation that he would not have to account for it. You who have had lots of experience of human life, rightly opened your mouth in absolute astonishment

---

134 Sir Campbell Stuart (1885–1972). Worked on propaganda in enemy countries during both world wars and in a number of other quasi-secret posts. Director of *The Times*. 1919–60.

21 February 1955   *Winston's return*   177

— the first time I ever saw you do so.

Money may save the Bay Street group at the next election, provided that those who put it up are certain that it will reach the voters.

I am delighted to hear that you are coming to England at the end of February. You would probably be happy here now. Our spring arrived in the middle of January and there is lots of sunshine and warmth.

(Sgd) Yours affly
Brendan

Bracken to Beaverbrook   Princes House,
21 February 1955   95, Gresham Street,
London, E.C.2.

My dear Max

Many thanks for your birthday message.

I shall have a lot to tell you when you get back at the end of this month.

The decision I mentioned in my previous letters is irrevocable and your hero will soon be taking over.[135]

The stock market here is in a great flurry and so it ought to be. Yields from industrial shares are ludicrously low and despite the Treasury's massive support of sterling which is costing us many millions of dollars a week, it continues to fall. Sterling is an Aunt Sally which no foreign exchange expert, particularly if he has crossed the Red Sea with dry feet, could possibly miss. There is a profit of 15% without any possibility of loss which is a most attractive proposition to these gentry.

Butler, who 'saved the £', is now very worried both about sterling and our export trade. When he was lunching at the Financial Times he held forth to us about his problems and the only comment my colleagues made after he had gone was that it was incredible that a man who had had the Treasury for nearly three years should be so naive in his approach to financial affairs.

I am much more worried by our industrial future than I am by the bungles of the Treasury. I reckon that it costs at least three times as much to replace ageing plant and equipment which though it earns good profits in boom times will disable us when a ferocious drive for exports is made by the United States, Germany

[135] Eden took over as Prime Minister on 5 April.

and Japan.

It is certain that our whole industrial life will be transformed when the Americans and Germans get ahead with their 'automation'. What a horrible word, but a purposeful one. I saw in a newspaper the other day that at the Ford plant in Ohio a chain of electronic brains and 'automation' machines worked by 250 skilled men, produced in one day double the work that was formerly done by 2,500 employees.

No one in Whitehall and few in British industry seem to have the faintest notion of the effects of the 'automation' developments on employment and production, and what is even worse, very few companies in England have sufficient cash reserves to finance the transformation they must make in their factories. Somerset House has seen to that.

I am greatly looking forward to seeing you at the end of the month.

(Sgd) Yrs affly Brendan

Beaverbrook to Bracken
19 March 1955
My dear Brendan,

Now that the great Prime Minister is ending his term of office in glory and splendour, his Resignation List will be, of course, the most important distribution of Honours that has taken place since the days of Drake and Raleigh.

As you know, he has offered me various Honours from time to time. While I have greatly esteemed and highly valued the distinction that the mere offer confers on me, I decided long ago that I would rather be de-peered. Unfortunately that's beyond his power.

But there is an honour that I greatly desire. It is a simple Knighthood for Mr. E.J. Robertson, the Chairman of the EVENING STANDARD.

Throughout the years he has been a steady supporter of the Prime Minister and he has been always the guardian in the columns of the paper of policy control in relation to Churchill.

If such an Honour should be conferred upon him, I would have a far finer glow of joy and pleasure than I recall as my sensation when I was myself knighted in 1911.[136]

Yours ever,

---

[136] Beaverbrook's appeal was to no avail.

8
EDEN AND SUEZ
1955–1956

On 5 April 1955, Churchill finally resigned. He was succeeded by Anthony Eden. The event went largely unremarked due to a newspaper strike, but it was certainly the end of an era for Bracken and Beaverbrook because virtually their last link with the corridors of power was finally gone. Nonetheless, Bracken still seems to have kept himself well informed.

The Eden Government was dominated by the Suez crisis, which finally forced the Prime Minister's premature resignation in January 1957. However, the Suez Crisis only began in earnest in the summer of 1956; the first year of Eden's Government promised much.

Bracken to Beaverbrook	Princes House,
15 April 1955	95, Gresham Street,
	London, E.C.2.

My dear Max

.... It now looks as if the N.P.A.[1] are faced by what may be a long-drawn out war of attrition. I must say I don't think much of the generals commanding our forces. Esmond[2] neither by experience nor temperament is a seasoned warrior and Burnham's[3] natural quality is to call a retreat. Hard it is that the newspapers which are regarded as one of the most lively of British industries should be in such a state of paralysis or impotence.

1 Newspaper Proprietors Association. The print unions went on strike for almost a month, preventing the publication of any national newspapers.
2 Lord Rothermere.
3 Lord Burnham, proprietor of the *Daily Telegraph*.

19 April 1955   *Eden and Suez*   181

No one is willing to try to bring out a paper or to take any other action to show that we are none other than rather mangy bullocks on their way to the abattoir. If we were to attempt to surrender now 13 other Trade Unions would dictate terms to the newspapers.

Many of our difficulties are due to the utterly inadequate organisation maintained by the N.P.A. Altham, the secretary, is a very conscientious and rather superior clerk. Their labour adviser is in the words of F.E. Smith 'distinguished by his all-round inferiority'. The newspapers were damn fools to have allowed Valentine Holmes to go to the Shell Oil Company. They ought to have given him £15,000 a year to act as executive chairman of the N.P.A. and in order to sweeten Lord Rothermere he ought to have been catapulted into the Presidency.

I grieve greatly over our old friend W. To be divorced from the red boxes which have been his life for so long and to have to act as a spectator of great affairs must inevitably deeply depress him. One of these days Eden must get rid of his multitude of advisers and decide for himself to have an Election as soon as possible. Time is not on the side of the Tories.

(Sgd) Yours aff.
Brendan

Beaverbrook to Bracken
19 April 1955
My dear Brendan,

.... I would like to have your views on the election.[4] I should think it will turn on peace, the bomb, negotiations on the highest level. Bevan, I imagine, will go for 'no bomb' during his campaign.

The Tories are very sure of their win.[5] If by any chance they don't pull it off they will not be in a position to repeat their indignation meeting after the election of 1945. Or if they do repeat it, the substance of their complaints will be different. Last time they complained of too much support from the 'Daily Express'. This time possibly not enough assistance.[6]

We have had a run of tremendous weather here. I have been

---

4 One of Eden's first decisions as Prime Minister was to announce the date of the next general election, held on 26 May.
5 The Conservatives won an overall majority of 60 seats.
6 Some Conservatives had blamed Beaverbrook and his over-aggressive

My Dear Max   *19 April 1955*

nineteen days at Capponcina with unbroken sunshine. God Almighty's hand waters the land sometimes by night but never by day.

I am leaving on the 29th of April and staying in London over the Election.

I am sorry for Churchill. Yet he has had such a wonderful sunset that we may be sure the afterglow will brighten the Universe.

Pat Hennessy has just left me and I miss him.

I am working on the Lloyd George papers at present, and I turn up the most extraordinary situations. For instance, he appointed Northcliffe to a Washington post in 1917. In order to get the job through he represented that Balfour, who was in Ottawa, approved of the appointment.

In fact, Balfour sent cables of protest.

The reason for wanting Northcliffe on the other side of the world was the intention to appoint Churchill to his Government.

Could I induce you to come out to New Brunswick in the month of October? The weather is cool there at that time, and I would like you to visit the University.

                                             Yours ever,

Bracken to Beaverbrook   Princes House,
21 April 1955   95, Gresham Street,
                                                 London, E.C.2.

My dear Max

.... You ask me my views about the Election. Let me begin by giving you Woolton's estimate, which is that the Tories will have a majority of 38. Woolton is a shrewd old shop-walker and gets quite good advice from the chief area agents.

You know better than I that it is impossible to give any exact electoral forecast.

To my mind the Tory fortunes depend upon Eden and Bevan. If Eden can persuade the public that he is a real leader, lots of votes will come to him and I think he is going to take immense trouble to create this impression.

Bevan, if he is shrewdly followed by reporters to small meetings where he would not expect much coverage, may easily make a few speeches which would do the utmost harm to the Socialists.

Eden ought to be well able to take care of issues such as peace

    newspaper tactics for their defeat in the 1945 election.

and negotiations on the highest level. If he is wise he will quote Eisenhower's declaration that he is willing to go anywhere to meet 'those behind the Iron Curtain who are genuinely seeking peace'.

The bomb is a different affair, but I think that the people who say don't use it in any circumstances will certainly not vote for the Tories, and so I think Eden will be well advised to pipe down on the bomb unless Bevan can make it a central election issue. If he were to do this of course Attlee and Morrison and most of the Labour Party are committed to the manufacture of the bomb and Bevan will have succeeded, to the advantage of the Tories, in showing the discords that exist in the Socialist Party.

If you are in London on the 29th or 30th I would love to have a talk with you: I start for South Africa on Sunday, May 1st.

I think there is every chance of my being able to go to New Brunswick in the latter half of October. I should greatly like to spend sometime with you at the University and then I can travel back to Britain by way of the United States.

(Sgd) Yours affly
Brendan

Beaverbrook to Bracken
19 November 1955
My dear Brendan,

One day Mrs Churchill, as I understood, asked me if I would like to have Sutherland's portrait of Churchill.[7]

I would like it very much. Do you think they would give it to my gallery in New Brunswick?

I would undertake to place the good Sutherland beside it, and — if it is desired — I will not let the picture be set up during the lifetime of our great hero.

Will you put the proposition direct to them on my behalf ?

I hate to bother you, but I do want to have a complete collection of Churchill. In fact, I am thinking of calling the gallery after him. But, of course, I would ask for permission first of all.

---

7 The famously controversial portrait by Graham Sutherland had been presented to Churchill by Parliament on the occasion of his 80th birthday in 1954. Churchill, and his wife, had both taken an instant dislike to it. Beaverbrook's request to bring his friend Sutherland's work to Canada was to no avail as Clementine Churchill secretly burned the picture in 1956.

And with affectionate good wishes,

I am,
Yours ever,

Bracken to Beaverbrook
21 November 1955

Princes House,
95, Gresham Street,
London, E.C.2.

My dear Max

Many thanks for your letter.

I agree that Millar is the most appropriate successor to Robertson.[8]

I sent you a letter to the Waldorf Towers thanking you very much for your hospitality in New Brunswick. I hope you got it as it is an attempt on my part to tell you of the pleasure and happiness I derived from my visit to Fredericton.

One of these days I will write you a long screed about happenings in politics. This government seems to be an avid collector of troubles. Butler has got himself into a hell of a mess and holds that everyone is wrong save himself. Aneurin Bevan is a much milder critic of our banks than is the Chancellor of the Exchequer. Butler's nerve is withering and I think if he could extricate himself from the Treasury he would jump at the opportunity of being Leader of the House.[9] But I can see no quick way of his doing this.

Macmillan has become a pompous posturer and will be a growing liability to Eden.[10] One of Eden's minor Ministers, Boyd Carpenter,[11] is likely to get the Government into a lot of trouble. The folly of allowing Thomas of the B.O.A.C.[12] to take a part-

---

8 In July 1955 E.J. Robertson had a stroke from which he never fully recovered. Millar did not succeed Robertson as general manager of Express newspapers; instead, the kingdom was divided between Tom Blackburn and Max Aitken.

9 In the December reshuffle, Butler was duly moved from the Treasury to become Lord Privy Seal and Leader of the House of Commons.

10 The latter was indeed true. So much so, that in the December ministerial reshuffle Macmillan was moved from the Foreign Office, where he had been showing dangerous signs of independence, to the Treasury.

11 John Boyd-Carpenter (1908–). Conservative politician. Minister of Transport and Civil Aviation 1954–55, Minister of Pensions and National Insurance 1955–62.

12 British Overseas Airways Corporation.

time job with Ferguson and the appointment of Rennell to be his deputy can hardly be exaggerated. B.O.A.C. is facing mortal competition from the Yanks and it sorely needs a tough full-time boss cast in the mould of Pat Hennessy. Boyd Carpenter is a pleasant little fellow, but is almost devoid of common sense....

Yours aye
Brendan

Bracken to Beaverbrook   Princes House,
17 January 1956   95, Gresham Street,
                                                     London, E.C.2.

My dear Max

When Jimmy Dunn was at your house at Fredericton I thought he was justified in prophesying that he would live to be a hundred.[13] He had the freshness of complexion which belongs to a sea captain and moderation governed all his physical doings. To you he was such a familiar that his going out of this world must be a wrench: in terms of geography he was part of your life's landscape.

In many ways Jimmie was an original, his liveliness, his foibles and his consuming interest in everything that was new mitigated the dulness of living in an over-standardised age. There was no measurement that quite fitted him and of him it is true to say that we are not likely to ever meet his like again. The baronet was unique and had some of the endearing qualities of Don Quixote.

Politics here are likely to be exciting during the next twelve months. Eden has made up his mind to try to brave the tidal wave of inflation, but like his supporters and critics he is justifiably uncertain of how to set about it. He has made a good if rather negative beginning by pushing Butler out of the Treasury. The public here are under the illusion that Butler either through weariness or timidity bolted from the Treasury. He often talked about the weight of his burden and the oppressing length of his days at the Treasury, but when the time for decision came he wanted to hold on. Eden, without any great knowledge of financial problems, had the wisdom to see that when Butler's luck had

---

13 Sir James Dunn died on 1 January 1956, leaving $65 million. Beaverbrook married his widow, Christofor, on 7 June 1963 at the age of 84. Beaverbrook liked to boast that she was the first lady friend he had had who was richer than himself: 'She must love me for myself alone'.

turned he was not the sort of man who could ride the storms that loom ahead.

As there was every reason for getting rid of Macmillan from the Foreign Office it was inevitable that he should be parked on the Treasury. It is undoubtedly a desperate appointment, but our financial affairs are in a pretty desperate condition. You have more experience of British Government formation than anyone alive and so you need no telling of the difficulty of providing for an ambitious and potentially dangerous leading colleague. The Treasury was the only carrot that would have led Macmillan to go quietly from the Foreign Office.

Quite apart from the problem of finding an adequate post for Macmillan, Eden had no range of choice in appointing a successor to Butler. I can't think of anyone in his Government who would be acclaimed as a daring pilot in our present extremity. Most of his colleagues are worthy mediocrities.

I don't think it is an exaggeration to say in the words of Swift that for more than a quarter of a century the officials of the Treasury have had the misfortune to be perpetually mistaken. They were wrong about the gold standard in 1924, they were totally wrong in the way they met the scarifying depression of the 1930's, they were wrong about Bretton Woods, the second American loan, the management of our attenuated gold and dollar reserves and the inflexible fiscal and trading policies they have ordained for a succession of Socialist and Tory Ministers since the war ended. And they now have no clue to the solution of the problem of how to rebuild our dwindling reserves and to encourage British exporters to show more resourcefulness in competing with the Yanks, the Germans and the Japanese.

In the world we live in currency might be described as a psychological problem. If you can get the world to believe in the £ sterling (and there are good reasons for doing so) all sorts of forces now operating profitably against the £ will turn in its favour. Financial orthodoxy is beyond our means and so we must fall back on a combination of bluff and resourcefulness. Macmillan may be the witch doctor we need — at any rate he for a while will give the appearance of being one — and may in our present circumstances be the best possible boss for the Treasury. He is a person of very little judgement and I can't forgive him for his gross disloyalty to

Churchill.[14] But our need now is for a financial Mary Baker Eddy and Macmillan has plenty of affinities with that most successful lady. And so let us hope for the best.

I have just been reading the Annual Report of the Massachusetts Institute of Technology. I notice that they are spending a good deal of money on geological fieldwork in Nova Scotia, which is, so far as we know, a much less mineralised area than New Brunswick.

The present market value of M.I.T.'s funds is $117 million and so they might have a margin to spare to help the School of Geology in the University of New Brunswick. As Clarence Howe is one of the members of the M.I.T. Corporation do you think you could invoke his aid to have some sort of tie-up with your University?

(Sgd) Yours ever
Brendan

McMillan (sic) gave a little party for financial pundits last night. He ranted at great length about the evils of deflation. He cursed the bankers and blessed cheap money. He reminded them that he had crossed the floor of the House of Commons because of the Tory Party's backwardness & declared he would not hesitate to do it again.

Never since the days of Charles Townshend[15] has the Treasury known a more unstable master.

Beaverbrook to Bracken
23 January 1956
My dear Brendan,
The death of Jimmy Dunn has distressed me a very great deal. I

14 This is probably a reference to Macmillan's rumoured attempt to persuade Churchill to stand down as leader of the Conservatives in 1947. Although other Tories, such as Halifax, occasionally made efforts to persuade Churchill to do so, there is no firm evidence that Macmillan ever made any such attempt in that year. However, he had been impatient with Churchill's leadership since 1952 and did write to him in 1954 urging him to relinquish the premiership before the end of the summer.
15 Charles Townshend (1725–1767). Chancellor of the Exchequer 1766–1767. He was responsible for the notorious tea duty that provoked the Boston Tea Party, which ultimately led to the loss of the American colonies.

have lost Bickle,[16] Ross,[17] Killam,[18] McCullach,[19] and now Jimmy Dunn. All I have got left in Canada is Fraser Winslow.[20]

I don't know what is going to become of his wife. She has written me to say that she wants to go to a convent. It would be a piece of folly. Besides, she wouldn't like the food there. And she would certainly quarrel with the Mother Superior.

What a depressing picture you give me of the Treasury. And unhappily, only too true.

I am obliged for your suggestion about the Massachusetts Institute of Technology. I have already written to Mackay, and I think we are on the way.

You remember Macmillan served with me.

He will do strange things and I am sure he will live to perpetrate a great deal of mischief.

I would rather have Butler.

And with affection and devotion and looking forward to my return early in March.

Bracken to Beaverbrook
8 February 1956

Princes House,
95, Gresham Street,
London, E.C.2.

My dear Max

Millar told me about his Gainsborough problem and I arranged with Gibson[21] of the National Gallery to have the picture examined. The experts describe it as a rather crude fake.

As a Calvinistical Presbyterian you will be displeased to hear that the Kirk of Scotland have imported their next moderator from England. You have, however, the consolation that he is a minister of the church of which you are an elder. I think you know Scott. The only thing that may be said against him is that he has been

[16] J.P. Bickell (1884–1949). An old Canadian friend, Chairman of International Nickel.
[17] W.D. Ross (1883–1947). Canadian financier from Toronto
[18] Isaak Killam (1885–1955). Started as a clerk in Beaverbrook's investment company, Royal Securities Corporation, and died leaving more than 150 million dollars.
[19] George McCullogh (1905–1952).
[20] Unidentified.
[21] William Pettigrew Gibson, keeper of the National Gallery 1937–60. Bracken was a Trustee of the National Gallery from 1955 until his death, reflecting a life-long interest in fine art.

swayed by the Archbishop of Canterbury to believe that marriage is a sacrament. You Calvinists had better resurrect John Knox....

Anything may happen in the High Church of St. Giles since the Episcopalian bishop in Edinburgh was allowed to stalk into the kirk arrayed in his full canonicals to marry the daughter of a Scottish duke.

I have a bad cold–even an eskimo would find London chilly.

(Sgd) Yours
Brendan

Gibson wishes you to know that he is always willing without fees or other rewards to get you good advice about any purchases designed for the University of N.B.

Beaverbrook to Bracken P O Box 1029,
13 February 1956 Nassau,
Bahamas

My dear Brendan -

So very many thanks for helping me over the Gainsborough. It is a shocking affair. The same man sold me the Constable, but of course in this transaction I had the assurance of Gibson that I was making a sound purchase. So I rest happily.

I am extremely obliged to Gibson for the offer to help me. I will turn to it at once as soon as I reach London.

I have lost all hope for the Scottish Church. It is departing from the 'faith of our fathers'. I am going to join the 'We frees'.

That Moderator whose name is Scott should be put on trial for heresy.

I shall be home in London soon.

And with affectionate
good wishes,

Bracken to Beaverbrook Princes House,
15 February 1956 95, Gresham Street,
London, E.C.2.

My dear Max

Your prophecy that your former Under-Secretary would make trouble for Eden has been swiftly proved. He sent in his resignation yesterday on a cunningly contrived issue which would have gravely embarrassed his boss and would have given your former Under-Secretary the credit for being the only virtuous and strong man in government. A trust (sic) has been patched up, but how long it will last is anybody's guess.[22]

Unfortunately for E. he has given this man a job which puts him plumb in the centre of the political stage and one may be sure that he will make the fullest use of his nuisance value.

(Sgd) Yours affly
Brendan.

Beaverbrook to Bracken   P O Box 1028
21 February 1956   Nassau
Bahamas

My dear Brendan,

I am so pleased to get news of political events in London. I am shut off from my usual line of communication, and I feel that I am a real isolationist.

Be sure that Macmillan will make trouble if he has the power. As long as he is kept in order he will be all right. When he gets up he will be all wrong.

I am very pleased about the picture. And I have telegraphed, accepting your kind offer to look after the cleaning and the framing of it.

I hope you will give me word of any other pictures you notice that may be worthy of a place in the Fredericton collection. My object is to have eight Old Masters. Already I have about four. I am not counting the Hogarth in the four.

I shall see you soon. And so happily,

THE SUEZ CRISIS. On 26 July President Nasser of Egypt unilaterally nationalised the Suez Canal, thus precipitating the Suez crisis. As this was supposed to be an international right of passage, the British and French Governments immediately began to prepare military plans to seize the Canal back if diplomatic efforts failed. A War Cabinet was

---

[22] At the beginning of February, Macmillan threatened to resign as Chancellor unless he was allowed to cut food subsidies on bread and milk in order to help stem the continuing flight from the pound. Eden was adamantly opposed to this. Eventually, a compromise was reached whereby these cuts were phased in gradually. For a full account, see Horne, *Macmillan 1894–1956* (London: Macmillan, 1988) pp. 379–386.

formed, consisting of Eden, Selwyn Lloyd (Foreign Secretary), Lord Salisbury (Lord President of the Council), Harold Macmillan (Chancellor of Exchequer), Lord Home (Commonwealth Secretary) and Sir Walter Monckton (Minister of Defence). From the very beginning, however, the British Government was dogged by two factors; its own lack of clear strategic thinking as to the ultimate aim of military action and, more importantly, the lukewarm response of the United States to the prospect of military action, which later hardened into outright hostility.

The months of August and September were occupied with diplomatic conferences and political manoeuvres designed to resolve the crisis peacefully. This diplomatic round began in England with the London Conference of 16–23 August, but it soon became obvious that neither side would budge on the main issue — that is, the ownership of the Suez Canal. The only constructive proposal that ever had any chance of being accepted by all parties was that put forward by U.S. Secretary of State John Foster Dulles, namely the Suez Canal Users' Association, mentioned in Bracken's first letter of the crisis. However, once this idea ran into difficulties, a military climax became virtually inevitable.

The long delay between the beginning of the crisis and the point of military action did not favour the British Government. As time went on, so the military, political and legal problems facing the British and the French in the event of military action seemed to become ever more intractable. As the Government prevaricated and hesitated, so dissension began to appear in the ranks of the Conservative Party. Anthony Nutting, Minister of State at the Foreign Office, resigned and Monckton only stayed at his post out of a sense of patriotic duty so as not to cramp military action at the eleventh hour; at the same time the Labour Party swung heavily against any armed assault on Egypt. By the beginning of October Eden's position was becoming increasingly untenable — his bellicosity was not matched by action and his negotiating lacked the essential ingredient of flexibility. It was in this situation that he grasped at a plan devised by the French by which Israeli forces would invade Egypt and French and British expeditions would force a landing in Egypt to 'separate' the combatants and 'safeguard' the canal – thus providing a specious legal reason to invade Egypt. This was kept completely secret: until long afterwards none of the major players in the game ever admitted to the existence of this secret pact which was known as the Sèvres agreement, after the clandestine meeting of 22 October between Israeli, French and British representatives who agreed the plan.

On the morning of 30 October Israel accordingly attacked Egypt and on the same day a British invasion force set sail from Malta to strike at Egypt from the sea. Amidst a rising chorus of world disapproval, British paratroopers dropped over the canal Zone on 6 November. But the Americans now threatened economic sanctions against Britain and France if they did not immediately stop an expedition that Washington regarded as little more than reckless Imperialism of the old school, and under this pressure and the universal condemnation of the United Nations Eden ordered a cease-fire at 5 p.m. on 6 November. The Suez operation had thus come to a halt in humiliating circumstances only a little more than 24 hours after it had begun.

The following weeks were dominated by Britain and France's attempts to extricate themselves from Suez with minimum loss of face, but there was no doubt that Suez was a heavy blow to British prestige and self-esteem and to the confidence of the Conservative Party.

Bracken to Beaverbrook
18 September 1956

Princes House,
95, Gresham Street,
London, E.C.2.

My dear Max

Many thanks for your message.

Dulles' Users' Committee[23] has created all sorts of problems for everyone in business in South Africa. The ports are already overcrowded and our American customers complain bitterly about delays from ports like Beira, Lourenço Marques, Durban, etc. If a lot of the Suez Canal traffic is to be diverted to African ports, U.C. will have much on its plate.

I shall not know whether I will be able to go to America until the beginning of November, but I will then cable you. If I do go I shall be in New York for a few days and will borrow a plane belonging to our business associates and fly to Fredericton and spend a couple of days with you and then go straight home.

I don't want to spend much time in the United States. The Americans are a very fine people, but one is apt to get into arguments with them about some of the ways they have treated John Bull since the end of the war. One oughtn't to do this in their

---

[23] The Suez Canal Users' Association (SCUA) was the brainchild of Secretary of State John Foster Dulles. It was to replace the Suez Canal Company as an international canal Users organization which would determine the sum of money that the users would give to the Egyptians for the use of the Canal.

own country.

Yours ever
Brendan

Bracken to Beaverbrook
19 October 1956

Princes House,
95, Gresham Street,
London, E.C.2.

My dear Max

I went to St. Thomas's Hospital to have a little operation to get rid of three or four abscesses in the jaw. The wonderful doctors there used a new American antibiotic on me which made me understand the meaning of those words so often used by coroners, 'rigor mortis'. I have been as stiff as a telegraph pole for days on end. I am getting better now, but I doubt if I shall go to America.

Your 'doubtful' pictures have been moved to Arlington House and by arrangement with Max I am bringing Gibson there one day next week.

Harold Macmillan jumped the gun when he enunciated his wonderful Britain plus a part of Europe free trade area.[24] Our government is so alarmed by the prospect of being left out of this curiously contrived arrangement that they are willing to toy with the idea.

There is, I am told, fierce opposition from industrial bosses who are large contributors to the Tory Party and I expect that Macmillan and Thorneycroft will battle for time.

If this mortal decision is taken it will be best described as a shotgun wedding after which no one can count the consequences. If Macmillan and Thorneycroft are unmindful of their party's past, what can one say of people like Julian Amery[25] and Lennox Boyd who are fostering a plan for offering membership of the Commonwealth to nations willing to join without any commitment.

---

24 At the Conservative Party Conference at Llandudno Macmillan had outlined Britain's response to the proposed European Common Market, which would come into being on 1 January 1958. Britain did not join the Market, but joined a European Free Trade Area instead.
25 Julian Amery (1919–). Leo Amery's son and Macmillan's son-in-law. A Conservative politician, he served in a number of junior ministerial posts during the 1950s and 1960s. On the 'Imperial Wing' of the Party, he was the most prominent advocate of a tough line against Nasser and leader of the 'Suez Group' of Conservative M.P.s, but also an enthusiastic Europeanist.

                                                  Yours affly
                                                  Brendan

Bracken to Beaverbrook   Princes House,
5 November 1956   95, Gresham Street,
                                                  London, E.C.2.

My dear Max

   As I was ill your office sent the two 'questionable' pictures to Gibson asking for his judgement.

   While Gibson thinks that one picture is fairly attributed, he speaks with contempt about the other. But as the picture has been sent to him at the National Gallery he feels that his official position precludes him from offering any advice in a matter which might lead to controversy or be brought into the Courts.

   While he is very willing to offer an opinion on the wisdom of purchasing a picture, he doesn't want to have any controversy with dealers. I can understand this and I am asking him to suggest the name of an expert who will in a professional capacity sign a judgement on these pictures. Do you approve of this course?

                                               (sgd) Yours affly
                                                        Brendan

Postscript

   Your book[26] has had splendid reviews.

   Eden's toughness has astonished the Socialists. His Cabinet is very docile, fearing as members do that if they cross his path they will be treated like Nasser.

   Eden, so far, has shown a lofty contempt for all his critics. The Socialists who thought he was a charming milksop now hold him to be a blood lusting monster. Vanity can be a great toughener.

Beaverbrook to Bracken   PO Box 1028
13 November 1956   Nassau
                                                         Bahamas

My dear Brendan,

   So very many thanks for your letter of November the 5th.

   I am now in the land of sunshine.

   I am obliged to you for the information about Gibson and the pictures. I wish he might tell me which picture is fraudulent. I am not going to bring him into any controversy; certainly not

---

[26] Men and Power.

without asking his consent. But in any case, I can conduct my own controversy.

I hope that the National Gallery will give me help in my attempt to collect pictures for New Brunswick. It ought to be an institution looking with fatherly interest on such a project as I am launching, and I hope the Gallery will give me encouragement to turn to it whenever I find it necessary to do so.

I think that Eden was doing wonderfully well until he gave order to cease fire. At that moment he committed his country and himself to damnation. Max does not entirely agree. And, of course, he is running the papers now.

I wish you would come here.

And with affectionate
good wishes,
I am,
Yours ever,

Bracken to Beaverbrook
22 November 1956

Princes House,
95, Gresham Street,
London, E.C.2.

My dear Max

Many thanks for your letter.

You may be sure that the National Gallery will do all it can to foster the University of New Brunswick's Art Gallery. Gibson, who likes your company and applauds your enthusiasm for your gallery, tells me he is only too delighted to advise you, but in a dispute about the attribution of a picture after it has been bought he can obviously take no part as he is a public official. I can't get hold of him at the moment, but his doubts about one of these pictures are not that it is a fake, but he feels that something has been done to it.

Sutton, who is a very good art expert, is coming to lunch with me tomorrow and I shall ask him to suggest somebody who can give us an independent professional opinion. When I get it you shall have it by air mail.

This government is, as you know, in a hell of a mess. Eden's illness is not diplomatic: he is suffering from exhaustion. But it doesn't affect his resolution or his obstinacy.

Until a week ago Macmillan, whose bellicosity was beyond description, was wanting to tear Nasser's scalp off with his own finger nails. He was like that character in O'Casey's play who cried:-

Let me like a hero fall, My breast expanding to the ball.

Today he might be described as the leader of the bolters.[27] His Treasury officials have put before him the economic consequences of the Suez fiasco and his feet are frost-bitten. You will remember that only ten days ago he declared that the financial cost of the Suez Canal operation would be small. He now finds that it will probably wreck his credit restriction policy as the cost of living is bound to go up through increases in commodity prices and transport costs. Furthermore, there is a desperate shortage of diesel oil. Unless we can get supplies long distance buses upon which the public rely rather than on the railways, will have to be laid

---

[27] Harold Wilson was later to say of Macmillan's rôle in the Suez Crisis that he was 'First in, First out'.

up. But this is only one of the many shortages that have impelled our Ministers to contemplate giving into the United Nations' demand that they should bundle our troops out of Egypt without ceremony and in the face of the jeering minions of Nasser.

The Government may bring themselves to do this, but if they do there will be a tremendous yell of rage from a large section of the public which always wanted to scrag Nasser. They believed that this could easily be done by the soldiers without any possible inconvenience to civilians at home. There is enough spirit left in the English to yell with rage if we appear to be bolting from Suez.

Furthermore, at last night's meeting of the 1922 Committee it was made clear to Heath[28] that between 30 and 50 Tories would not support the Government in a scurry from Suez. And so if the Government intend to bolt they will have to depend on Socialist votes. You know better than anyone in this world how impossible it would be for a Government to stay in office when it has to depend on the Opposition's voting strength. A big abstention in any Suez division would bring down Eden's government as quickly as Chamberlain was brought down.

The Government haven't yet decided to bolt, but a large part of the Cabinet is not willing to believe that there is no other alternative. But under Butler's chairmanship they are a dithering lot. A blast of public anger and the certainty of large scale Tory abstentions in the Lobby might make them stand up to the United Nations. You can't predict what our Ministers may do. They are best described by a remark made by Mr. Gladstone on one of his colleagues — 'An injection of water would strengthen his constitution'. I don't know what is going to happen.

Here is a piece of private information for you. In a short space of time your Lordship in your capacity as a resident of both Jamaica and the Bahamas will have a Governor-General to grace the new Federation. An eager aspirant for this post is no less a person than the Governor-General of your native land, Vincent Massey.[29] I don't know whether he will get it or not. He is 71, but a tough little hen and he likes the notion of continuing to be His Excellency. If he does get the job of governing the West In-

---

28 Edward Heath (1916–); Conservative Politician. Conservative Chief Whip 1955–9, Leader of the Party 1965–75, Prime Minister 1970–74.
29 Vincent Massey (1887–1967) Canada's first native-born Governor-General, 1952–59.

dies, would Canada reciprocate by taking our Lord Mountbatten who could do so much less harm in Ottawa than he has done in India and is doing here?

Yours affly
Brendan

The collusion charge also upsets some Ministers. A Tim Healy is required to handle this. Diversion is the only tactic.

Beaverbrook to Bracken
2 December 1956
My dear Brendan,

I am now in New York, and I plan to go back to Nassau on December the 15th.

I am so grateful to you for your letter giving me the political news.

I find myself out on a limb in Nassau. New York is not much better.

The Americans are exceedingly hostile to Britain. The only reason they hold on to us is because of the need for support in their impending war with Russia.

Do give me more news as the situation develops.

I have a very poor opinion of Harold Macmillan. There is no use in asking you to come to Nassau. But there is no harm in it either.

Do you think Britain will ever recover?

Bracken to Beaverbrook   Princes House,
7 December 1956   95, Gresham Street,
                                 London E.C.2.

My dear Max

Thank you for your letter.

I am replying on the afternoon of the second day of the vote of censure on the government when forecasters are at variance about the number of Tories who will abstain.

My experience of the Tories leads me to believe that they are inclined to talk a lot of hot air in committee rooms upstairs and to obey the Whips when they are shepherded into the lobby. I shall be surprised if more than 10 to 15 Tories abstain, and the figure may be less.³⁰

This hapless Government's gyrations defy description. The best way of describing their Suez adventure is to call it another Jameson Raid.³¹ No one can ever estimate the economic and financial consequences of their action. Macmillan, who has been an absentee from the Treasury, as he has been busily posturing on platforms as the scourge of Nasser, has now returned to the bosom of his gloomy officials. They have almost scared him from his bread and butter and so the financial measures he is taking to rectify the Suez fiasco are almost as silly as the adventure. To ask for a waiver on the interest of the American debt could hardly be more silly in the light of the Government's recent estimate of their holdings in American industrial securities. By asking for this waiver they encourage the bears of sterling everywhere and it will cost them more dollars to support the pound than the amount they hope to get under the waiver.

Macmillan is telling journalists that he intends to retire from politics and go to the morgue. He declares that he will never serve under Butler. His real intentions are to push his boss out of No. 10 and he has a fair following in the Tory Party.The so-called Canal die-hards think better of him than they do of Eden or Butler.

The Express correspondent, Marks, who is, as you know, well disposed to Eden, seems to be under the assumption that he intends voluntarily to relinquish the Prime Ministership.

Eden has no intention of giving up No. 10. I should say he was the least rattled of all his ministers. He writes cheerful letters from Jamaica and doesn't seem the least bit perturbed by all the storms that blow over him. There is nothing wrong with him physically, but he was very tired, hence his holiday.³²

If it was a mistake for him to go away at the present time (and I now think it probably was) I was one of the people who advised

30 Bracken was right; only 15 Tory M.P.s, mainly from the Suez Group, abstained in the division on the censure debate.
31 The 'Jameson Raid' of 1895 was a bungled attempt by the British in Southern Rhodesia to surprise the Boers with a swift march on Johannesburg. The 'raid', one of the most famous examples of reckless imperialism, was an abject failure.
32 On 23 November Eden flew to Jamaica to recuperate after Suez. He stayed at Ian Fleming's house, Goldeneye.

him to go.³³ It shows how poor an adviser I am! But as he told me that he fully intends to brazen this out, I though he might as well get physically fit before facing the litter of problems that lie ahead.

Whitehall is scared by the British Embassy in Washington's re-iterated statements that the American Government has decided on a radical reorientation of policy. Our Ambassador avers that Eisenhower and his advisers now believe the only way of preventing Russia from dominating what is called the Afro-Asian Group will be for America to put herself at the head of that curious assortment of nations. It is argued that if America produces a Marshall plan for Asia and Africa the inhabitants thereof will avoid the snares of the Kremlin. A subsidiary but by no means unimportant argument is that if the ever-increasing production of the United States cannot be wholly absorbed by the Americans they can dump it on the Asiatics and the Africans.

I know that some people in the State Department have long since lost interest in NATO and have wanted America to be a titular leader of the non-political powers.

Lennox-Boyd's doings puzzle me greatly.³⁴ He has complete evidence that nothing can stop civil war in the Gold Coast and he is agreeing that immediate self-government should be offered that opulent colony. This is one of the most cynical political actions known to me.

I wish you were here.

(Sgd) Yours affly
Brendan

P.S. I still think you were right to back Eden. He is the best of the Tories. I don't say that is terrific praise, but it is something. The alternatives are the crackpot Macmillan or Butler, who is a curious blend of Gandi and Boss Tweed.

Beaverbrook to Bracken
11 December 1956
My dear Brendan,
I am so pleased to get your letters.

---

33 Eden's biographer, Robert Rhodes James, writes:'Eden's departure to Jamaica had been a fatal mistake...'(p.587).
34 Alan Lennox-Boyd was Secretary of State for the Colonies, 1954–59.

This is a hard life here where so much is going on and I am always on the fringe.

One good thing, however, is that Max is on his own. He has acquitted himself wonderfully well.

You have proved to be a prophet, as usual, in predicting the rebellion of Tories upstairs and their submission in the lobbies.

I have had two telegrams from Eden. They asked me, in effect, to go to Jamaica. But it was not possible for me to leave here. So I suggested we meet in New York on his way to London. This morning he tells me he is travelling home direct.

I am sure Macmillan will fail in his conspiracies and Britain will have further terrible failures if he becomes Prime Minister.

I don't know why Marks went so far astray. He predicted 35 rebels, Eden's resignation and Macmillan's accession.

I agree with you that Eden was foolish to go to Jamaica. Any place except the West Indies would have gone down a bit better. He might have tried the South of France.

It is tragic to see the separation between Canada and Britain. Much worse than a quarrel with the United States.

Fortunately, the Press of Canada and also the people are against their Government. But I don't suppose they will turn the administration out.

Again my thanks for writing me,

Your affectionate friend

9

THE LAST HURRAH
1957–1958

On 9 January 1957 Eden resigned as Prime Minister on the grounds of ill-health. His sojourn in Jamaica had merely delayed the inevitable. A poll was taken of the Cabinet to find his successor, and Harold Macmillan kissed hands as Prime Minister on 10 January. Eden departed for a holiday in New Zealand on 18 January; the last person to see the Edens off was Brendan Bracken.

Bracken to Beaverbrook Princes House,
23 January 1957 95, Gresham Street,
 London, E.C.2.

My dear Max

The main reason for Eden's departure is not the one circulated by politicians and the Press. The reason is political, but as it involves a secret stuffed with dynamite I can't put it in a letter.[1] This seems melodramatic, but alas, it is only too true as you will agree when you hear it. If Eden had been of tougher fibre he could, I am sure, have brazened it out.

Health, of course, played a part in the decision, but I think his illness is more due to the effect of mind upon body than to the patchwork done by the surgeons and doctors.

My Lord Salisbury's intervention in Eden's affairs was conclusive. Eden's authority in the Cabinet had diminished considerably after the somersault about Suez. This was due to the opposition, if intense wavering can be called opposition, lead by Macmillan. At the beginning of our invasion of Egypt Macmillan breathed

---

1 This is presumably a reference to the secret Sévres agreement.

23 January 1957 203

fire and slaughter against Nasser and his tribe. When the Americans declared there would be no oil forthcoming for Britain and the Treasury officials started totting up the cost of an oil famine, Macmillan was all for obeying the behests of Eisenhower and Dulles.

The President was in a great state of rage against Eden and sent him some scarifying messages. Eisenhower's indignation was due more to personal pique than to any fervent belief in the United Nations. He felt that his electoral prospects might be seriously damaged by a war in Egypt.[2] It certainly was awkward for him because he had been declaring that the position in the Middle East had greatly improved and so far as the old gentlemen had any policy it was one of peace in our time — quite a good slogan for a renewal of the tenancy of the White House.

Naturally, the Suez fiasco greatly lowered Eden's prestige. He could, I think, have got over this were it not for the spate of criticism of his departure for Jamaica. He returned in high spirits which only lasted for a few hours because scarcely had he arrived in Downing Street than a deputation lead by Salisbury and Butler informed him that while the Cabinet were willing to carry on under his leadership until Easter, if it was then clear that his health was not fully restored they felt a new head of the government would be necessary. If Churchill had had such a greeting from his colleagues he would have told them to go to the furthermost part of hell, but as you know very well Eden has none of Churchill's pugnacity.

Butler greatly fancied his chances of succeeding Eden, but they were blighted by the advice offered to the Monarch by Eden, Churchill and Salisbury. Most of the Tories in the House of Commons were agin Butler. They blamed him for the Suez scuttle, whereas Macmillan had a far greater responsibility. Nor was Macmillan slow in his siege of Number 10. He let it be known that in no circumstances would he serve under Butler and he did some powerful private canvassing. Of Butler, therefore, it may be truly said in the words of Coleridge — 'For I have lost the race I never ran'.

You may have noticed the New York times leader on Friday was

---

2 Eisenhower was in fact re-elected as President on 6 November 1956 with a majority of nearly 10 million votes.

headed 'An Egyptian Hitler' and that Sulzberger Junior (their foreign editor), a nephew of the old boy, has been writing excoriating attacks on Dulles. The Yanks are finding Nasser the worst client they have had for many a long day and the evangelistic Eisenhower's naive belief that you can solve all problems through the United Nations is, I am told, withering rapidly.

Your friend, Arthur Sulzberger, the publisher of the New York Times, is here at the moment and he says that Dulles is to depart in June.³ This will be a very good thing, but a lot of damage has been done, some of it irreparable.

(Sgd) Yours ever
Brendan

Beaverbrook to Bracken
29 January 1957
My dear Brendan,
 I am very glad to get your letter.
 It is little I hear of the political situation in Great Britain and I long for news.
 I can guess from your mention of political secrets, stuffed with dynamite, just what happened. Political assassination has become a habit in great Britain, for, of course, Churchill himself was a victim.
 I think Eisenhower had a right to complain about the conduct of Britain and France on the eve of the election in the U.S.A.⁴
 Churchill would have taken that political situation into account. Eden should have been prepared to delay until after election day.
 For my part, I make no complaint about his concealing his intentions from the Americans.
 It is my view that Macmillan was the wrong choice for Prime Minister. If Butler was to be turned down, then a younger man should have been chosen.
 I am expecting Sir Patrick Hennessy here next Saturday week and for my part I am looking forward to landing in England early in March with all the prospects of political conversation bringing me up to the hour in the most wonderful drama since the last

---

3 Dulles stayed as Secretary of State until 1959.
4 The Suez operation coincided with the American Presidential Election on 6 November.

war.

Again my thanks. And with affectionate good wishes, deploring the misfortune which interferes with your visits warm climates,

I am,
Yours ever,

Bracken to Beaverbrook
4 February 1957

Princes House,
95, Gresham Street,
London, E.C.2.

My dear Max

I am sending you under separate cover /by Air Mail/ a very portly volume of Alanbrooke's Memoirs.[5]. Before you get the book you may see some extracts which appeared in last Sunday's 'Times'. They are deceptive inasmuch as they contain copious tributes to Churchill, whereas most of the book is given over to fierce criticism.

The book is a cunning affair. Arthur Bruant (sic) who is an experienced writer, reminds readers hundreds of times that Alanbrooke is really responsible for the strategy of the war. Brooke doesn't often make this claim himself, but comes near to doing so.

Bryant often says Churchill has many of Marlborough's quality, whereas Alanbrooke persists in declaring him to be a menace to all strategy.

Anyone who reads this book may well be forgiven for coming to the conclusion that Alanbrooke won the war by keeping Churchill in a strait waistcoat.

(Sgd) Yours affly
Brendan

For many years the control of the Financial Times has been under the shadow of death duties. If anything happened to Oliver Eyre the paper would have to be sold. One of the Cowdray private Trusts has offered a price for above the market value and I strongly

---

5 Field-Marshal Sir Alan Brooke (1883–1963), Chief of the Imperial General Staff, 1941–45. The eminent historian, Sir Arthur Bryant, wrote his biography — essentially a study of the war based on diaries and autobiographical notes of Alan Brooke. There were copious extracts from these sources in the two volumes, *The Turn of the Tide, 1939–43* (published in 1957), and *Triumph in the West, 1943–45* (1959).

pressed for acceptance.

The Eyre family will make a vast profit. I don't make a cent but that does not worry me. A good business is the ownership of the F.T. Ellerman made a big profit by selling to Camrose. He made a much bigger one by selling to the Eyres. They make twice as big a profit by selling to Cowdray.[6]

The 'dynamite' I mentioned in my last letter is collusion not assassination by colleagues. They were willing, of course, to stab. But our friend brought himself down & needless remorse unnerved him. Secret this!

Beaverbrook to Bracken
9 February 1957
My dear Brendan,
Very many thanks for your letter.

I have been reading Bryant's book for some little time. It is a monstrous publication. This man Alanbrooke is the most egotistical and self-satisfied General that ever served in the British army for a long time. He outstrips Jack Sealy.[7]

It may be that Churchill has many of Marlborough's qualities. It is quite certain that Alanbrooke has many of the qualities of the late beloved Sam Hughes.[8]

I see that Alanbrooke has been preparing for attacks. That is quite wise on his part.

I am longing to hear news of politics.

I am sorry that Cowdray has bought the Financial Times. It

---

6 The Eyre family sold the paper to the Pearson group under the control of the Third Lord Cowdray. The Eyre family was paid £720,000 for their shares in the paper. David Kynaston has written of this transaction that '... it was not an exorbitant price, granted that the paper (including St. Clements Press) was already making a pre-tax profit of some £550,000'. Sir John Ellerman had owned the paper from 1905 to 19, Lord Camrose from 1919 to 1945 and the Eyre Trust from 1945 to 1957. See David Kynaston, *The Financial Times : A Centenary History*, pp. 252 – 254, for details of this episode.
7 J.E.B. Seely (1868–1947), who was Asquith's Secretary of State for War until he resigned over the Curragh Incident in 1914. He was a brigadier-general commanding the Canadian Cavalry Brigade from 1915 to 1918.
8 Probably Lt-General Sir Sam Hughes (1853–1921). A Canadian soldier, vigorous propagandist for the British empire and M.P.

would have been much better in the hands of the Eyre family.

Beaverbrook to Bracken
1 April 1958
My dear Brendan,
In acknowledging this magnificent set of engravings on behalf of the University of New Brunswick, I am grateful for the books and also for the giving by you.

It is long now that our friendship has blossomed and strengthened, and for me it has been a precious possession.

It is my hope that for the rest of my life, which must be brief, I may have the opportunity of closer association and more intimate companionship.

The University will also acknowledge the books.

And with good regards,
I am
Yours ever,

Bracken to Beaverbrook Princes
10 April 1958 House,
95, Gresham Street,
London, E.C.2.

My dear Max
Winston was quite right to put off his American visit. If he were to cross the Atlantic now he would have to submit to a number of Press conferences and I doubt very much if he is in a position to do so. Furthermore, I think that an invitation to stay with the much harassed, rather discredited President is much less valuable now than when it was issued!

Eisenhower is a goose — an agreeable goose — who makes a good chairman of a meeting provided he has a tough guide such as Bedell Smith.[9] He is lost in politics.

(Sgd) Yours ever
B.

---

9 General Walter Bedell Smith (1895–1961). American General, was Eisenhower's chief of Staff in the Mediterranean, 1942–4, and Western Europe 1944–5. U.S. Ambassador to Soviet Union, 1946–49.

Beaverbrook to Bracken
13 April 1958

My dear Brendan,

So many thanks for your letter.

I saw Churchill at the airfield and talked with him for a while.[10] He was clear in his head though not firm on his feet. He said he was going to America and I offered to make the sea journey with him. I have had a telegram today saying 'I am laid up again. Writing.'

I am sure he is wise to cancel the journey. He would find Eisenhower in a very gloomy mood. America is terribly depressed. They are in a slump and not a recession. I fear it will be a long time before they come out of it too.

It is time the newspaper manufacturers reduced their prices. They need stimulation I think.

I do wish I could persuade you to come here. I can't give you a favourable account of the weather but bad things go and good things come. It is past time for the good things!

If you know of any method by which I can persuade you to take a favourable view of the journey here I wish you would let me know. I have no visitors and I give up much time to my attempt to complete 'unfinished business'.

With affectionate good wishes.

Bracken to Beaverbrook Princes House,
21 April 1958 95, Gresham Street,
 London, E.C.2.

PRIVATE

My dear Max

Many thanks for your letter.

Alas, Winston is not very well. Moran has been at Chartwell for four or five days and his normal imperturbability seems rather dinted. He told me he would like to come up and have a talk with me on Monday and I, of course, am at his service.

Our friend Winston is, of course, a medical marvel. He has disregarded all the normal life-lengthening rules and has witnessed,

---

10 Beaverbrook met Churchill at Nice Airport on 3 April. On 10 April Churchill succumbed to illness again.

doubtless with regret, but with some complacence, the burial of most of his doctors, save Charles. But the sun is Churchill's great life-maintainer and the lack of it has probably played some part in creating his present condition. After I meet Moran, I will give you a summary of our talk.

The vagaries of climate are indeed crazy. You will require a lot more credibility than you possess to believe the following weather report. Last weekend I went up to the North of Scotland to look at a little house by the side of a river where I thought I might spend part of the summer. Rivers and hills give me more pleasure than any other landscapes. I got to a place called Craigellachie, which is way beyond Aberdeen, on Friday and I had to discard my overcoat. It was one of the loveliest days I have known. Alas, I had to spend most of it in bed as the railway journey tired me, but on Sunday I went to look at the most beautiful house in the North of Scotland, Duff House, Banffshire (built by the elder Adam) and I was sitting out in the sun for five hours on end.

On Monday I went to Aberdeen to take the train home to London and that cold granite city was lit up by sun. I am told that during this weekend the weather in London was poorish. Weather is the great mystery of our time.

Contrary to doctor's expectations my health doesn't seem to improve. This wondrous cobalt radiation seems to have narrowed my throat to such an extent that I find it awfully difficult to swallow food. Believe it or not, the only thing I can eat happily is porridge — stuff I haven't touched since I left school. If I limited my drinking to lemonade I could set myself up as the champion of the simple life!

As a Somerset landlord and cheesemaker, you may be interested in the enclosed article. I bet you Lord Waldegrave doesn't produce a cheese like yours.

(Sgd) Yours affly
Brendan

P.S. Here is a photograph from last Sunday's New York Times which shows that when it suits the Holy Roman Church they can be quite civil to Mr. Khrushchev.[11] The Archbishop who is beaming upon him is no Quisling. He is, with the Pope's consent,

---

11 New York Times, April 13, 1958. The photograph shows Archbishop Joseph Groesz, Roman Catholic prelate, greeting Nikita Khrushchev

acting head of the Roman Church in Hungary. The head of the Church, Cardinal Mindszenty is still a refugee in the American Embassy. His host is, I understand, a prosperous glue producer from Cincinatti who is a pillar of the Rechabite Church and whose recruitment to the diplomatic service was facilitated by a large cheque to the Republican campaign fund. The Cardinal must often wonder whether a concentration camp is any worse than dwelling with such a bore.

Bracken to Beaverbrook Princes House,
29 April 1958 95, Gresham Street,
London, E.C.2.

My dear Max

Thank you very much for your offer to send me one of your noble cheeses. Alas, it would be wasted upon me. To turn one of your fine cheeses into a paste or a souffle is akin to sacrilege.

Furthermore, I have to act as my own cook and I am so hamhanded that I wouldn't be able to make a paste. My culinary qualifications are limited to making porridge and boiling an egg and I am not too good at either task.

Since Costello and his wife[12] retired I haven't been able to replace them. I have seen or heard from large numbers of German, Italian and other servants, but none gave me any feeling of confidence. Lord North Street is now run by charwomen, but that is better than having uncongenial servants. I dare say one of these days I may be able to find what I want, but all my friends tell me that good servants are now completely unobtainable. I was very spoilt by the fact that my poor Costello and his wife had been with me for more than thirty years and I shall never see their like again.

Moran had lunch with me today and was more gloomy than usual about our friend.

At the end of every tenth year your friend the Archbishop of Canterbury invites all the Bishops of the Episcopal Church at home and overseas to attend what is called the Lambeth Conference. I should think about two hundred of these holy men congregate in Lambeth and pass all sorts of resolutions about im-

at the start of a visit by the Soviet Premier to Budapest, the Hungarian capital.

[12] Bracken's long-standing butler and housekeeper.

9 May 1958   211

proving mankind. They always have a violent and uncharitable blast against the iniquities of divorce.

A couple of months ago I saw a small paragraph in the New York Times about the election of a new Episcopal Bishop in California. The gentleman chosen was a popular parson in New York who apparently found some difficulty in getting on with his wife, parted from her and has now remarried. I expect that he will be invited to attend the Lambeth Conference and if he comes here the Express really can preach a sermon to the Archbishop about the difference between example and precept. This Lambeth Conference takes place in July and the list of Bishops attending it will soon be available to the Press. If the Californian prelate is among them it is desirable to wait until he is actually in the country before preaching your sermon.

When are you coming back to England?

(Sgd) Yours affly
Brendan

Bracken to Beaverbrook
9 May 1958

Princes House,
95, Gresham Street,
London, E.C.2.

My dear Max

Many thanks for sending me such a noble cheese.

Many things have you accomplished during your eventful life and no one has been more active in controversy, but in your capacity as a cheese maker you will for ever be freed from all criticism.

You of your kindness asked me to go to a party you are giving for the Canadian premiers. I should be a wretched guest because as you know I can only eat slops and that would interfere with the arrangements for providing dinner for a large number of people. The first line of Burns's Selkirk grace should be said for me: 'Some hae meat and canna eat'.

Beaverbrook to Bracken
9 May 1958

My dear Brendan,

I have your letter, and I am so glad you enjoyed the cheese.

Arrangements have already been made for slops to be prepared for you at Dinner on the 29th May. Therefore, I hope very much that you will decide to join me that evening.

My Dear Max 9 *May 1958*

Yours affectionately,

Bracken to Beaverbrook
5 July 1958

Flat 121,
Grosvenor House,
Park Lane, W.1[13]

My dear Max

The more I think about our commitment to Jordan, the more depressed do I become.

It is said that two-thirds of the people of Jordan are against the King. The country itself cannot produce enough food to keep its people healthy and so it is a military and financial liability of the first order.

What worries me most is that I can see another *General Gordon* situation arising in Jordan in which our troops may lose their lives and King Hussein[14] and his small following may be extirpated. Nothing could be more discreditable to our good name or to what is left of our position in the Middle East.

The Headmaster of Harrow, who is a pretty cold fish and in whose house Hussein lived for four years, holds this 'lack land' monarch has quite a good brain. The Yanks and ourselves should buy him an estate in some pleasant part of the world. After all, he is only 22 years of age and could easily rebuild his life. He might well go to Harvard or Yale and get some higher educational qualifications.

In addition to getting our troops out of Jordan we must also try to offer sanctuary to the King's followers. The Yanks might well bear the expense of doing this and if necessary we should help financially. It couldn't cost us a vast sum of money, and might turn out to be a very cheap way of solving what may be a horrible problem.

Bracken to Beaverbrook
28 July 1958

Flat 121,
Grosvenor House,
Park Lane, W.1.

13 At the beginning of July, Bracken, by now mortally ill, was moved from Westminster Hospital to Sir Patrick Hennessy's flat overlooking Hyde Park. On the way his chauffeur drove via 8 Lord North Street, the last time he was to see his home.

14 King Hussein of Jordan (1935–). He was educated at Harrow, and acceded to the throne of Jordan on 11 August 1952, aged 17. Britain had traditionally had strong military and diplomatic links with Jordan.

5 August 1958

My dear Max

Thank you very much for sending me 'American Heritage'.

All you say about Hoover[15] is an understatement. He hates Britain mainly because of the criticisms of his financial integrity made by an eminent Edwardian High Court judge.

I don't know whether W.S.R. ever sent you the book published in Melbourne on Mr. Hoover's company promotions.

(Sgd) Yours affly
Brendan

Bracken to Beaverbrook
5 August 1958

Flat 121,
Grosvenor House,
Park Lane, W.1.

My dear Max

Many thanks for sending me the Birkenhead book on Kipling.[16] I have read the first half of the first volume and the book has come to fascinate me.

For some reason beyond my powers of thought I am getting very, very tired. It is becoming an effort for me now to walk a short distance. I must fight this with all my might. If I don't I could quickly enter into a life of invalidism. I don't share your optimism about the doctors' view of my condition, but it is obviously quite silly while one is in the world to depend upon people for too many services.

Yours affly
Brendan

P.S. If Joe could get him to do so, the man to write out a surgical preface is undoubtedly General Sir Louis Spears.[17] Since he was turned down in his hope of becoming a life peer he wants nothing from anybody *at the present time*. If Louis really got down to describing Eisenhower's qualities he could write something extremely good, in fact it might be quite uproariously funny. It was indeed one of the largest armies in history and should never have fought in the war. A synthetic general was needed to launch soldiers and armies of great pugnacity and here was Ike 'waiting to

15 Probably Herbert Hoover (1874–1964); President of the U.S.A., 1929–33.
16 Birkenhead's unpublished biography of Kipling.
17 Major-General Sir Edward Louis Spears (1886–1974); soldier; M.P. 1922–4, 1931–45; author.

hand'. To win the last election, and the one before, the Republicans needed a synthetic President who was all things to all men. Perfection was found in Ike. No one knew where he stood on anything. Ike, in fact, is the Dale Carnegie of generals as well as politics. A wonderful world we live in!

The following day, 6 August, Bracken's condition rapidly deteriorated. He died in the small hours of the morning of 8 August.

Bibliography

This is not an exhaustive bibliography, but is intended merely as a guide to the main literature about the lives and careers of Brendan Bracken and Lord Beaverbrook.

Brendan Bracken

Andrew Boyle, *'Poor, Dear Brendan'; The quest for Brendan Bracken* (Hutchinson, 1974)
Brendan Bracken; Portraits and Appreciations (Eyre and Spottiswoode, 1958)
Paul Einzig, *In the centre of things* (Hutchinson, 1960)
David Kynaston, *The Financial Times; A Centenary History* (Viking, 1988)
Charles Lysaght, *Brendan Bracken* (Allen Lane, 1979)
Kenneth Young, *The Diaries of Sir Robert Bruce-Lockhart, 1939–65* (Macmillan, 1980)

Lord Beaverbrook

Arthur Christiansen, *Headlines All My Life* (William Heinemann, 1961)
Tom Driberg, *Ruling Passions* (Jonathan Cape, 1977)
Tom Driberg, *Beaverbrook; A study in power and frustration* (Weidenfeld and Nicolson, 1956)
David Farrer, *G for God Almighty; A personal memoir of Lord Beaverbrook* (Weidenfeld and Nicolson, 1969)
Michael Foot, *Debts of honour* (Poynter, 1980)
David Low, *Autobiography* (Michael Joseph, 1956)
A.J.P. Taylor, *Beaverbrook* (Hamish Hamilton, 1972)
George Malcolm Thomson, *Vote of Censure* (Secker and Warburg, 1968)

On the political careers of Beaverbrook and Bracken

Sir John Colville, *The Fringes of Power* Vol. I (Sceptre, 1985)
Richard Cockett, *Twilight of Truth* (Weidenfeld and Nicolson, 1989)
Ian Mclaine, *Ministry of Morale* (George Allen and Unwin, 1979)
Martin Gilbert, *Winston S. Churchill* Vols. IV–VIII (William Heinemann, 1979-1988)
Lord Moran, *Churchill; The struggle for survival 1940–65* (Constable, 1967)
Winston S. Churchill, *The Second World War* Vols. I–VI, (Cassell, 1948–1951)
Stephen Koss, *The Rise and Fall of the Political Press in Britain* Vol 2. (Hamish Hamilton, 1984)

INDEX

Abdication crisis, 3; Beaverbrook's book on, 27.
Aberdeen, 209.
Acheson, Dean 142 and n.
Acland, Sir Richard 80 and n.
Adams, Brook 119 and n.
Adams, Henry, 119 and n.
Africa, 110, 127, 200.
Afrikaaners, 102.
Aitken, Max, 27, 61 and n., 65, 81, 108, 121, 150, 165, 193, 195, 201.
Alexander, A.V., 71 and n.
Alexander, Field Marshal Sir Harold, 126.
All Souls College, Oxford, 161.
Allingham, Gary, 78 and n.
Amery, Julian, 193 and n.
Amery, Leo, 160 and n.
Ampleforth School, 10, 17.
Anderson, Sir John, 81 and n., 129.
Apartheid, 74.
Asquith, H.H., 20.
Ashton-under-Lyne, 19.
Astor, John Jacob, 130 and n.
Atomic bomb, 117, 183.
Attlee, Clement, 24–5, 49 and n., 55, 63, 66–7, 69, 70–2, 74, 78, 84, 94, 99, 105, 110, 111, 114, 117, 123, 127, 129, 183.
Auchinleck, F.M. Lord, 77.
Australia, 2, 37, 164.

B.B.C., 74, 86, 150.
Baillie, Lady, 144 and n.
Baillieu, Sir Clive, 56.
Bagehot, Walter, 133 and n.
Baldwin, Stanley, 3, 18, 22, 36 and n., 39, 132, 168, 173, 176; Beaverbrook's projected book on, 159–163.
Balfour, A.J., 41, 163 and n., 182.
Balfour, Harold, 25–6.
Barrington-Ward, Robin, 6, 87 and n.
The Banker, 5.
Barry, Gerald, 82 and n.
Baruch, Bernard, 68 and n., 99.
Baxter, Beverley, 120 and n.
Beaverbrook, Lord (Sir Max Aitken), background and career 18–27; relations with Bracken, 1, 5–8, 12, 17, 28–9, 32–3; letters, 34–214.
Bedell Smith, General Walter, 207 and n.
Belgrade, 70.
Bell, Stanley, 138 and n.
Bennett, R. B., 27.
Bermuda, conference at, 147–8, 150–1, 156.
Bevan, Aneurin, 7, 75 and n., 98, 105, 114, 89, 122, 133, 151–2, 181–4.
Bevin, Ernest, 53 and n., 55, 168; clashes with Beaverbrook, 24; as Foreign Secretary, 59, 63, 66, 71, 73, 75–6, 78, 94, 104; and Korean War, 113, 116.
Bickle, J.P., 188 and n.
Birkenhead, 1st Earl of (F.E. Smith), 103, 181.
Birkenhead, 2nd Earl of, 31, 213.
Birkenhead, Lady, 103 and n.
Bishop's Stortford School, 2.
Blackpool, 58.
Bolton, Sir George, 136.
Bonar Law, Andrew, 19, 20, 40, 51, 132; and Baldwin's achieving Premiership, 162.

Boothby, Robert, 3, 174 and n.
Bournemouth, 15, 60, 72, 110, 127, 155.
Bowater, Sir Eric, 138 and n.
Brazil, 89.
Bretton Woods (conference), 22, 186.
Bridges, Sir Edward, 61 and n.
Bridgeman, W.C., 160 and n.
Boyd-Carpenter, John, 184 and n.
Boyle, Andrew, 1, 8, 28.
Bracken, Brendan, background and career, 1–18; relations with Beaverbrook, 19, 23, 25–6, 28–9, 30, 31, 32, 33; letters, 34–214.
Bristol, East (by-election), 120.
British Empire, 75, 97, 119; and Jamaica, 139, 174.
British Information Services, 156.
B.O.A.C., 184.
Brooke, Field Marshal Sir Alan, 205 and n., 206.
Brown, Bill, 61 and n.
Brownlow, Lord, 137 and n., 170.
Bryant, Sir Arthur, 205 and n., 206.
Bruce-Lockhart, Robert, 9, 10, 14, 18, 63 and n., 64–6.
Buchman, Frank, 21.
Burke, Edmund, 5.
Burnham, Lord, 87 and n., 180.
Butler, R.A.P., 14; 15, 26, 58 and n., 60, 95, 108, 129, 143, 144, 149, 157, 177, 184, 185, 188; and 1953 Budget, 136; and Suez crisis, 197, 199, 200; and Eden's resignation, 203.

Cadbury, Laurence, 85 and n, 128, 171–2.
California, 210.
Camlachie (by-election), 79, 89.
Camrose, Lord, 6, 16, 38 and n., 90, 103, 122, 138, 147, 164, 206.
Canada, 19, 32, 131, 141, 150, 201.
Cannes, 37.
Capponcina, La, 27, 112, 125, 175, 182.
Carey, Godfrey, 114 and n., 127–8.
Chamberlain, Sir Austen, 163 and n.
Chamberlain, Neville, 11, 22, 39 and n., 43–6, 113, 118.
Cherkley, 7, 27, 38, 100, 108.
Cherwell, 1st Viscount (Prof. Lindemann), 12, 23, 124 and n., 126.
Chile, 89.
Chinese, and Korean War, 116, 117.
Christiansen, Arthur, 21.
Churchill, Lady Clementine, 124 and n., 131, 139, 171, 183.
Churchill, Mary, 65 and n.
Churchill, Randolph, 104, 109, 176.
Churchill, Sir Winston, 36, 38, 39, 48, 51, 57–8, 63, 74–5, 86, 91–2, 96–9, 103–4, 107–8, 109, 113–5, 117–9, 124, 126–7, 129, 130, 132, 135–6, 139, 140, 142, 145, 153, 158, 162, 167, 168, 203–8; and relationship with Bracken, 1–8, 10, 11, 12, 14–5, 17; and relationship with Beaverbrook, 19, 20, 22–7; and friendship with both the above, 28–33; and the Gold Standard, 34; and 1953 stroke, 147–9; and Bermuda conference, 149–51; and resignation, 166, 172, 179, 180, 181–4, 187.
Churchill College, Cambridge, 20.
Church of England, 52.
Citizen Kane, 172.
Citrine, Sir Walter, 94 and n.
Clore, Sir Charles, 152 and n.
Coal Board, 94, 111, 133–4.
Coleridge, Samuel Taylor, 203.
Colonial Office, 127.
Columbia, 139.
Colville, Sir John, 6, 9, 25–6, 126, 171; and Churchill's stroke, 147–8.
Communists, 63; and Korean War, 112, and miners, 133, 139.
Conservative Party, (or Tories), 11, 14, 17, 19, 20, 21, 26, 51, 59, 68, 72–3, 79, 82, 84, 89, 90, 95, 98, 99, 101, 105, 106, 108, 110, 114, 120, 124, 126–7, 135, 157, 163, 165, 169, 181, 183, 187; Beaverbrook's and Bracken's disenchantment with, 31; and 1946 Conference, 58; and Suez crisis, 192, 197, 198, 200, 203.
Cooper, Alfred Duff, 13, 91,1 44.
Cooper, John, 122 and n.
Costello, Mr., 210. and n.
Cousins, Frank., 8.
Coward, Noel, 141.
Cowdray, Lord, 206.
Cranbourne, Lord (and 5th Marquess of Salisbury), 61 and n., 79, 89, 155;

and Suez crisis, 191, 202–3.
Creech-Jones, Arthur, 110 and n.
Cripps, Lady Isobel, 141.
Cripps, Sir Stafford, 25, 55, 64 and n., 67, 71, 75, 78; as Chancellor of the Exchequer, 81, 82, 86, 87, 94, 97, 109.
Crookshank, Harry, 60 and n.
Crosthwaite-Eyre, Simon, 5.
Crowther, Geoffrey, 5.
Cunard, Lady, 36 and n.
Cunningham, Lt. General Sir Alan, 53 and n.
Curzon, Marquess of, 28–9; and failure to become Prime Minister in 1923, 160–161.
Cyprus, 170.
Czechoslovakia, 45, 47.

Daily Express, 20–2 , 56, 111, 132, 157, 181.
Daily Herald, 80, 99.
Daily Mail, 20, 46, 137, 165.
Daily Mirror, 42, 85, 126, 137, 158.
Daily Telegraph, 6, 74, 137.
Daladier, Edouard, 46.
Dalton, Hugh, 10, 13, 25, 55, 71 and n, 81, 94, 129; resignation of, 77–8.
Darvall, Frank, 156 and n., 157.
Davies, Sir Daniel, 68 and n., 85, 151.
Davies, Clement, 129.
De Gasperi, Prime Minister of Italy, 147.
Delhi, 77.
Dawson, Geoffrey, 40 and n., 161.
Dawson of Penn, Lord, 96 and n.
Derby, Earl of, 25, 90 and n., 160.
Devonport (by-election), 109.
Dickens, Charles, 166.
Disraeli, Benjamin, 15.
Ditchley, 4.
Donne, John, 100.
Douglas, Lewis, 81 and n., 96–7, 127.
Drake, Sir Francis, 178.
Driberg, Tom, 22, 117 and n., 172–4, 176.
Dufferin and Ava, 4th Marquess of, 43 and n.
Dulles, John Foster, 142 and n., 159; and Suez crisis, 191, 203–4.
Duncan, Sir Andrew, 73 and n., 98.
Dunn, Sir James, 27, 115, 145–6, 185, 187.

Eccles, David, 95 and n., 96.
The Economist, 5, 16, 82,
Eden, Anthony, 3, 11, 13, 14, 18, 24–6, 57 and n., 60–1, 91, 99, 147, 157, 184–5, 186, 190; and Churchill's resignation, 171; and succession to Premiership, 180; and 1955 election, 182, 183; and Suez crisis, 191–2, 194–7, 199, 200, 201; and resignation, 202.
Edinburgh, Duke of, 84.
Edmonton (by-election), 98.
Egypt, 87; and Suez crisis, 191–2, 203.
Einzig, Paul, 5.
Eisenhower, Dwight D., 143, 214–5; and 1953 Bermuda conference, 148, 150–1; and Suez crisis, 183, 200, 203–5.
El Alamein, 25.
Elizabeth, Princess, 84.
Ellerman, Sir John, 206 and n.
Empire Free Trade Campaign, 22.
English Life, 5.
English-Speaking Union, 156.
Epsom (by-election), 82, 101.
Epstein, Jacob, 53 and n.
Evans, Trevor, 56 and n., 73.
Evening Standard, 20–21, 30, 103, 124, 178.
Excess Profits Levy, 137, 189.
Eyre, Oliver, 205–7.
Eyre and Spottiswoode, 4, 5.

Fawcett, Sir Luke, 153.
Federation of British Industries, 171.
Financial News, 5, 16, 40.
Financial Times, 6, 8, 10, 16, 17, 66, 90, 91, 96, 137–8, 145, 155, 177, 204.
First Lord of the Admiralty, 11, 13; Bracken as, 14.
Fleming, Sir Alexander, 64 and n.
Flynn, Ed, 57.
Flynn, Errol, 141.
Foot, Sir Hugh, 140 and n.
Foot, Michael, 7, 19, 21, 61 and n., 90, 109, 141.
Forbes, Alastair, 59, 167 and n.
Ford (motor company), 178.
Foreign Office, 10, 13, 135, 147, 163, 186.
Formosa, 176.
Forster, Sir John, 153 and n.

France, 87, 147; and Suez crisis, 191, 204.
Franks, Oliver, 130 and n.

Gaitskell, Hugh, 86 and n., 169.
Gandhi, 20, 75.
Garvin, J.L., 2, 6, 12, 28, 131.
Gas industry, 15, 77.
General election, of 1945, 7, 22, 26, 31, 55, 58, 73, 80, 97, 126, 181; of 1950, 101, 109; of 1951, 126-7, 171; of 1955, 182.
George III, King, 72.
George V, King, and Baldwin's accession to the premiership, 159-163.
Germany, 5, 177, 186.
Gestapo (election speech by Churchill), 26.
Gibbon, Edward, 134.
Gibson, William Pettigrew, 188 and n., 194-5.
Glasgow, 154.
Glasgow Herald, 108.
Gold (industry), 95.
Gold Coast, 110, 200.
Gold Standard, 186.
Goldie, Sir George, 40 and n.
Gordon-Walker, Patrick, 123 and n.
Gravesend (by-election), 80, 81.
Greenwich (by-election), 79.
Greenwood, Arthur, 49 and n., 81.
Gretton, John, 94 and n.
Gromyko, Andrei, 145 and n.

Hacking, Douglas, 43.
Haley, Sir William, 130 and n.
Halifax, 1st Earl of, 11, 25, 79 and n.
Hammersmith (by-election), 105.
Hannegan, Robert E., 57.
Harcourt, Sir William, 164 and n.
Harcourt, 'Lulu', 164 and n.
Harriman, Averell, 57 and n.
Harris, Wilson, 61 and n.
Harvard, 212.
Harrow (school), 212.
Havenga, Nicholas, 94 and n.
Head, Anthony, 173.
Heath, Edward, 197 and n.
Hennessy, Sir Patrick, 1, 18, 105 and n., 182, 185, 204.
Hertzog, James, 93 and n.
Hicks-Beach, 129 and n.

Hill, Dr. Charles, 89 and n.
History Today, 18.
Hitler, 45, 95, 166-7.
Hoare, Sir Samuel, 22, 46 and n., 47, 79.
Hodge, Alan, 16.
Hofmeyr, Jan, 93 and n., 100.
Home of the Hirsel, Lord, 191.
Hoover, President Herbert, 213 and n.
Hore-Belisha, Leslie, 43 and n., 44, 45, 66, 121, 155.
Horner, Arthur, 69 and n.
Horsburgh, Frances, 128 and n., 129, 165.
Hoskins, Percy, 30.
Houldsworth, Hubert, 111, 134 and n.
House of Commons, 3, 6, 15, 44, 60-1, 70-2, 76, 78, 84, 96, 126, 134, 147, 153, 172.
House of Lords, 15, 32, 75, 89; Bracken refuses to take seat in, 127.
Houston, Lady, 39 and n.
Hudson, Robert, 43 and n., 62.
Hungary, 209.
Hughes, Charles Evans, 98 and n.
Hull, Cordell, 39 and n.
Hussein, King, 212 and n.

Illustrated Review, 5.
India, 3, 35, 174, 197.
Inskip, Sir Thomas, 43 and n.
Institute of Directors, 8.
International Monetary Fund, 143.
Investor's Chronicle, 5, 42.
Ireland, 1.
Iron and Steel Industry, 15.
Ismay, General Sir 'Pug', 77 and n., 126.
Israel, 93; and Suez crisis, 192.
Italy, 89.

Jackson, C.D., 151 and n.
Jamaica, and Beaverbrook, 26, 32, 63, 68, 77, 83, 87, 110, 117, 122, 136-7; American influence in, 139; politics of, 174, 197; Eden's 1956 stay in, 199, 201-3.
Jameson Raid, 198.
Japan, 178, 186.

Index

Jebb, Gladwyn, 10.
Joad, Dr. Cyril, 67 and n.
Johannesburg, 73–4, 96.
Jones, Dr. Tom, 40, 168 and n.
Jones, Jesse, 130 and n.
Jordan, 212.

Kemsley, 1st Viscount, 41 and n., 61–2, 99, 122, 128, 132, 137, 137, 162, 164, 165.
Kenya, 110, 127–9.
Keynes, J.M., 7–8, 22, 136, 143.
Killan, Isaak, 188 and n.
Kipling, Rudyard, 3, 213; and Elsie Kipling, 103 and n.
Knickerbocker, Charles, 141 and n.
Knox, John, 107, 176, 189.
Korea, 111, 112.
Kruger, Stephen, 97 and n.
Krushchev, Nikita, 209.

Labour Party, 3, 14, 15, 17, 22, 54–5, 80, 126; and Suez crisis, 191, 194.
Lambeth Conference, 210–211.
Lambton, Lord, 104 and n.
Laski, Harold, 67 and n.
Layton, Sir Walter, 5, 39 and n., 82, 171–2.
Leathers, Lord, 59 and n.
Leicester (West), 3.
Lennox-Boyd, Alan, 134 and n., 167, 193, 200.
Liberal Party, 80, 113, 126, 129.
Linlithgow, Marquess of, 90 and n.
Liverpool Journal of Commerce, 5.
Lloyd, Geoffrey, 128 and n., 134.
Lloyd, Selwyn, 170 and n., 191.
Lloyd George, David, 20, 27, 182.
Lord Privy Seal, Beaverbrook as, 25, 51.
Low, David, 20–1.
Luce, Harold, 104, 143; and *Time*, 143; Anglophobia, 167.
Luce, Clare, 60 and n., 104, 143.
Lyle, Lord, 83 and n., 150, 151, 155, 159.
Lysaght, Charles, 1, 12, 30.
Lyttleton, Oliver, 53 and n., 149, 167.

MacArthur, General Douglas, 116 and n.
Macdonald, Sir John, 150 and n.
Macfarlane, Mason, 14.
Mackay, Hugh, 91 and n.
Mackenzie King, W.C., 91 and n., 142.
Macmillan, Harold, 15, 24, 26, 58 and n. , 68, 130, 135, 144, 184; at the Treasury, 185–8, 189; and Suez crisis, 191, 193–4, 196, 198, 199, 200, 201, 203; as Prime Minister, 202, 204.
Macmillan, Lord, 48 and n., 156.
Maharajah of Kashmir, 76.
Maisky, Ivan, 53 and n.
Malan, Daniel, 93 and n., 95.
Malaya, 127.
Malenkov, Georgi, 151 and n., 158.
Malta, 192.
Manchester Daily Despatch, 132.
Manchester Guardian, 66, 132, 141, 165.
Manley, Norman, 174 and n.
Marrakesh, 119.
Marshall Plan, 81, 87, 99, 106, 200.
Margesson, David, 11, 107 and n., 111.
Massey, Vincent, 197 and n.,
Mathew, Francis, 18.
Mau Mau, 136, 141, 148.
Maxwell-Fyfe, David, 62 and n.
May, Erskine, 110.
McCormick, Robert, 103 and n.
McCullough, George, 130 and n, 188.
McNair, John, 91 and n.
McNeill, Hector, 123 and n.
Men and Matters column, 16–7.
Mendes-France, Pierre, 167 and n.
Mieville, Sir Eric, 77.
Millar, A.G., 38 and n., 87, 184, 188.
Miners Union (N.U.M.), 133–4.
Minister of Aircraft Production, 23–4, 49, 51.
Minister of Economic Affairs, 75.
Minister for Fuel and Power, 15.
Minister of Production, 24.
Ministry of Economic Warfare, 13.
Ministry of Housing, 135.
Ministry of Information, 156, 175; Bracken as Minister, 12–4, 30, 49, 62; Beaverbrook as Minister, 20.
Ministry of Labour, 24; Monckton as Minister, 135.
Ministry of Pensions, 135.
Ministry of Raw Materials, 135–6,

155.
Ministry of Supply, 51, 70, 117.
Molotov, V.M., 78 and n., 158.
Molyneux, Edward, 141 and n.
Monckton, Sir Walter, 120 and n., 121, 135, 168; and 'appeasement' of Unions, 153; and Suez crisis, 191.
Moran, Lord, 4, 14, 32, 86, 125, 208–9, 210; and Churchill's stroke, 147–9.
Morgan, Evan Frederick, 5.
Morison, Stanley, 150 and n., 174, 176.
Morning Post, 36.
Morocco, 82.
Morrison, Herbert, 55, 59 and n., 60–1, 66–7, 71, 73, 75–6, 89, 94, 95–6, 100, 108, 110, 114, 123, 129, 175, 183.
Morrison, W. 'Shakes', 41 and n., 44.
Moscow, 23-4, 112.
Mosley, Sir Oswald, 83 and n.
Mountbatten, Lady Edwina, 141.
Mountbatten, 1st Earl of, 76 and n., 77, 82, 154, 173, 197.
Munich (agreement), 45, 47, 113.
Murdoch, Keith, 37 and n.
Mussolini, Benito, 46.

Napoleon, 83.
Nassau, 26, 115, 143, 155, 168, 198.
Nasser, President, 191, 195–7, 199, 203, 204.
Nathan, Lord, 88 and n.
National Gallery, 194–6.
National Government, 45.
National Labour Party, 44.
National Liberal Party, 44.
Nationalization, 15.
N.A.T.O., 200.
Nazi Germany, 3, 22, 42, 45–7.
Nehru, Pandit, 141.
New York, 76, 133, 136, 174, 198, 201, 211.
New York Times, 149, 203, 209–210.
New Zealand, 11, 202.
News Chronicle, 39, 82, 85, 171–2.
News of the World, 137.
Newspaper Proprietors Association, 35, 180–1.
Newton, Gordon, 171.
Nigeria, 111.
Norman, Montagu, 93 and n.
North, Lord, 72 and n.

Northcliffe, 1st Viscount, 21, 39 and n., 40, 174, 182.
Nutting, Sir Anthony, 170; and Suez crisis, 191.
O'Casey, Sean, 196.
O'Donnell, Charles, 141 and n.
Observer, 2, 131.
Oppenheimer, Sir Ernest, 96 and n.
Orange Free State, 73, 96, 102.
Owen, Frank, 21, 41 and n.
Oxford University, 3.

Paddington (North), 3, 14, 29, 53, 105.
Pakistan, 77.
Parliament Act, 79 and n.
Parliament, 3, 5.
Parnell, Charles, 36 and n.
Peerage, 15.
Peron, President, 85 and n., 95,
Persia, 139.
Plummer, Sir Leslie, 171 and n., 172.
Political Warfare Executive, 10.
Pollitt, Harry, 58 and n., 59, 68.
Portal, Lord, 59 and n.
Pravda, 143.
Presbyterianism, 27, 84, 102, 107, 108, 174, 176, 189.
Press Council, 131.
Prime Minister, Churchill as, 11, 15, 178; Bonar Law as, 20; Chamberlain as, 43; Attlee as, 78; Macmillan as, 201, 204.
Prime Minister of New Brunswick, 104.
Primrose League, 67.

Queensberry, 11th Marquess of, 25–6.
Quinlon, Gordon, 52.

Raleigh, Sir Walter, 178.
Randall Committee, 157.
Rent Restriction Act, 153, 157.
Reynolds (family), 139, 141.
Rhodesia, Northern, 110.
Robertson, E.J. 21, 49 and n., 108; and honours, 178, 184.
Roosevelt, President, 24, 120.
Root, Elihu, 98 and n.
Rosebery, 5th Earl of, 164 and n.
Ross, W.D., 188 and n.
Rothermere, 1st Viscount, 20, 22, 38 and n., 39, 87.

Rothermere, 2nd Viscount, 137, 180.
Royal Air Force, 118.
Royal Commission on the Press, 20, 87.
Royal Empire Society, 7.
Royal Festival Hall, 17.
Royal Society of Literature, 157.
Royds, Admiral Sir Percy, 44 and n.
Runciman, Walter, 39 and n., 43.
Russia (Soviet Union), 53, 78, 119, 145, 147, 159, 198; and Beaverbrook, 22–4; and Korean war, 113.

St. Andrew's University, 176.
St. Laurent, Louis, 91 and n.
Salisbury, 4th Marquess of, 25, 160 and n., 161–3.
Samuel, Harold, 152 and n.
Samuel, 1st Viscount, 128 and n.
Sandys, Duncan, 134 and n., 9.
Savoy (Hotel), 152.
Scotsman, 8, 32, 172, 209.
Sealey, J.E.B., 206 n.
Sedbergh School, 1, 10, 17.
Sèvres agreement, 191.
Shaw, G.B., 157.
Shawcross, Hartley, 123 and n.
Sheean, Vincent, 9.
Shinwell, Emmanuel, 64 and n., 71, 75, 94, 115; and 1947 power crisis, 69.
Simon, Sir John, 45 and n.
Simpson, Edward, 39.
Sinclair, Archibald, 49 and n., 83, 128, 157.
Singapore, 24.
Smuts, General, 73, 93 and n., 93, 95–7, 100, 101.
Soames, Christopher, 130 and n.
Socialists, 55–6, 60, 62, 65–7, 70, 74, 76, 78, 79, 81–2, 84, 91, 95–6, 98–9, 105–9, 110, 113–5, 123–4, 135, 152–3, 158, 165, 168, 183, 195.
South Africa, 5, 16, 73–4, 90, 92, 94–5, 100, 101, 167, 171, 192.
Spears, General Sir Louis, 214 and n.
Stalin, Josef, 63 and n., 112, 117, 147–8.
Stamfordham, Lord, 160 and n.
Stanley, Oliver , 122 and n.
Steel Bill, 98–9.
Steel Board, 59.

Stoke Newington (by-election), 83.
Stokes, Richard, 50 and n., 116.
Strachey, John, 64 and n., 75, 89, 98, 108.
Strakosch, Sir Henry, 5, 6, 16, 73.
Strathcona and Mount Royal, Lord, 43 and n.
Strikes, 97, 153.
Stuart, Sir Campbell, 176 and n.
Stuart, James, 62 and n.
Suez Canal Users Association, 191–3.
Suez Crisis, 180, 191–2, 196–9, 202.
Sunday Dispatch, 137.
Sunday Express, 20, 29, 36, 81.
Sunday Telegraph, 138.
Sunday Times, 99, 138, 205.
Sulzberger, Arthur, 115 and n., 141, 149, 204.
Sulzberger (Junior), 204.
Sunderland, (by-election), 158.
Surtees, Robert, 166.
Sutherland, Graham, 183.
Swinton, 1st Earl of, 149 and n.
Sykes, Sir Frederick, 161 and n.

Tanganyika, 110.
Tanner, Jack, 59 and n.
Taylor, A.J.P., 21, 25.
Thackeray, William, 166.
Thorneycroft, Peter, 128 and n., 193.
The Times, 6, 18, 49, 135, 161; and death of Barrington-Ward, 130.
Tobruk, 24.
Townshend, Charles, 187 and n.
Trades Union Congress, 59, 71, 78, 153–4, 171, 181.
Transport Commission, 94, 134.
Transport and General Workers Union, 8.
Transvaal, 73.
Tredegar, Lord, 5.
Tree, Ronald, 4.
Trollope, Anthony, 166.
Truman, Harry S., 80 and n., 112, 142.
Turner, Sir James, 165 and n.

Union Corporation, 5, 16, 73, 88, 90, 96, 136, 170.
United Nations, 112, 116, 149, 192, 197, 203, 204.
United States of America, 74, 80, 81, 82, 99, 118–9, 131, 133, 139, 170,

172, 173, 177–8, 183, 185–6, 208–9, 212; and 1945 loan, 57, 67, 70, 74, 106, 136; and Korean War, 111–3, 116–7, 123; and foreign policy, 139, 142, 141, 144; and 1953 Bermuda Conference, 147–150, 157, 159; and Indochina, 166; and Suez crisis, 191–3, 198–9, 200, 201, 203–4.

University of New Brunswick, 18, 26–7, 32, 102, 149, 182–3, 187, 195–6, 207.

Vienna, 76, 111.

Walkenden, Evelyn, 78 and n.
Ward, Lady Penelope, 8–9.
Wardell, 108 and n., 120, 150.
Washington, 23–4, 83, 112, 143, 182; British Embassy in, 199.
Waterhouse, Colonel Sir Ronald, 160 and n., 161–3.
Webb, Maurice, 84 and n.
Wellington, Duke of, 176.
Weech, William, 1.
White, Harry Dexter, 143 and n.
Williams, Francis, 21.
Winchell, Walter, 83 and n.
Wilson, Harold, 17, 106 and n.
Wilson, Sir Horace, 12, 49 and n.
Wilson, President Woodrow, 49, 174 and n.
Winant John, 80 and n.
Windsor, Duke of, 98, 109, 132, 151.
Windsor, Duchess of, 65.
Winslow, Fraser, 188.
Winster, Lord, 8.
Wiseman, Sir William, 174 and n., 176.
Wontner, Sir Hugh, 152 and n.
Wood, Kingsley, 11.
Woolton, Lord, 14, 75, 79 and n., 80, 101, 109, 133, 154, 182.

Yale, 212.
Young, G.M., 132 and n.